THE ART OF
SINCLAIR LEWIS

THE ART OF
SINCLAIR LEWIS

by D. J. Dooley

UNIVERSITY OF NEBRASKA PRESS · LINCOLN

To Marie

Contents

INTRODUCTION ix

1. The Troubadour from Sauk Centre 3

2. Opiates for the Tired Business Man 17

3. The Revolt Against Main Street 57

4. Aspiration and Enslavement 97

5. An Alien View of America 139

6. Defending the Republican Virtues 175

7. New Life and Endless Exile 207

8. The Author, the Critics, and the Nightmare World 235

SELECTED BIBLIOGRAPHY 269

ACKNOWLEDGMENT 279

INDEX 281

Introduction

In 1936, when the bibliophiles' magazine *Colophon* asked its readers to name the living American authors they considered to have the best chance of being thought "classics" in the year 2000, Sinclair Lewis easily led the list. In a similar poll conducted in 1948, Lewis was ranked second to Eugene O'Neill. Yet Lewis's reputation has declined to such an extent that Mark Schorer, toward the end of his monumental biography, seems to doubt whether it was all worth while; and his rather sour final judgment is "He was one of the worst writers in modern American literature . . . ."[1] This conclusion is not prepared for, since Schorer treats Lewis's books chiefly as events in his life; we could hardly wish for a more comprehensive view of Lewis's deficiencies, but we are left wondering how many other recent American writers did what E. M. Forster attributed to him: lodged a piece of a continent in our imagination. Schorer takes Lewis as "a prime example of that characteristic phenomenon of American literature—the man who enjoys a tremendous

[1] Mark Schorer, *Sinclair Lewis: An American Life* (New York: McGraw-Hill, 1961), p. 813.

and rather early success and then suffers through a long
period of decline and deterioration . . . ."[2] The success
and the decline are admirably described in Schorer's
book, but after we have finished it we may still be left
pondering the nature of the achievement.[3]

There is a remarkable range of opinions concerning
what Lewis did or tried to do. "Main Street is the climax
of civilization," begins the ironic prefatory note to the
book which made Lewis famous; the note concludes,
"Would he not betray himself an alien cynic who would
otherwise portray Main Street, or distress the citizens by
speculating whether there may not be other faiths?" The
position of the author seems clear enough: here is the age-
old appeal of the satirist asking his reader to adopt an
"enlightened" perspective. The man whom Main Street
would regard as an alien cynic is, of course, only an
ordinary reasonable man who has not suffered from the
limitations of a small-town environment, an ordinary man
who sees it as his duty to expose the foolish and the
vicious. So Lewis has been seen by Vernon L. Parrington
as an American Diogenes, by Carl Van Doren as a man
of outspoken courage telling the true story of the American
village, and by Robert Spiller as an honest man crying
out against the blindness and hypocrisy which destroy
elemental human values.[4]

[2] From Schorer's description of his biography as given on the dust
jacket.

[3] In a critical study of Lewis which has appeared since his biography
(*Sinclair Lewis*, University of Minnesota Pamphlets on American Writers,
No. 27 [Minneapolis, 1963]), Schorer has made an excellent brief estimate
of Lewis's merits and defects and of his place in literature. The pamphlet
gives a somewhat more favorable impression of Lewis than does the biography, even though Schorer says in a foreword that the general evaluation
in the two is the same.

[4] Most of the views of Lewis referred to in this paragraph will be discussed, and their sources identified, later on; their sources are also given
in the bibliography.

But it is not easy to determine what really was Sinclair Lewis's attitude toward America, and especially toward the Middle West, which was his favorite subject. T. K. Whipple saw him as a Red Indian stalking his foes; J. Donald Adams denied that there was acid in his satire and called attention to his prodigal love for mankind. Edgar Johnson has described him as out to bring down the whole of modern America from Gopher Prairie to the glittering pinnacles of business; Alfred Kazin has stressed his boisterous good fellowship with the very people he caricatured. He has been seen by many critics as primarily an anatomist of society, an anthropologist, a collector of specimens; Frederick J. Hoffman, however, refutes the notion that Lewis gives an exact and mimetic transcription of American life, and for James Branch Cabell the pleasure of reading Lewis was that "of seeing a minim of reality exaggerated into Brobdingnagian incredibility." To Edward Wagenknecht he was primarily a satirist, to Percy Boynton an expositor, to Constance Rourke a fabulist in the American tradition. For Carl Van Doren he was the voice of the liberal decade before 1929, and for Henry Seidel Canby the standard-bearer of a code of individualism coming from the heroic age of the frontier; for Maxwell Geismar, on the other hand, he was a writer who mistook a small arc for the entire circle of human experience and therefore was truly the last provincial of American letters. Finally, for Mark Schorer he was a novelist trapped in his own hallucination of the world as a trap, with no concept of realizable values toward which he or his society might aspire.

How did Lewis see himself? Variously, as the mood took him. He could even describe himself as a yearner after quaint ivy-clad cottages and a "romantic medievalist of the most incurable sort."

Lewis's examination of American society in the 1920's

was so vigorous and impressive that he gave "Main Street" and "Babbitt" special meanings which these terms continue to possess; confirmed Europeans in their worst prejudices about the United States—indeed gave them a new stereotype for the American; and taught Americans a new way of looking at themselves and their country. If the story of his life is a pathetic one, it is not entirely a story of failure; he cannot be dismissed as a writer of meretricious best sellers who had his decade of popular success and is now best forgotten along with his books. Even if we were to accept Schorer's judgment that he was one of the worst writers in modern American literature, we would have to accept the accompanying opinion that we cannot imagine modern American literature without him. If we can no longer be certain that his novels will be regarded as classics in the year 2000, they do possess their literary merits; furthermore, they are worth examining partly because of their strengths and partly because of their curious weaknesses—weaknesses which can be traced sometimes to the writer's paradoxical personality and sometimes to the middle-class milieu of which he was the chronicler and perhaps the prisoner.

The present study does not pretend to be exhaustive or definitive; it is an introduction to Lewis and a contribution to the continuing debate over his place in American letters. The critical opinions which have already been mentioned, plus a number of other assessments of individual novels or of Lewis's career as a whole, will come in for examination, either as evaluations which are noteworthy in themselves or as starting points for further critical discussion. Van Wyck Brooks said of an early Lewis novel, *The Trail of the Hawk*, that it foreshadowed Lewis's later work in certain ways, for one saw in it the kind of world that he was to measure society by and the kind of man that he was to choose as a hero. Such considerations justify a chronological approach here, even though this approach has already been used in a number of studies of Lewis: the more important novels of the 1920's need to be read in the light of the themes discussed and the techniques employed in their less important predecessors. For the sake of placing the novels in their biographical context and of telling a connected story, I have related briefly the events of Lewis's life. There is a great deal of biographical material on him to be found in *From Main Street to Stockholm*, the collection of letters between Lewis and his publisher during the 1920's; in *The Man from Main Street*, the Sinclair Lewis reader edited by Harry E. Maule and Melville H. Cane; in the reminiscences by Lewis's two wives, Grace Hegger Lewis, who told of her life with Lewis in *With Love from Gracie*, and Dorothy Thompson, who wrote two very revealing articles for the *Atlantic Monthly*, in addition to the letters and diaries which provide the basis for Vincent Sheean's *Dorothy and Red*; as well as in many other books and articles. Consequently, though I have looked to Schorer as a guide, I have not relied on him as much as may be thought; and my view of Lewis is not precisely his.

In an excellent review of *Dorothy and Red*, Steven Marcus, reflecting Schorer's opinion, describes Lewis as "that remarkable modern phenomenon, a man who had apparently no inner life; he was incapable of reflection or self-examination ...," and, after observing that Lewis's endless suffering and the fact that he was a writer were the two most authentic things about him, goes on to say, "It was altogether typical ... that the suffering did not get into the writing, that he was quite unable to express his anguish in the one form of expression available to him."[5] In reply, one might first question whether

[5] Steven Marcus, "American Gothic," *New York Review of Books*, January 9, 1964, pp. 3–5

Lewis's anguish could have been so intense if he had had no inner life. Second, does not the comment indicate (as Schorer does toward the end of his book) a wish that Lewis had been not merely a better writer but a different kind of writer—a novelist of the subjective life? Sometimes one feels that Lewis is being tried, as Johnson said of Shakespeare, by the laws of some country other than his own. Third, would it not have benefited Lewis to look outside himself to some external source of value? Paradoxically, the only myths for which he had any reverence kept him firmly locked within the prison of self.

Main Street and Babbitt soon became standards of judgment, so that it became the task of every literate American to prove that there was nothing of Main Street, nothing of the Babbitt, about him. Yet Lewis the "alien cynic" was also a local patriot and even a local booster; an ardent rebel who distrusted most of the revolutionary literary, social, and political movements of his day and sometimes longed for a return to pioneer, even Puritan, virtues; a man unwilling to profess the faith of Main Street and yet uncertain whether any other faith was adequate to judge it or supplant it. It soon became clear that in his novels he was not really setting western naiveté against eastern sophistication, not ridiculing the standards of the small town or medium-sized city according to the standards of the metropolis, and certainly not attacking America by European or cosmopolitan standards. When he was asked for some indication of his standpoint, he responded by giving his readers an example of heroic behavior, the dedication of a scientist to his science. But his example raised as many questions as it answered; his heroic soul had to free himself not merely from restrictive conformity and corrupting commercial pressures, but virtually from human values and society itself. In Martin Arrowsmith rugged American individualism reached its apogee: he lived as a hermit in the woods.

For Lewis the freedom of the 1920's became the freedom to ignore family responsibilities, to go wherever fancy or alcoholic whim took him, and to praise or blame the Babbitts and the Gantrys according to the caprice of the moment. It became the despairing flight from place to place, each sanctuary becoming a prison as soon as attained, which Schorer describes so vividly. Holding to no standard but this unchartered freedom, Lewis became erratic and unpredictable in his personal behavior, and inconsistent in the handling of the themes, characters, and situations in his books. The ambiguities in his novels, therefore, have a connection with his conception of liberty. The story of Sinclair Lewis's futile endeavor to find satisfaction for his spirit by rushing from somewhere to nowhere, until he died alone and unknown in an alien land, is a parable for our times.

One aspect of his concept of freedom was an Alice-in-Wonderland carelessness about words: occasionally he made them mean what he wanted them to mean. Satire he called "one of those back-attic words into which is thrown everything for which no use can be found."[6] But this did not prevent him from writing a whole series of satirical novels and presenting a whole gallery of satirical characterizations, almost invariably belonging to the class which he considered enslaved by conformity. Many critics have pointed out that his middle-class world was a nightmare world; at times his vision resembles that in *The Waste Land* of people walking meaninglessly around in a ring, or the Orwellian image of drawn and cowed people in an Airstrip One. But his florid, loud-mouthed representatives of the class which spins not and toils chiefly at

[6] Attributed to Lewis by C. Harley Grattan in "Sinclair Lewis: The Work of a Lifetime," *New Republic*, CXXIV (April 2, 1951), 19.

salesmanship proved to be richly varied and full of life and gusto. Lewis was never happier than when a Marduc or a Pickerbaugh, a Windrip or a Blausser, had sprung full-blown into existence in the world of his imagination and begun to wax eloquent. These were characters to be treated with satiric humor; some of them were menaces, some of them were conspiring to destroy all freedom and all individuality, but except in his gloomier moments, Lewis never believed that they would succeed. He kept his faith in the American Dream.

THE ART OF
SINCLAIR LEWIS

1. The Troubadour from Sauk Centre

HARRY SINCLAIR LEWIS was born in Sauk Centre, Minnesota, on February 7, 1885. The third son of Dr. Edwin J. and Emma Kermott Lewis, he was perhaps of Pilgrim stock on his father's side, and at least descended from Americans for generations back; his mother was the daughter of a physician, dentist, and veterinarian who had come from Canada. Did his mother's early death, when he was only six, produce the gritty dissatisfaction with the world which was to turn Sinclair Lewis into a satirist? Possibly so; but he was not deprived of maternal affection, for his father's second wife, Isabel Warner Lewis, treated him with sympathy and understanding, and became in effect a mother to him. It was the father, however, who was the dominant influence in the home; and almost every account of Dr. Lewis stresses what a stern, difficult, and puritanical man he was. Mark Schorer places a great deal of emphasis on the appalling regard—not affection—which Lewis had for his father all through his life; parental tyranny, he thinks, was the cause of the mental disorder of Lewis's later years. The eccentric behavior, emotional instability, undue conceit, suspiciousness, and lack of self-control had either this origin or at least, in Lewis's mind, this excuse.

Lewis also dwelt on the fact that his brothers Fred and Claude were nine and seven years older than he, and that to Sauk Centre he was "Claude Lewis's red-headed kid brother." He was the small boy who was always trying to keep up with the gang and was always being left behind. Even as an adult he remained the "kid brother" who had to prove himself; his second wife, Dorothy Thompson, said that an enormous inferiority complex and a desire to call attention to himself, as a compensation for his inabilities, persisted throughout his life.[1] One would have expected that time and success would have lessened this feeling of inadequacy, and that the Nobel Prize medal would have been to Sinclair Lewis a symbol of achievement which his brother could not match. But Lewis had his generation's respect for physical science; Claude had followed his father into medicine and become a highly respected surgeon, and Sinclair was never sure that his own work was equally important. In 1947 he wrote that for sixty years he had been trying to impress his brother Claude; it had been his chief object and his chief failure.

Lewis referred to himself as a "product of the pioneer forests and wheatfields of Minnesota." Neither Sauk Centre nor the state was thirty years old in 1885, so he was born into a region which had vivid memories of pioneer days; he could recall hearing of men who, during the Sioux Uprising of 1862, had "dogtrotted a hundred miles over swamp-blurred trails to bring the alarm to the nearest troops," and of settlers who were scalped within

[1] Dorothy Thompson, "The Boy and Man from Sauk Centre," *Atlantic Monthly*, CCVI (November 1960), 48.

sight of stockades.[2] Now the Indian wars were over and the frontier had virtually disappeared; the heroic challenges of pioneering which had confronted the white man ever since he first landed in North America were at an end, and the spirit of enterprise which had expressed itself in such adventure had to find new outlets. Lewis was sufficiently aware of this necessity to make it a major theme in several of his novels. In addition, he never ceased wondering at the speed with which an Indian-haunted wilderness was transformed into a complex civilization: Minneapolis, he wrote, grew from a single cabin to a city of 400,000 in just seventy-five years. He lived through the most important transitional period in midwestern life.

If Sauk Centre had come into existence at a turning point in history, it was not aware of the fact; and if Lewis sometimes thought of it as a pleasant place in which to spend one's early years, this was only in retrospect and at a distance. When he wrote of his boyhood days there, he usually strove to be whimsical and amusing; furthermore, one set of recollections contradicted another. Although he once said that he was entirely normal and not at all ill-adjusted, his other accounts and outside evidence prove that he was awkward, self-conscious, and very much driven into himself. In later years he both hated and loved his native town. When he took his first wife, Grace, to visit it in 1916, he had not been back for eight years; his second wife was never there at all during the thirteen years of their marriage. Yet he chose to be buried in Sauk Centre, beside his father.

In a "Self-Portrait" written in 1927, Lewis described his boyhood as utterly commonplace "except for a love of

[2] "Minnesota, the Norse State," *The Man from Main Street: Selected Essays and Other Writings, 1904–1950*, ed. Harry E. Maule and Melville H. Cane (New York: Random House, 1953), pp. 273 and 278.

reading not very usual in that raw new town."[3] He became a voracious reader at an early age, perhaps seeking in books, as Dorothy Thompson suggested, an escape from an environment which was not uncongenial but whose demands he could not meet.[4] According to legend, he read every book in the town library, was found sprawled with a book on the lawn which he was supposed to be mowing, and even pulled out a book at a dance and ostentatiously began reading it. He read indiscriminately, but his special favorites, according to his own recollection, were the novels of Scott and Dickens. The itch for scribbling soon followed that for reading; it attacked him, he said, when he was about eleven, and his early hero was the town newspaper editor. Sauk Centre had two newspapers, in fact, and he worked on them in turn during the summers of his seventeenth and eighteenth years; he described his experiences later, with more humor than accuracy, in "I'm an Old Newspaperman Myself" and "You Meet Such Interesting People."[5] Thus his first published writing consisted of items of local news. His early efforts at self-expression, however, took him out of the world around him into the world of romance. A variety of unsympathetic magazines, ranging from *The Youth's Companion* to *Harper's*, became the targets for what he later described as the effusions of a wild romanticist— "banal and imitative verse, all about troubadours and castles as sagely viewed from the eminence of a Minnesota prairie village."[6]

"His mind was as swift as light," wrote Dorothy Thompson.[7] But Lewis's early teachers were less impressed by his mental agility than by his subversion of order. As

[3] *The Man from Main Street*, p. 49.
[4] "The Boy . . . from Sauk Centre," p. 47.
[5] Reprinted in *The Man from Main Street*.
[6] *The Man from Main Street*, p. 49.
[7] "The Boy . . . from Sauk Centre," p. 47.

time went on, his work improved, though his conduct did not; and he had sufficient desire for learning to begin the study of Greek on his own and to arrange for special instruction in it outside school. Long before he completed high school, he determined to go to college; moreover, he insisted that it be an eastern college. Although his father wanted him to attend the University of Minnesota, Lewis's own first choice was Harvard; it seems to have been his father who made the final decision in favor of Yale. In preparation for university, he spent some months, beginning in September, 1902, at Oberlin Academy in Ohio.

Oberlin remained in his mind as a place where smoking was forbidden and class parties were opened "with a powerful prayer by some student in training as a Y.M.C.A. secretary."[8] Under other names, it is depicted satirically in several of his novels, most notably *Elmer Gantry*. But the Lewis who entered Oberlin did not scoff at its evangelism. Though there was little religious feeling in his family—they were Congregationalists, but the religious sentiment went no deeper than the father's opinion that religion was a good thing for the community—and though some biographical accounts emphasize his early "unwillingness to accept ready-made opinions, his iconoclasm about accepted dogmas such as Jonah and the whale,"[9] he apparently underwent a conversion. From the first, he described himself as favorably impressed by Oberlin's muscular Christianity. In fact, he practiced it himself: like Elmer Gantry he pumped a handcar, in bitter winter weather, to a nearby town where he taught Sunday school. For a time he wanted to become a missionary, preferably to some very demanding region of the world such as Africa.

[8] "My First Day in New York," *The Man from Main Street*, pp. 56–57.

[9] "A Sketch of the Life of Sinclair Lewis," in Stuart P. Sherman, *The Significance of Sinclair Lewis* (New York: Harcourt, Brace, 1922), p. 21.

This religious enthusiasm soon disappeared; it was certainly gone well before the end of Lewis's first year at Yale. William Lyon Phelps, who was one of his professors, related that at the university Lewis was universally known as "Red," partly because of his hair and partly because of his radical opinions, "which he took no pains to conceal."[10] The comment suggests that he was a misfit at Yale; in Phelps' judgment, he was not really disliked but looked upon as an amiable freak. Schorer, on the other hand, considers that he was friendless and isolated; he was continually trying to make an impression on the leaders of the undergraduate community, and each time he was rebuffed—thrown back among the strays and the eccentrics. Nevertheless, he received encouragement from some of the faculty members, especially Phelps and another English instructor who was destined to become a distinguished scholar, Chauncey B. Tinker. His one clear ambition was to write; he kept submitting contributions to the Yale *Literary Magazine* and the *Courant*, and in March, 1904, he became the first member of his class to have something published in the *Lit.* It was a poem on Launcelot, in the manner of Tennyson, and it began

> Blow, weary wind,
> The golden rod scarce chiding;
> Sir Launcelot is riding
> By shady wood-paths pleasant
> To fields of yellow corn.

In spite of his radicalism, he remained very much the naive romanticist.

[10] William Lyon Phelps, *Autobiography with Letters* (New York: Oxford University Press, 1939), p. 658. Lewis's independence and radicalism are emphasized in reminiscences of him as a college student by two of his Yale friends: William Rose Benét, "The Earlier Lewis," *Saturday Review of Literature*, X (January 20, 1934), 421–422, and Leonard Bacon, "Yale '09," *Saturday Review of Literature*, XIX (February 4, 1939), 13–14.

Instead of returning to Sauk Centre at the end of his freshman year, Lewis worked for a brief time as a waiter in a Harvard dining room and then sailed from Portland, Maine, to Liverpool on a cattle boat. This was a quixotic type of adventure, since it involved eleven days of subsisting in filthy conditions, eating unpalatable food, and doing backbreaking work on a rolling ship, all for the reward of spending eight days in England without the means to see it. When he landed again in the United States, he was penniless, and he had to spend his first night ashore in the Portland railway station.

Although he was full of ambition to get back to college, the ambition soon faded and he went into a sophomore slump. Both the *Lit* and the *Courant*, however, published stories and poems by him, and a widely read magazine, *The Critic*, accepted an article pointing out similarities between a recent best seller by Katherine Cecil Thurston and an older novel by Israel Zangwill. Lewis was paid twenty dollars for the article, and it was noticed—though its allegation of plagiarism was deprecated—by the book section of the New York *Times*. Exhilarated by this success, Lewis began churning out poems, short stories, and whimsical essays in profusion, and sending them on the rounds of the magazines. During the summer of 1905, he was at home in Sauk Centre; he found it dull. Yet by this time he had learned from Hamlin Garland's *Main-Travelled Roads* that it was possible to write of the Midwest realistically. He began to think that the very dullness he experienced, the product of what he called the "village virus," might provide the subject for a novel.

Because of his contributions to the *Lit* and the *Courant*, Lewis was on the editorial boards of both in his third year of college. In three "Editor's Table" essays from the *Lit* which are reprinted in *The Man from Main Street*, he is seen lecturing his fellow students on their limited knowledge of New Haven and its history and on their failure to recognize that the greatest contributions to college life were probably not being made by the "typical Yale men" but by the heretics and dissidents. The editorials convey an image of their writer as a proud and independent spirit who would make no compromise with the mediocre or the ignoble. The proud and independent spirit, however, would do incredibly abject things for the sake of getting something into print. The verse which he sent to magazines became more and more banal; in the autumn of 1905 he began securing three-dollar successes with cute little rhymes—"elephantinely kittenish," Schorer terms them—on subjects such as a pussy and a puppy and a doll in the midst of a wash-tub sea.

The following summer he made another cattle-boat trip to England; this time he was able to do several weeks of sight-seeing. He returned to Yale in an unsettled mood; and in late October he and a friend, Allan Updegraff, decided to leave the university altogether and to go stay at Helicon Hall, Upton Sinclair's experiment in communal living on the Palisades near Englewood, New Jersey. Lewis's parents had the shock of seeing their son leave college in his final year, and for a radical colony under the direction of a notorious socialist. At Helicon Hall, Lewis worked as a janitor; in a somewhat facetious account of the experience, "Two Yale Men in Utopia," which appeared in the New York *Sun* on December 16, 1906,[11] he described his bungling attempts at manual labor and revealed that he lasted just a month in the colony. Then he and Updegraff tried their own experiments in living, in some of the seedier districts of New York City. Both of them failed to make a go of it. When free-lancing proved unprofitable, and a job as a trans-

[11] Reprinted in *The Man from Main Street*, pp. 61–69.

lator for *Transatlantic Tales* dull and menial, Lewis left New York for Panama, traveling steerage, in the hope of getting work on the construction of the Canal. This venture came to nothing, however; only by good fortune was he able to return to New York, and by Christmas he was again in New Haven. He was readmitted to Yale through a special faculty vote, and in June, 1908, after completing a full year's work in little more than one semester, he received his degree. By that time he was sufficiently reconciled to academic life to think of taking a Ph.D. in English, but his real ambition was still to be a writer.

Lewis once expressed regret that the period had been so short in which he had been "a patently useless, irregular, undependable young man, wandering and getting fired, earning almost nothing and seeing almost everything."[12] This phase of his life began when he left home in July, 1908, to take an editorial job with the Waterloo, Iowa, *Daily Courier*. It was not long before he was trying to save enough money to take him to New York; the paper was very glad to see him go. In New York he found employment with the Joint Application Bureau of the Charity Organization Society and the Association for the Improvement of the Condition of the Poor; this was his first encounter with the alphabetical agencies which were to figure so largely in his novels. Rescue came through "two kind women who wrote sentimental mountaineer novels";[13] Grace MacGowan Cooke and her sister Alice MacGowan, whom he had met at Helicon Hall, wired him from Carmel, California, asking whether he would care to go there as their secretary. Having sold a story to *Redbook* magazine for seventy-five dollars, he was able to buy a ticket to California on a day coach.

[12] "I'm an Old Newspaperman Myself," *The Man from Main Street*, p. 88.

[13] Grace Hegger Lewis, *With Love from Gracie: Sinclair Lewis: 1912–1925* (New York: Harcourt, Brace, 1955), p. 20.

Carmel was then comparatively undiscovered; Lewis called it "the nearest to a young writer's paradise that I have ever seen" and said that he spent "six months in Arcady," six months as "a citizen in a Californian mirage."[14] He shared a cottage or shack with an aspiring poet and fellow Yale man, William Rose Benét; since their rent was only fifteen dollars a month and they were frequently invited to picnics on the beach, their expenses were minimal. Either because his employers were undemanding or because he neglected the work he was supposed to do for them, Lewis was able to concentrate on his own writing. But in his writer's paradise, significant themes did not grow on trees: beyond concocting some short-story plots which he sold to Jack London, he produced nothing except potboilers. Through the Cookes, he gained an entree to *Nautilus*, a magazine devoted to New Thought, the philosophico-religious movement which emphasized mental healing, the "creative power of constructive thinking," putting oneself in tune with the infinite, and so on; for this magazine he wrote a short story and a serial, both full of syrupy optimism. When the opportunity to write was given him, the results made it questionable that he would ever rise above the level of Grub Street.

His idyllic life at Carmel soon ended, however—the Cookes came to realize that he was not justifying his title of secretary; and Lewis worked for two months on the San Francisco *Bulletin* and for a slightly longer period as wire editor for the Associated Press. From both positions he was dismissed for incompetence. "So I went back East," he wrote, "to Occupy a Responsible Position, on a magazine called *The Volta Review*, a journal for teachers of the deaf . . . ."[15] The "Responsible Position" paid fifteen dollars a week; it was offered to Lewis by the

---

[14] *The Man from Main Street*, p. 88.
[15] *Ibid.*, p. 96.

editor, a Yale friend named F. K. Noyes. The work was dreary, Noyes was hard to get along with, and Lewis stood it for only six months. Then he moved to New York, to the first job he was to stick at—that of manuscript reader with the Frederick A. Stokes publishing company.

Between 1910 and 1915 Lewis was, as he put it, "a very prosaic and unenterprising editor in New York, acquiring a wife, and a conviction that he never would, never could, learn to compose anything more imaginative than advertisements for bad novels . . . ."[16] During his two-year period with Stokes, he was moved into publicity work, which he entered with much more zest than the comment above would have led us to anticipate. In October, 1912, he became assistant editor of *Adventure* magazine, at twenty dollars a week; the following August he was astonished to receive an offer of sixty dollars a week to edit a syndicated book page for newspapers. When the syndicate came to an end in the uncertainties surrounding the beginning of the First World War, he was hired by George H. Doran as editorial assistant and advertising manager. Doran's was a well-known publishing house with a distinguished list of authors, among them Arnold Bennett, Compton Mackenzie, Somerset Maugham, and Hugh Walpole. In spite of his own statement to the contrary, Lewis had good novels to deal with as well as bad, and he proved to be a very enterprising booster of them. After several false starts, he seemed to have found his métier.

What had happened to his radicalism? In 1911 he had joined the Socialist party; his socialism, however, seems to have been inspired by Wells and Shaw, whom he could read, rather than by Marx, whom he could not. It was an outgrowth of his dissidence rather than a clearly formulated political creed; Dorothy Thompson was later

[16] *Ibid.,* p. 50.

to describe him as "basically apolitical."[17] Although he was living in Greenwich Village, he did not share its mentality; he had no sympathy with most of its *avant-garde* causes. Margaret Anderson discovered this when she came from Chicago to seek support for her *Little Review;* she could not interest Lewis in her proposed magazine of experimental writing, and she received a lecture from him on the danger of being remote from the common herd and neglecting the psychology of the average person. He made his best friends not from among the bohemians and the radicals but among his associates in the publishing business such as Alfred Harcourt and Harry Maule; their main concern was not the overthrow of the system but personal advancement within it. His radicalism was tempered as well by the fact that he was now a married man.

In September, 1912, when Lewis was still with Stokes, he met a girl in a freight elevator; her name was Grace Livingstone Hegger, and she worked in the *Vogue* office in the same building. Though Carl Van Doren assures us that Lewis's romantic fantasies did not outlast his boyhood,[18] he was still so much a romantic when he began to court Grace that he cast himself in the role of "Jacques the Jester" or "François the Troubadour" begging his "silver maiden," his "faraway princess," to throw open her casement and listen to his songs. Grace had still another role for him, that of "Best Playmate"; together they went "daventuring" on weekends, for Lewis could, like O. Henry, see New York as Baghdad on the Subway and find it fascinating to explore. As time went on, he talked less of châteaus in Provence and more of little cottages somewhat nearer. In her book *With Love from*

[17] "The Boy . . . from Sauk Centre," p. 42.

[18] Carl Van Doren, *Sinclair Lewis: A Biographical Sketch* (Garden City: Doubleday, Doren, 1933), p. 34.

Gracie, the first Mrs. Lewis gives a revealing picture of Lewis during the years when he was preparing for and writing his most important novels; at the same time, her book discloses something of the vanity, frivolity, and pseudo sophistication which Lewis put into the character of Fran in *Dodsworth*. When Mrs. Lewis tells us that she chose a French maid partly because it pleased her to give orders in French before guests, and when she appends to a picture of herself and her son in riding dress the comment that for her to ride in the Bois when the chestnuts were in bloom was to fulfill a dream of years, one wonders how she could ever have been compatible with a man who said that his one consistent attitude was an old-fashioned American hatred of bunk. The truth seems to be that Lewis was not consistent even in his dislike of putting on airs; he was almost as much himself when he cultivated a monocle, a gray Homburg, and cream linen spats as when he ridiculed such symbols of elegance. For a time the princess remained aloof and unyielding; but when, a year after they had first met, Lewis brought her a copy of his first novel and showed her that it was dedicated to her, she realized the sincerity of his affection and began to reciprocate it. They were married on April 15, 1914, in an Ethical Culture meeting house. Their first home was not a white cottage but a brown bungalow in Port Washington, Long Island.

The book dedicated to Grace was actually Lewis's second. In August, 1912, Stokes had published an adventure story for boys, *Hike and the Aeroplane*, written by Lewis under the pseudonym Tom Graham. He had ground it out to order during the previous summer, in the shortest possible time. It was hack work, written only for the money, but it testified to the strength of his ambition. Even though he had become a successful huckster of books—at this time, according to his wife, "no one was writing cleverer book jackets or planting publicity more adroitly than Sinclair Lewis" [19]—he was making a strenuous effort to carry on with his own writing, and the two hundred dollars he received for *Hike* enabled him to spend the month of July, 1912, at Provincetown completing the first draft of a more serious attempt at fiction. After it had been rejected by several other publishers, the manuscript was accepted by Harper's in June, 1913, and in the following February it was published under the title *Our Mr. Wrenn*. Sinclair Lewis the novelist was launched on his career.

[19] *With Love from Gracie*, p. 67.

2. Opiates for the Tired Business Man

"THE TIRED BUSINESS MAN will find just the right antidote for weariness in *Our Mr. Wrenn*, a gently satiric novel by Sinclair Lewis." [1] This about the future author of *Main Street* and *Babbitt*? This about H. L. Mencken's ally in the excoriation of the "booboisie"? If the anonymous critic in the *Review of Reviews* was correct in his judgment, Lewis did not always manifest the dissatisfaction with American conditions and the earnest desire for change which are so often considered characteristic of him. In fact, he exhibited as much complacency as rebelliousness in the novels before *Main Street*.

The subtitle of this first novel, *The Romantic Adventures of a Gentle Man*, recalls H. G. Wells; the debt to the author of *Kipps* and *The History of Mr. Polly* is obvious throughout. Mr. Wrenn is a sales-order clerk in a New York office, a pathetic little man trying to fulfill his romantic dreams in a hostile world. Like Kipps, he secures release from monotonous routine but finds his new way

[1] *American Review of Reviews*, XLIX (1914), 628.

of life as restrictive as the old one: Mr. Wrenn takes a trip to England, which for him is only "a cold and friendless prison." Like Kipps, he finds that money introduces him to people outside his own class; in England, a frustrated would-be artist named Istra Nash leads him into the arty world which Lewis terms "hobohemia." Just as Kipps is befuddled by anagram teas and bewildered by polite manners, Mr. Wrenn is thrown into inarticulate agony when he is asked his opinion about the sins of the eternal bourgeoisie or the current Rodin vogue. Like Kipps, he wants to marry above his station, but he is eventually brought "To a Happy Shore" (the title of the last chapter), where a romantic marriage supplants his dreams of Arcady and Mandalay.

Our Mr. Wrenn seems to have the same thesis as *Mr. Polly*—that if you do not like your life you can change it. But Wells' picture of life has one important difference from Lewis's. Mr. Polly alters his mode of existence by finding an idyllic haven; he withdraws from the economic hurly-burly altogether. Indeed, Wells introduces a "highbrow gentleman" into his book to point out that, until the whole scheme of things is revised, there will always be thousands of small shopkeepers like Mr. Polly living marginal existences. Similarly Kipps, at the end of his vicissitudes, muses on how rum the world is; money comes and money goes, and the Kippses of this world cannot control it—or their circumstances. But Mr. Wrenn can control his. During his trip to England aboard a cattle boat, his character changes marvelously: he loses his meekness, becomes "one of the gang," beats up a tormentor twice his size. When he returns to America he sees it with new eyes, and he realizes that life in it need not be drab. He is not compelled to remain in his old boardinghouse, which is run by a tyrannical slattern; he can have a decent home, meet congenial friends, and hope to find a wife. Even the humdrum office routine can be changed, and business can become a joyous adventure: he embarks on a campaign to increase his firm's business in the South and carries it off successfully. Opportunity comes to the man who is alert; by the end of the book, the new Mr. Wrenn is on his way to becoming, if not a captain of industry, at least a subaltern. If Lewis takes from Wells the theme of the little man helpless before the complexities of the modern world, he ignores or distorts the implications Wells draws from the theme.

A difference in tone between the two writers is also noticeable. Lewis is not quite so sympathetic to his central character as Wells is to his; he is much more patronizing. Into Mr. Wrenn he has put something of his own experiences of loneliness and yearning; but he cannot present these emotions honestly, and takes refuge behind a curtain of superciliousness. Whereas Wells convinces us of the depth of his feeling for the little man, the plaything of social forces, Lewis's Mr. Wrenn never becomes more than the plaything of his author.

Before we move off into the wonderland where small men beat up big men and go on walking tours with fabulous redheads, there is a considerable amount of realistic writing. Mr. Wrenn's boardinghouse is made almost as repulsive as George Orwell's in *The Road to Wigan Pier*. But if the unpleasantness of Mr. Wrenn's life is effectively conveyed, the weight of social criticism in the book is not sufficient to make it appear the author's major concern. "One puts the book down in a pleasant frame of mind," wrote the *Nation*'s reviewer, "with the feeling of having wandered a while in an odd and delightful world of make-believe."[2] A novel which gives such an impression is a very different thing from the novel Wells would have written, even though Arthur B. Coleman described *Our*

[2] *Nation*, XCVIII (1914), 266.

Mr. Wrenn as "all Wells."[3] Wells saw the novel as part of what he eventually called his "Open Conspiracy" against society; it was to be "the social mediator, the vehicle of understanding, the instrument of self-examination, the parade of morals, . . . the factory of customs, the criticism of laws and institutions and of social dogmas and ideas."[4] If Lewis at times viewed the novel as a parade of morals and an instrument of self-examination, he never looked on it in such a comprehensive way as Wells. Furthermore, it is doubtful that he would have agreed with what Wells went on to add—that the chief purpose of a novel was "the ventilation of the point at issue," and that the novelist should not "sweep under the mat for crumbs of characterization . . . ."

It seems necessary, then, to qualify any generalization about Wells' influence on Lewis. No doubt in at least some of his novels Lewis's first consideration was the exposure of some social ill; no doubt he felt, as Wells did, that society needed to be reconstructed. He had assimilated ideas then freely circulated, and he had taken over, especially from Wells and Thorstein Veblen, the

[3] In his doctoral dissertation entitled "The Genesis of Social Ideas in Sinclair Lewis (New York University, 1954), Arthur B. Coleman declares that in his first five novels Lewis relied on Wells, Shaw, Garland, Veblen, and Mencken for all of his important characters, all of his important themes, and all of the ideas of any sort. He puts special emphasis on Lewis's debt to Wells and Veblen. On Veblen's influence he is particularly interesting; but though he substantiates many of his claims, I feel that he overstresses the influences of all of these writers on Lewis. For example, he describes the hero of Lewis's second novel in these terms: "Carl is the Veblenian engineer, with a good deal of the Wellsian scientific socialist and the Shavian superman potential." I cannot feel that the description is meaningful.

[4] The terms are taken from the "Digression about Novels" in Wells' *Experiment in Autobiography* (London: Gollancz, 1934), especially pp. 492 ff. Though this statement of principles was written many years later, by the time of the writing of *Our Mr. Wrenn*, Wells' concept of the novel had already become clearly apparent through his own novels, his controversy with Henry James, and his discussion "The Contemporary Novel," a version of which appeared in the *Atlantic Monthly* in January, 1912.

notions of a warfare between creative and acquisitive instincts and of the necessity to find a new social framework which would liberate rather than enslave man's potentialities. Van Wyck Brooks could see in Lewis a mind which "had something in common with the . . . circle of [Randolph] Bourne," and perceived behind Lewis's novels "the hovering presence of this image of a world with which the author was always comparing the visible world as it was . . . ."[5] But when Brooks adds, "For Lewis the treatment was secondary, while he devoted all his care to the documentation of the all-important subject,"[6] he is clearly in error. Wells was so much imbued with a sense of the subject that he wrote, "I am a journalist . . . . I refuse to play the artist. If sometimes I am an artist it is a freak of the gods. I am journalist all the time and what I write *goes now*—and will presently die."[7] Lewis viewed the matter differently. "If you have it in you to produce one thunderingly good novel, one really big novel, just one," he wrote, "your place in American literature will be safe for the next hundred years."[8] Wells was a reformer first and a novelist second; though Lewis might wave the banner of reform, sometimes very

[5] Van Wyck Brooks, *The Confident Years, 1885–1915* (London: Dent 1953), p. 297. Bourne died in 1918 at the age of thirty-two; his *History of a Literary Radical*, edited by Brooks, appeared in 1920. Lewis shared many of the views expressed in Bourne's famous essay "The Puritan's Will to Power," which was published in *Seven Arts* in April, 1917, but the lineaments of the intellectual, as Bourne drew them a few months later, are not those of Lewis at all. This second essay by Bourne, "Below the Battle," appeared in *Seven Arts* in July, 1917, and is reprinted in Henry F. May's *The Discontent of the Intellectuals: A Problem of the Twenties*, "Berkeley Series in American History" (Chicago: Rand McNally, 1963), pp. 14–19.

[6] *The Confident Years*, p. 301.

[7] *Autobiography*, p. 623.

[8] "How I Wrote a Novel on Trains and Beside the Kitchen Sink," *The Man from Main Street: Collected Essays and Other Writings, 1904–1950*, ed. Harry E. Maule and Melville H. Cane (New York: Random House, 1953), pp. 201–202.

vigorously, his main ambition was not to change the world but to write the great American novel.

When Perry Miller sought to discover the major influences upon Lewis, he found that the one writer from whom he could be said to derive was Dickens. There was little to be gained, Miller learned, by asking him about the realists and naturalists: "He had read here and there, but most of them meant little to him, except for Shaw and Wells, who to him were primarily writers that showed what might be done with Dickensian exaggeration in a modern situation."[9] As Martin Light observes, Lewis could find in Dickens both social commentary and a reforming impulse, but he was less attracted to these than to Dickens' evocation of a social milieu through the creation of a great number of memorable characters.[10] Only two years before *Mr. Wrenn*, Wells had made an oblique attack, in a discussion of contemporary fiction,[11] on the notion that the novelist was primarily interested in character; Lewis apparently followed the Dickens who wrote, "I thought of Mr. Pickwick, and wrote the first number . . . ."[12] Lewis declared in 1924 that

> of all the topics in the world, the most interesting is humankind, people and what they are like . . . . That is why fiction—the recounting of human customs—is the most popular form of writing; that is why, in fiction, a garrulous account of human foibles is more stirring than the trickiest melodrama or the sublimest philosophy.[13]

[9] Perry Miller, "The Incorruptible Sinclair Lewis," *Atlantic Monthly*, CLXXXVII (April 1951), 32.

[10] Martin Light, "A Study of Characterization in Sinclair Lewis's Fiction" (Ph.D. dissertation, University of Illinois, 1960), p. 4.

[11] In "The Contemporary Novel," which was first delivered as a lecture to the *Times* Book Club. See note 4, above.

[12] Preface to *Pickwick Papers*, "Oxford Illustrated Dickens" (London: Oxford University Press, 1947), p. xi.

[13] "A Pilgrim's Progress," *The Man from Main Street*, p. 165.

Very few of the characters in *Our Mr. Wrenn* are presented in a satiric light. When they are, the author's view of them is far from radical; it is often even philistine. Intellectuals prove easy targets; there is a Stanford professor of English, for example, who writes poetry which he files under the letter *p*. Istra Nash, the cigarette-smoking hellion of a type to be caricatured by many twentieth-century novelists, receives more charitable treatment than one might expect: she is shown as restless and unfulfilled, and therefore more pathetic than ridiculous. But her friends, overflowing with advanced chatter about the arts they practice either badly or not at all, are handled savagely:

> Then came the superradicals, to confuse the radicals who confused Mr. Wrenn.
> For always there is a greater rebellion; and though you sell your prayer-book to buy Bakunine, and esteem yourself revolutionary to the point of madness, you shall find one who calls you reactionary. The scorners came in together—Moe Tchatzsky, the syndicalist and direct actionist, and Jane Schott, the writer of impressionistic prose—and they sat silently sneering on a couch [119–120].[14]

Lewis makes little effort to individualize his arty types; they remain only grotesque names associated with grotesque attitudes. Some of the other characters are portrayed with similar crude exaggeration, but more fully and vividly:

> Mrs. Zapp was a fat landlady. When she sat down there was a straight line from her chin to her knees. She was usually sitting down. When she moved she groaned, and her apparel creaked. She groaned and creaked from

[14] *Our Mr. Wrenn* (New York: Harcourt, Brace, 1923). For each novel, the edition quoted from will be specified in a note to the first quotation, and all page numbers in brackets or parentheses will refer to that edition.

bed to breakfast, and ate five griddlecakes, two helpin's of scrapple, an egg, some rump steak, and three cups of coffee, slowly and resentfully. She creaked and groaned from breakfast to her rocking-chair, and sat about wondering why Providence had inflicted upon her a weak digestion. Mr. Wrenn also wondered why, sympathetically, but Mrs. Zapp was too conscientiously dolorous to be much cheered by the sympathy of a nigger-lovin' Yankee, who couldn't appreciate the subtle sorrows of a Zapp of Zapp's Bog, allied to all the First Families of Virginia [3].

This description tells us a great deal about Lewis's methods. Obviously he is creating a character in two senses of the word—both an imaginary person and an odd or eccentric person; and he is using what Walter Allen considers the normal English method of character creation and what Lord David Cecil calls the normal English method before George Eliot. Allen explains it in this way:

A French novelist, inventing a miser or hypocrite, is interested in the quality of miserliness or hypocrisy. An English novelist is much more likely to stress the comic aspects of miserliness or hypocrisy, so much so, indeed, that both he and his readers may be in danger of forgetting the vice in their appreciation of the idiosyncrasies which are its result. [15]

Lewis undoubtedly followed Wells and his other beloved master, Dickens, in endeavoring to secure humorous effects by gross exaggeration of physical details. At the same time, the laconic third sentence has a home-grown flavor; Mrs. Zapp is a decayed representative of the southern aristocracy; and the total effect is distinctively American. The passage suggests that the writer belongs

[15] Walter Allen, *The English Novel* (London: Phoenix House, 1954), pp. 285–286. See also David Cecil, *Early Victorian Novelists* (Harmondsworth: Penguin Books, 1948), Chap. VIII, especially p. 227.

to the tradition of American satire described by Constance Rourke as that of Mark Twain, Bret Harte, and Artemus Ward.[16] The satire is vulgar, earthy, and broadly absurd; it is blunt and obvious and good-naturedly cynical; sometimes it relies upon understatement and sometimes upon exaggeration. A typically American position is suggested by the assault on pretension, that of a man of the people, a defender of custom and common sense, a scoffer at innovation and theory and the trappings of culture.

It is strange to find Lewis also in the tradition exemplified in his time chiefly by the hundred or more novels of Horatio Alger and at a later time by the writings of Norman Vincent Peale—the tradition which emphasizes that virtue, industry, and the proper amount of self-confidence bring guaranteed material rewards. Even Mr. Wrenn, ineffectual as he appears to be, can find satisfaction for most of his desires within the existing system. We are tempted to think that Lewis was writing down to his audience and falsifying his beliefs. But *Our Mr. Wrenn* was not a potboiler; the product of the most strenuous effort, it was the best Lewis could do at the time he wrote it, and years later he wrote in a copy which he inscribed for a friend that it was the only book of his which he had ever loved. It was not out of keeping with his character for him to write a story showing the rewards of industry; in some moods, he was quite prepared to write parables befitting the Puritan tradition. We expect, and find, satire of Puritanism in Lewis, but from his father he inherited a considerable respect for the Puritan virtues. When Dorothy Thompson observed, "How many characteristics of his father the author-son displayed!" it was just after she had given some examples of Dr. Lewis's sense

[16] Constance Rourke, *American Humor* (New York: Harcourt, Brace, 1931), pp. 283–285 particularly.

of duty, scrupulousness regarding debts, and hatred of slackness.[17] In his second novel Lewis said that it was his hero's destiny to restore the "wintry Pilgrim virtues" to his native land.

Lewis's America, then, is an open society in which the honest, industrious, imaginative man can find prosperity. In part, as his description of the "ragged vacant lots" of New York and "the tame grassy shore of a real-estate boomer's suburb" shows, he possesses the Wellsian vision of a muddled world which badly needs straightening out. He also follows Wells in urging the application of scientific principles in all departments of life. But he usually rebels at the notion of institutions or organizations which will put the findings of rational investigation into practice in society. Paradoxically, if like Wells he preaches emancipation from hidebound custom and convention, he does not imitate Wells in rejecting codes of behavior imitated from the past; he is really guided, as Henry Seidel Canby points out, by a code of individualism stereotyped from the heroic age of the frontier.[18] The cultural myths which derived from the impact of a new and unspoiled land upon its settlers, such myths as those described by Henry Nash Smith in his *Virgin Land* and by R. W. B. Lewis in *The American Adam*,[19] are deeply imbedded in his mind. A belief that the character of America is defined, not by streams of influence from the past, or by cultural tradition, or by the nation's place in an Atlantic or a world community, but by responses to the challenges offered by the American continent itself; a faith in prog-

[17] "The Boy and Man from Sauk Centre," *Atlantic Monthly*, CCVI (November 1960), 44.

[18] Robert E. Spiller *et al.*, *A Literary History of the United States* (New York: Macmillan, 1948), II, 1222.

[19] Henry Nash Smith, *Virgin Land* (Cambridge: Harvard University Press, 1950), especially p. 186; R. W. B. Lewis, *The American Adam* (Chicago: Chicago University Press, 1955), especially pp. 1 and 5.

ress; a distrust of the foreign; a conception of the American as a new man, free from the burden of mankind's guilt-ridden past, a figure of great potentialities at the start of a new history; a belief that class distinctions should be inadmissible in the United States—these are some of Lewis's most enduring convictions. It is on the basis of his hopes for America that he satirizes its shortcomings.

The conservatism of *Our Mr. Wrenn* might seem belied by an article entitled "Relation of the Novel to the Present Social Unrest: The Passing of Capitalism" which Lewis wrote for the *Bookman* (November, 1914). Surveying the English and American literary scenes, he states that almost every important writer presents the individual conflicts of his characters against the background of an imminent struggle over capitalism. The article is not polemical, however, and it avoids positive commitment. Lewis indicates a desire for change when he says that the conditions described in Frank Norris's *Octopus* will no longer be tolerated if enough young men ask themselves the how and the why of society; but he is just as prepared to see a new capitalism, a new autocracy, or even a new anarchism as he is to see the triumph of socialism. In his survey, he gives the place of honor to Wells; in fact, he awards him the "somewhat perilous" title of the greatest living novelist. Hazardous as this judgment was, Lewis provided an even better example of his failure to discriminate in 1917, when, dedicating a novel to the "splendid assembly" of young British writers, he described them all—such diverse figures as Compton Mackenzie, Oliver Onions (the disciple of Romain Rolland), Gilbert Cannan (the disciple of Samuel Butler), and D. H. Lawrence—as followers of H. G. Wells.

This period of his life was described by Grace Lewis as the only time her husband cherished the idea of a home and of roots. In the domestic bliss of Port Washington, the two of them read the surprisingly appreciative reviews of *Mr. Wrenn*. With this encouragement, he kept at his writing. In the *American Magazine* for April 1921, he told "How I Wrote a Novel on Trains and Beside the Kitchen Sink." On weekends, and weekday mornings when he could manage to get up an hour early, and during his morning and evening commuter trips, he worked away at his second novel. He emphasizes here, as he always did, that writing is hard work; the person with the necessary determination will somehow find the time to make the requisite number of black marks on white paper. If the story as he tells it is somewhat heightened, there is no questioning the extraordinary stamina, concentration, and will power which enabled him to write this second novel, four hundred pages long, in just over a year, while he was carrying on a full-time job with Doran's. He was doing his best to live the American success story.

Though it is dedicated to a group of "optimistic rebels," *The Trail of the Hawk*, which was published in September 1915, shows little more radicalism than *Our Mr. Wrenn*. Once again it is a Horatio Alger story: the small-town boy, Carl Ericson, wins fame as an aviator and marries the daughter of an aristocratic New York family. Yet he is described as a born rebel against conventions. While he is at Plato College, he takes the side of a socialistic professor in a controversy, and is shamefully expelled. The professor's social doctrine is derived almost entirely from Wells; in a lecture, he unfolds the simple vision of Wells' *Anticipations*: "The great vision of the glory that shall be, not in one sudden millennium, but slowly advancing toward joys of life we can no more prevision than the aboriginal medicine man could imagine the X-ray!" [20] His socialism is a rallying cry rather than a clear political

[20] *The Trail of the Hawk* (New York: Harcourt, Brace, 1923).

program, and it does not differ markedly from Rotarianism: "If we would take thought all together, and work together, as a football team does, we would start making a perfect world" (81). In any case, socialism is not a major motivating force in the novel. Though Carl Ericson is an opponent of the leisure class, his interest in social reform does not go beyond a desire for freedom from unreasonable restrictions and freedom to contribute to progress through his inventions. The book does not satirize the American system, but endeavors to define its essence:

> Since Carl Ericson . . . was the divinely restless seeker of the romance that must—or we die!—lie beyond the hills, you first see him in action . . . . But equally, since this is a serious study of an average young American, there should be an indication of his soil-nourished ancestry.
>
> Carl was second-generation Norwegian; American-born, American in speech, American in appearance, save for his flaxen hair and china-blue eyes; and, thanks to the flag-decked public school, overwhelmingly American in tradition. When he was born the "typical Americans" of earlier stocks had moved to city palaces or were marooned on run-down farms. It was Carl Ericson, not a Trowbridge or a Stuyvesant or a Lee or a Grant, who was the "typical American" of his period. It was for him to carry on the American destiny of extending the Western horizon; his to restore the wintry Pilgrim virtues and the exuberant, October, partridge-drumming days of Daniel Boone; then to add, in his own or another generation, new American aspirations for beauty. [5–6].

Behind this passage lies a variant of the frontier myth. As many critics have noted, American writers have depicted a succession of frontiers of different types. Lucy Lockwood Hazard, for example, has divided her study *The Frontier in American Literature* into literary treatments of regional pioneering, industrial pioneering, and spiritual

pioneering.[21] In *The Trail of the Hawk*, Lewis is inquiring
what outlets for the pioneering spirit can be found in
twentieth-century America. He is asserting that the period
of almost boundless opportunity has not passed, that
there is still an opening into a freer, more abundant life
than has previously been known, and that the search
for this life calls forth the best in man. If the geographical
frontier has vanished, he believes, other frontiers will
have to be found, or the American spirit will become a
stunted, wasting thing. Furthermore, though he complained about the clamorous insistence of Americans on
hustling nowhere in particular,[22] he admires the hustler
rather than the contemplative man; his hero must be a
restless seeker, a doer, a man of action.

Satire often takes the disillusioned view that opportunities for heroism have disappeared. This is not Lewis's
opinion. Such age-old themes of romance as the perilous
journey, the crucial struggle, and the overcoming of
seemingly insurmountable obstacles are to be met in his
novels, even though he tries to find new settings for them.
He sees the need of a new type of folk hero to replace
such legendary figures as Natty Bumppo and Davy
Crockett; a decade before Lindbergh became the embod-
iment of the myth, Lewis makes the hero of *The Trail of
the Hawk* an aviator. In *Tono-Bungay*, Wells' hero Remington had been both a flier and an inventor as Carl Ericson
was to be, but Remington's primary function was that
of commentator and social critic. Moreover, Lewis's central character is not only the new man but the new
American. The passage quoted above ends with the idea
of specifically American responses to experience, new ways
to fit a new nation.

[21] Lucy Lockwood Hazard, *The Frontier in American Literature* (New York:
Crowell, 1927), pp. xvii–xviii.

[22] *The Man from Main Street*, pp. 205–206.

Carl's wanderlust impels him onward, not necessarily to higher and better things, but to experiences which are new and different. After he has risen from packer in a department store to part-owner of an automobile repair shop, he hears of the first successful flights of Curtis and the Wright brothers; he recognizes instinctively that here is the career for which his whole undisciplined nature has been longing. His conquest of the air might reasonably serve as the climax of his story. Instead, Lewis sends him on to new frontiers which are tame in comparison—so tame that the reader finds it hard to understand Lewis's excitement over them. When Carl invents and markets something called a Touricar, he is acting as a Veblenian engineer and contributing to progress through technology; far from ridiculing the myth of perpetual advancement through industrial development, Lewis accepts it enthusiastically. Finally Lewis brings Carl to still another frontier, the frontier of business forms. As in *Mr. Wrenn*, romance occurs where it is least expected; those who have eyes to see can easily find it in the world of business. Partly because of marriage, Carl becomes a caged hawk for a time, confined to an office job and a New York apartment. In the end, however, he flies away to freedom; when we last see them, he and his wife are on the way to Buenos Aires, where he is going as "Argentine Republic manager for the Van Zile Motor Corporation, possessed of an unimportant salary, a possibility of large commissions, and hopes like comets." The "socialism"' of the book seems to have evaporated; no Chamber of Commerce president could wish for a better vindication of his principles. In the modern world, the frontier spirit may find expression in such obviously hazardous activities as flying airplanes, but there is no need to seek it in them: it is also the spirit of daring which causes a man to leave a safe office job and take something on a commission basis.

If there is satire in the book, then, it is not directed at blind faith in material or technological progress, or at boosting and bustling; rather, it is aimed at whatever impedes the free movement of the Carl Ericsons, especially the small town, the small college, and the restrictive social groups:

> The school-bound child—taught by young ladies that the worst immorality was whispering in school, the chief virtue, a dull quietude . . . [22]. Life at Plato was suspicious, prejudiced, provincial . . . [62]. They were all so uniformly polite, so neat-minded and church-going and dull [245].

Yet this novel, like the previous one, offers little to outrage the tired business man. One possible way of escape from dullness and provincialism is a bohemian way of life, but it is sharply ridiculed. The opposing point of view—that the poet has less to offer humanity than the automobile dealer who introduces the city dweller to the beauties of nature—is presented with the author's full sympathy.

For his attack on convention, Lewis is satisfied to employ characters who are no more than puppets. An example is S. Alcott Wood, president of Plato College, given the damning attributes of being a conservative, a Bible reader, and an opponent of socialism. He is valorous in the pulpit, timorous outside it:

> President Wood was an honest, anxious body . . . . He was given to being worried and advisory and to sitting up till midnight in his unventilated library grinding at the task of putting new wrong meanings into perfectly obvious statements in the Bible. He was a series of circles—round head with smooth gray hair that hung in a bang over his round forehead; . . . round little stomach in a gray sack-suit; round dumplings of feet . . . . A harassed, honorable, studious, ignorant, humorless, joke-

popping, genuinely conscientious thumb of a man. His prayers were long and intimate [106].

Lewis draws his figure in a certain shape to illustrate his point: the reader is to have impressed upon him, in every way possible, the fact that President Wood is a nonentity. The passage shows that Lewis is willing to forsake realism for exaggeration; it is a good example, in fact, of his use of his satiric resources. The movement is drawling and the words relished and lingered over, as in "putting new wrong meanings ...." The effect is secured, not by wit or by pithy descriptive phrases, but by an accumulation of grotesque details; the strokes are broad, the irony unsubtle. When the President comes to speak, he delivers some of the satiric monologues which are to become Lewis's stock in trade, and they reveal his limitations in the broadest and most obvious way.

But the characters embodying qualities which Lewis wants to ridicule are not always simple caricatures. Mrs. Cowles and her daughter Gertie, social lionesses in Joralemon, Minnesota, who contrive to remain lionesses in New York by acquiring a circle of trivial-minded acquaintances, are more complex creations than President Wood. Although Lewis is ruthless in exposing their snobbery, he shows us that they are as much to be pitied as blamed, made narrow by their small-town environment. In Carl's eyes, Gertie stands for the conventionalism which wants to put restraints on him; to Gertie, Carl is the only person who can rescue her from a desperate situation, the only hope she has of achieving fulfillment in life. Both she and her mother are particularly pathetic in the scene in which Gertie loses her self-control completely (Chapter 23). The interesting thing is that Lewis creates these women as types of weakness and folly, but is unwilling to maintain a satiric point of view toward them. The satirist could present them unsympathetically, but the novelist, inquiring into the causes of their irrational or antisocial behavior, begins to understand and sympathize.

Similarly Lewis has all the materials for caricature at hand in his portrayal of Ruth Winslow, Carl's wife, but refuses to use them. In many Lewis novels, the hero comes from the Midwest and the heroine from the East. He is unsophisticated but enterprising, a projection of Lewis himself. She resembles Grace Hegger, possessing a settled taste which may reject what is vigorous and alive because it seems coarse, and an awareness of social position which may incline toward snobbery. He burns with ambition to make or do something, not simply in order to improve his own position, but to contribute to social progress; her ambition may be to accumulate the symbols of prestige valued by the leisure class, so she may do her best to get in his way. Since Ruth comes from an old, established New York family, dominated by a dowager aunt who acts as a stout bastion against outsiders, Lewis could have made her a social butterfly, a prize secured with difficulty and not worth having. Instead, she is made to find her own atmosphere narrow and uninteresting, and to take an interest in settlement houses. She is almost as restless as Carl, and it is in an endeavor to find something new and exciting that she first meets him.

As Martin Light observes, the importance of play has not been stressed in criticism of Lewis, though it is as pronounced a strain in him as realism.[23] Play means games, make-believe, fantasy, and escape into nature; it is the answer which the characters give to oppressive reality. Brought together by a mutual love of whimsy, Carl and Ruth are playmates for each other, and their final escape is associated with their refusal to surrender their dreams, give up play, and accept their environment. Carl declares

[23] Light, "Characterization," p. 139

that people do not run away from slavery often enough, if more of them did the world would be better off: "Perhaps if enough of us run away from nice normal grinding, we'll start people wondering just why they should go on toiling to produce a lot of booze and clothes and things that nobody needs" [407]. Are booze and clothes to be irrelevant in the new society? The book concludes with little evidence of hard thought on social problems; instead it becomes an eccentric defense of escapism.

Reviewing the novel in *The Bookman*, Frederic Taber Cooper wrote, "It is improbable, to be sure, almost burlesque, yet so joyous, so spontaneous, so kaleidoscopic in its varied scene and shifting action, that one needs must accept it with indulgent credulity."[24] Most of the other reviewers were equally indulgent; the novel brought little profit to Lewis, but it brought him praise. Still determined to become a successful professional novelist, he felt himself more and more hampered by his publishing job. Unexpectedly, he found a means of release from it: he discovered the knack of churning out salable short stories. According to Grace Lewis—there are different accounts—she encouraged him to turn to stories as a change from novels, and he quickly finished off a story called "Nature, Incorporated" and sent it to the *Saturday Evening Post*. He had written it as a lark, hardly hoping that it would ever be published, but he soon received a letter from George Horace Lorimer welcoming him to the *Post* family and enclosing a check for five hundred dollars. By December, 1915, he had sold three more stories to the *Post*, and his rate of payment, his savings, and his prospects were sufficiently encouraging for him to take the decisive step of resigning from Doran's.

In his first letter Lorimer had written, "Now that you

[24] Frederic Taber Cooper, review of *The Trail of the Hawk, Bookman*, XLII (1915), 214.

have made a start with us I hope you will follow the example of Irvin Cobb, Bob Fitzsimmons and Miss Phoebe Snow and start in to become a household word."[25] Lewis did become, if not a household word, at least a highly successful manufacturer of light fiction for the mass-circulation magazines. In his most productive period, from the beginning of 1917 to the end of 1919, he published forty short stories, enough to give him a comfortable income. Critics who have sampled them usually describe their quality, on average, as wretched, and Robert Cantwell used them as evidence that Lewis had turned out as much journalistic rubbish as any good novelist ever signed his name to.[26] Lewis, however, did not admit that they were rubbish; in 1921 he maintained that "even in my magazine stories ... I have steadily sought to work out a means of doing as honest work as the powerful negations of the magazine editors would permit."[27] Nevertheless, he was usually prepared to go very far in flattering philistia. If some of the stories show that he was handicapped by editorial taboos—the *Post* objected to profanity and to ladies drinking, and would tolerate no disrespect for home or mother or the advertising industry—many others reveal Lewis indulging his native whimsicality and sentimentality. The chief interest of the stories, consequently, lies in their handling of themes, settings, and types of character to be developed more fully in later novels.

"Nature, Incorporated" had to do with the introduction of an outsider, a Boston real estate man, into a fake back-to-nature colony on Cape Cod. As Grace Lewis remarks, a

[25] Grace Hegger Lewis, *With Love from Gracie* (New York: Harcourt, Brace, 1955), p. 71.

[26] Robert Cantwell, "Sinclair Lewis," *New Republic*, LXXXVIII (1936), 298.

[27] Letter to Carl Van Doren, October, 1921, quoted in *The Man from Main Street*, p. 138

character incongruous to the setting was usually sure-fire, and Lewis employed the device often. Another example, and one of his best-known stories, "Young Man Axelbrod,"[28] about a sixty-five-year-old Scandinavian immigrant who leaves his farm to go to Yale, exhibits a second characteristic which Mrs. Lewis points out: Lewis's sympathy for older people. Though he was incapable of creating a believable child and never at ease with the language of people in love, he did have an understanding of the elderly, and many of his best short stories dealt either with the very old or with people who felt old age creeping upon them.[29] "Number Seven to Sagapoose," which appeared in the *American Magazine* for May, 1921, presented a Mr. Rabbitt who thought of himself as "nothing but an old deuce of spades." This admission, the similarity of his name to Babbitt, and his occupation of traveling salesman may lead us to expect that he will be treated satirically. But Lewis depicts him as a "Plain Man" full of the plain man's common sense; his job has given him a thorough knowledge of human nature and its offers him many opportunities for dispensing sensible advice. One person whom he helps is a young man with medical ambitions, a precursor of Arrowsmith, especially in his forsaking—under Mr. Rabbitt's influence—a lucrative practice for experimental work. This story, like many of Lewis's others, follows a circular pattern: as it leaves Mr. Rabbitt sighing that he is an old fool who never influences anybody, the reader is left with a warm feeling toward him and the homely moral that we little know the effect which we may have on those around us.

When he employed realistic observation, met the demands of his fictional situation honestly, and controlled

---

[28] First published in *Century Magazine*, June, 1917; reprinted in Lewis's *Selected Short Stories* (New York: Doubleday, Doran, 1935).
[29] *With Love from Gracie*, p. 91.

his whimsy, Lewis could be readable and interesting; replying to the criticism that his stories were chiefly brisk and amusing chatter, he was able to list a number of them which did not fit this description.[30] Even a banal story with a contrived ending, such as "The Hidden People," might possess some genuine feeling; it conveyed, though in awkward terms, a young man's loneliness in New York. Here the discovery of a playmate and prospective wife is linked with the discovery of a world unknown to college graduates like the hero:

> His heart beat with something bigger than any emotion he had ever associated with this mysterious, interesting race of women. He was hoping to rise from his social class, of smug little talkers, to her class of the Hidden People who do the world's work and give without ceasing.[31]

Portraying the loss of upper-class condescension and snobbery and the selection of the genuine over the artificial, this is the story of the development of a mature perspective on life. A similar choice has to be made by the owner of a novelty store in "A Matter of Business";[32] he can either handle a line of highly profitable but trashy dolls or continue to subsidise a skilled craftsman whose dolls are works of art. Eventually he repudiates the ethics of the Boosters' Club and takes the genuine over the gimcrack.

The conflict between beauty and utility occurs in other stories as well. In "A Woman by Candlelight," a traveling salesman seems happy enough or resigned enough at the prospect of tying himself to a girl who is the typical product of a mediocre environment, until he meets Miss

[30] Letter to Carl Van Doren, October, 1921, *The Man from Main Street*, pp. 138–139.
[31] *Good Housekeeping*, LXV (September 1917), 139.
[32] *Harper's Magazine*, CXLII (March 1921).

Weeks, a Gopher Prairie milliner who is bold enough to try to satisfy her aspirations for beauty in her own way.[33] He has always responded to the romantic appeal of the faraway; Miss Weeks, on the other hand, teaches him to recognize the splendor of the open prairie around him. Yet he is afraid of trusting his own aesthetic responses, afraid of using any standard except utility:

> Because they did belong to the new settlements they could not keep up the strain of rhapsodizing. It didn't seem to Wilbur quite decent to talk about beauty. As though the label on a tomato can had any use except to make it sell![34]

The conception of America as a pioneer country, apparent in many of Lewis's stories and novels—in "The Hidden People," hero and heroine sat hand in hand before the fire, "the youngsters who were American pioneers, not in the West but in the city"[35]—is presented in "A Woman by Candlelight" through Miss Weeks' appraisal of Gopher Prairie's state of civilization: "Our towns aren't beautiful—not yet. Maybe they will be when they stop trying to be showy." Under the guidance of Miss Weeks, the hero develops a detached and critical point of view; he can now see how silly and pretentious are the values of his other girl friend—they are symbolized by the ornate mansion in which she lives—and how menacing is the standardized person he recognizes her to be: "She was a stranger to him; and always would be, though they were married with bell, book and candle. But he could say nothing. He was afraid of the serene power of commonplaceness in her."[36] Although it moves towards a predictably

---

[33] First published in the *Saturday Evening Post*, July 28, 1917; reprinted in Schorer's collection of Lewis's short stories, *I'm a Stranger Here Myself* (New York: Dell, 1962).

[34] *I'm a Stranger Here Myself*, p. 61.

[35] "The Hidden People," p. 139.

[36] *I'm a Stranger Here Myself*, p. 71.

happy ending, this story and others show that Lewis was dealing in his short fiction with one of the main themes of his novels—the nature of twentieth-century civilization in the United States.

For Lewis, if not for Grace, freedom from the routine of a job meant freedom to travel; after he left Doran's he was almost incurably peripatetic for the rest of his life. Early in 1916, they took a cottage near St. Augustine, Florida, and Lewis settled down to write; but as before, writing did not come easily when he had the leisure for it. The *Post* rejected a number of short stories as well as a short serial, "The Innocents," which he had written in two weeks; the magazine thought that it was too sentimental. Florida was not entirely unprofitable, but by March Lewis was in Chicago, meeting people, exploring the city, and gathering material, while his wife remained behind in the South, sick with influenza. When she joined him, they went for an extended visit to the family home in Sauk Centre. The strain of introducing his bride to his home town was something which Lewis would not easily forget; to it was added the difficulty of living under the tyranny of Dr. Lewis, who demanded that they be on time for meals, invaded their privacy, and showed little interest in his son's writing except for the money it brought in. On the other hand, it is clear that Lewis and his wife could not accept the village as they found it, but deliberately tried to outrage its sense of propriety—and succeeded in doing so.

They stayed long enough for Lewis to rent an office overlooking Main Street and begin work on a new novel. Then suddenly he and Grace were off on another adventure—Lewis's version of the pioneers' trek westward—a trip in a Ford touring car from Sauk Centre to Seattle over a highway that sometimes was no more than two ruts through the wheat fields. He was seeing America at first hand; during their four months on the road, he and Grace passed through a thousand and one Gopher

Prairies. From Seattle they went to San Francisco, and then down to Carmel. Lewis had planned to spend the winter in his writer's paradise, but his reception there was disappointing. For various reasons—a major one being that Grace was pregnant and wished to be near friends and doctors in New York—they returned to the East after two months.

They were back in New York in time for the publication of Lewis's next novel, *The Job*, in February, 1917. A feminist document, it was subtitled "An American Novel," perhaps to indicate that it was not modeled on Wells' *Ann Veronica* (1909). *The Job* was in fact set firmly in the American scene and pervaded by American sentiments, not the least of them a greater optimism about current conditions than Wells expressed. Ann Veronica achieves personal fulfillment only because she is an unusual person; before she attains it, events have forced her to face the facts of a woman's position in the world, "the meagre realities of such freedom as it permitted her, the almost unavoidable obligation to some individual man under which she must labour for even a foothold in the world." But in Lewis's America escape from the doll's house into a free and full life entails chiefly an effort of the will: America is still the land of almost infinite possibilities, and it offers a woman many alternatives to a parasitic state of existence. Far from showing his heroine, Una Golden, as the victim of conventional restraints upon the second sex, Lewis turns her into a feminine Horatio Alger character; through initiative, hard work, and a shrewd grasp of opportunities, she rises from an eight-dollar-a-week typing job to a managerial position in a hotel chain, and creates for herself the kind of life which she wants to live.[37]

But the Horatio Alger element emerges only toward

[37] *The Job: An American Novel* (New York: Harper, 1917). Coleman, in "The Genesis of Social Ideas in Sinclair Lewis," p. 26, notes similarities

the end of the story. Lewis begins with an entirely different theme, that of the *deracinée*, the uprooted woman. His central character is not a humorous little caricature or a strongly individuated person; instead, he emphasizes her typicality: on any subway train you might see "a score of mild matter-of-fact Unas." She is a "thoroughly commonplace, small-town girl" imbued with "the village idea of virginal vacuousness." In the manner of the documentary writer, with a great deal of editorializing on the theme, Lewis studies an important social phenomenon: the movement of girls from the small town to the metropolis in the quest of work, adventure, and emotional fulfillment. A cheerful or sentimental tone is really precluded by the evidence which he turns up; the book is in part an exposé of a situation and an indictment of the forces which have caused it. Lewis is concerned with "women whom life didn't want except to type its letters about invoices"; anticipating a number of twentieth-century dramatists, among them Arthur Miller, he asserts that such a bourgeois theme is as valid material for tragedy as the story of Clytemnestra. Curiously, after making the claim he turns his story into a tragicomedy: everything turns out well, and everyone lives happily ever after.

The novel conveys forcefully the importance of "the job" for a person in a commercialized society. The view of life as a trap, suggested in the first chapter of *Our Mr. Wrenn* but mercifully altered in the second chapter, is here presented with bleak emphasis. "The job" means an impersonal and mechanical routine; Una Golden, typing out form letters over and over again, is only a will-less instrument—during the working day, which consumes a large part of her time and nearly all her energy, she must

---

between *The Job* and Garland's *Rose of Dutcher's Coolly* as treatments of the "new woman" theme, the problem of a woman in carving out a career for herself in a world dominated by men.

forget that she is a sentient human being. Bringing this passive prisoner of routine into contact with a rebellious spirit is an obvious plot line: Una meets Walter Babson, a young man surprisingly like Lewis in his flamboyancy, his spontaneity, his taste for Shaw and Wells, and his shy quoting of Tennyson, but whose typicality is nevertheless emphasized—he is one of the "million hall-room boys who want to be geniuses." These two are "children of the city, where there is no place for love-making, for discovering and testing each other's hidden beings"; in the commercial metropolis, nature is steel-bound. When spring makes its "scornful, lusty demand," Una can only cry out to be spared from it; when it becomes insistent she has to fall back on "We'll be good," a cliché which Walter ridicules as the perfect expression of the American woman, but which he cannot subvert. Since marriage or any other continuing relationship is impossible for them, Walter goes out of Una's life by taking a job a thousand miles away from New York.

The next step is for Lewis to drive Una into the arms of a "typical American business man"; because he seems to offer her a refuge from her slavery, she marries Julius Edward Schwirtz, a coarse and garrulous paint salesman. On her wedding night she realizes that she has only exchanged one kind of prison for another, and in two years of living "amid the blank procession of phantoms who haunt cheap family hotels" nothing happens to make her believe that life possesses either beauty or meaning. But when Julius Edward loses his job and she has to go to work again, she gains a certain independence from him—an independence which she refuses to surrender when he can again support her. Once more she is depen-dent on the job, but she is no longer shown as entrapped or enslaved. The theme now becomes, as Stuart Sherman put it, the development of an intelligent and purposeful feminine will.[38] Una steadily climbs up the business ladder, and through a sentimental twist in the plot she is given back her Walter Babson. Evidently in *The Job* Lewis was trying to capture the true nature of life in America. Both his reading and his personal experience told him that many people in his society led narrow and frustrated lives. He refused to believe, however, that most Americans were oppressed by a sense of futility and powerlessness; his realism, like that of Howells, was sunny, so that, having conjured up a vision of bleak despair, he concluded upon a note of hope. He presents two different visions of America, visions ultimately irreconcilable with each other.

The portrayal of Schwirtz, the bloated commercial traveller, exemplifies Lewis's ambivalent attitude. Grace Lewis thought that the characterizations in *The Job* were sharp and unrelentingly realistic, because Lewis had found something to hate; reviewing a reissue of the novel in 1923, Henry Longan Stuart wrote that Lewis viewed Julius Edward in "the cold light of a perfect distaste."[39] The repugnance is qualified, however. First of all, the salesman's rambling, slangy monologues are amusing, even though they illustrate his hypocrisy and moral confusion. Moreover, though he is shown as drunken, slovenly, lecherous, and diseased, he is still called an "honest fellow" at one point. And in his last quarrel with Una, we are suddenly invited to feel sympathy for him. Una, who has plenty of reasons for hating him, abruptly breaks off the argument by saying that they would never understand each other if they talked for a thousand years; she con-

---

[38] *The Significance of Sinclair Lewis* (New York: Harcourt, Brace, 1922), p. 8.

[39] *With Love from Gracie*, p. 101; Henry Longan Stuart, "Novels from the Grub Street Days of Sinclair Lewis," New York *Times Book Review*, April 22, 1923, p. 3. Mrs. Lewis's explanation for the ambivalence in the novel is that Lewis allowed himself to be swayed by the editors at Harper's into giving the story an unreal, unconvincing happy ending (p. 109).

gratulates herself on being free again, but congratulates him too and calls him a "poor, decent man." Again the movement is from a satiric to a novelistic perspective; yet Lewis establishes a standard by which Julius Edward must be convicted of indecency and then in effect declares that this standard is to be ignored.

The presentation of the business world is also ambivalent. There is a great deal of satire, from Una's first impression of the "savage continuity" of toil in an office and her feeling that if she transgressed unknown rules "they" would crush her, to her view of the caste system at Pemberton's, where florid, large-chinned executives talk easily of "shifts in policy" which may throw four hundred people out of work, and bright young men who may some day be beatified into chiefs vow "to adhere to the true faith of Pemberton's, and not waste their evenings in making love, or reading fiction, or hearing music, but to read diligently about soap and syrups and window displays . . ." [231]. Arthur B. Coleman finds the basis of Lewis's criticism in Veblen; in fact, he describes Chapter XIV of *The Job* as little more than a popular account of Veblen's point of view as it is expressed in the *Theory of Business Enterprise*. The marching out of ponderous battalions to sell a brass pin, the sacred rite of composing dull letters and filing them solemnly away—such forms of nonsense result from the acceptance of the pecuniary principle in business. The strongest Veblenian echo, however, comes in Lewis's exemplification of the qualities which a person develops in this system either to emulate others or simply to survive.[40] Yet in spite of all the criticism, it becomes clear very early that if there is an ideal in the book it is that of Big Business:

> For "business," that one necessary field of activity to
> which the egotistic arts and sciences and theologies and

[40] Coleman, "Genesis," pp. 30–33.

military puerilities are but servants, that long-despised and always valiant effort to unify the labor of the world, is at last beginning to be something more than dirty smithing. No longer does the business man thank the better classes for permitting him to make and distribute bread and motor-cars and books. No longer does he crawl to the church to buy pardon for usury. Business is being recognized—and is recognizing itself—as ruler of the world [25].

It is startling to find Lewis relegating theology, all the arts, and all the sciences to a position of subservience to business. It is equally surprising to find him, in the next paragraph, rejoicing in the application of systems and charts and the scientific mind to industry, and describing "the vision of an efficiency so broad that it can be kindly and sure . . . ." In Veblen's terms, Lewis is praising the parasites upon the industrial system and confusing them with its real working force, the technicians.[41] The passage gives additional evidence of the lack of logical consistency in Lewis's handling of ideas.

The novel presents an argument, common to Wells and Veblen, that mankind is operating at only a fraction of its potential and that it must realize that it needs a revision of all its clumsy, outworn procedures. Still this argument is put in the mouth of a businessman, characterized as benevolent by his name, Mr. Fein. "The only possible ground for optimism about the human race that I can see," he says, "is that in most all lines experts are at work showing up the deficiencies . . . ." But while the Wellsian utopia is evolving, Mr. Fein, and by inference Lewis, advocate nothing more revolutionary than being patient and cultivating one's garden:

[41] See, for example, Chapter VIII, "Industrial Exemption and Conservatism," in Veblen's *Theory of the Leisure Class* (New York: Macmillan, 1899).

"I'm not at all sure that there's any higher wisdom than doing a day's work, and hoping the subway will be a little less crowded next year, and in voting for the best possible man, and then forgetting all the Weltschmertz, and going to an opera. It sounds pretty raw and crude, doesn't it? But living in a world that's raw and crude, all you can do is to be honest and not worry" [309].

Here we have another measure of the ideological distance between Lewis and Wells. Lewis's emphasis on old-fashioned benevolence recalls Dickens—his Mr. Fein is as philanthropic as the Cheeryble brothers in *Nicholas Nickleby*—but this recommendation to "be honest and not worry" demonstrates a greater degree of complacency than Dickens would have tolerated, and it certainly would have made Wells despair. In his review, Henry Longan Stuart described *The Job* as the first in a legitimate dynasty of fine novels; in it, he wrote, Lewis "assumed the mantle of an authentic message and method," and he stated that Lewis's success dated from the time he began to arraign America.[42] But only three years before *Main Street* and five before *Babbitt*, Lewis was capable of describing business as the highest form of human activity. His indictment of a system which imposes a loveless routine upon human beings loses its force because the defense counsel is given the better of the argument.

Lewis had two novels published in 1917: *The Job* was followed by *The Innocents*, which was serialized in the *Woman's Home Companion* prior to book publication. In the dedicatory introduction, it was described as "a story for lovers," "a tale for people who still read Dickens and clip out spring poetry and love old people and children ...."[43] Neither Lewis nor his publishers thought it worthy of inclusion in lists of his works during the 1920's,

[42] "Novels from the Grub Street Days of Sinclair Lewis," p. 3.
[43] *The Innocents* (New York: Harper, 1917).

but it illustrates certain continuing motifs in his writing. It concerns an elderly couple who, after leading happy but restricted lives, engage in two adventures. First they establish a tearoom on Cape Cod; when it fails for lack of patronage by the bohemians and socialites—who, of course, are satirized—they make the incredible decision to hike across the United States in midwinter. "It is earnestly recommended to all uncomfortable or dissatisfied men over sixty," pontificates the author, "that they take their wives and their mouth-organs and go tramping in winter . . . ." After all the writing he had done, Lewis had not lost his sentimentality and his pseudo medievalism: his elderly couple falls in with and reforms a gang of tough hoboes, and Pa becomes King of the Bandits. The newspapers get hold of their story, and fame accompanies them as they continue their journey. At Lippittville, Indiana, Pa receives an offer to take over a shoe store. He accepts, and with astonishing rapidity he becomes a successful businessman and a pillar of the community. When their severely respectable son-in-law comes to rescue them and put them in an old people's home, the oldsters humiliate him properly; for the occasion Ma appears in a gown like a herald's cloth-of-gold tabard and wears a platinum *lorgnon*. Just as in the other early novels, the plot turns on the success myth; Lewis sets forth the thesis that any broadening of experience such as the Innocents undergo will almost automatically provide an opportunity for advancement. He suggests as well that the progress of America is due to people who use their initiative as these two do. It is also notable that the pot of gold at the end of the rainbow is found after a quest, a launching out into the unknown, and that it is located not in the sophisticated East, but in the Midwest, among decent small-town people.

According to *With Love from Gracie*, the birth of his son Wells in July, 1917, meant to the father chiefly a threat to his freedom to travel. When his wife complained that she felt like a rootless, homeless nomad, Lewis rebuked her with a reminder that she had promised the baby would make no difference to their wandering. So began two years in which she tried to prove to her husband that his family was not going to tie him down. They spent the winter of 1917–1918 in St. Paul, where Lewis worked with Daniel Reed on the dramatization of one of his *Saturday Evening Post* stories, "Hobohemia" (the play was produced without great success in February, 1919). During the summer of 1918 they were on Cape Cod, the next winter back in Minneapolis, and the summer of 1919 in Mankato, Minnesota. His work during these years convinced Lewis that he could write a major novel and brought him a sympathetic publisher. When his friend Alfred Harcourt resigned from Henry Holt and Company in the spring of 1919, Lewis urged him to establish his own firm and promised to write for him. So began the partnership of ebullient author and patient editor which the letters collected in *From Main Street to Stockholm* document.

The fact that Lewis invested two thousand dollars in the new firm of Harcourt, Brace and Howe in the summer of 1919 is evidence enough to destroy the myth that Lewis had received no financial or critical encouragement before the publication of *Main Street* and that to write the novel he had to go badly into debt. Carl Van Doren, for instance, in describing Lewis's poverty during these years, says that Lewis was "obliged ... to finish his sixth, and first successful, novel on borrowed money," and follows with a lyrical outburst: "He could be magnificent on nothing."[44] Actually, in 1919 Lewis, besides selling stories and articles to other magazines, had what must be close to a maximum possible number

[44] *Sinclair Lewis: A Biographical Sketch* (Garden City: Doubleday, Doran, 1933), p. 35.

of appearances in the *Saturday Evening Post*: seven short stories, a serial entitled *Free Air*, its continuation *Danger— Run Slow*, and a series of articles called "Adventures in Autobumming." Lewis's handling of the serial illustrates his skill in exploiting commercial possibilities; he sold it to the *Post*, at Harcourt's suggestion began writing a continuation to make it a book-length work, sold the continuation to the *Post*, sold the movie rights to Famous Players, and had the completed work published in book form.

Free Air was described by Stuart Sherman as a "modern fairy-tale" written by "a masterly realist on a lark . . . ." [45] Yet Lewis took it seriously enough to ask Ellen Eayrs, Harcourt's assistant, whether it would be "perfectly insane and egotistic" to send a copy to the Pulitzer Prize committee, "suggesting that the dern thing is a study in 'the wholesome atmosphere of American life' etc ?" [46] It presents themes and characters already familiar in Lewis's fiction—wanderlust, snobbery, the rich girl, the up-and-coming mechanic hero. Though it is vigorous and interesting, it is full of faults: Lewis completely fails to make his snobs believable human beings or even distinctive representatives of various types of snobbery. Yet it has its appeal; the *New Republic* reviewer, puzzled by the charm of a novel with a banal plot and banal characters, decided its distinction lay in the author's catching "the sweep and exhilaration of the great open country over which his characters wind their way" and characterized it as "an Odyssey of the Northwest." [47]

The story deals with a transcontinental automobile trip and the romance which grows out of it. While they

[45] *Significance*, p. 10.

[46] Letters to Ellen Eayrs, November 12, 1919, *From Main Street to Stockholm, Letters of Sinclair Lewis 1919–1930*, ed. with an intro. by Harrison Smith (New York: Harcourt, Brace, 1952), p. 18.

[47] Anonymous review of *Free Air*, *New Republic*, XXI (1920), 275.

are traveling west, Claire Boltwood and her wealthy father meet a young garage owner, Milt Daggett, in a small Minnesota town. Dropping everything, Milt follows them across the country, always managing to turn up in the nick of time to rescue them from muddy roads and motorized bandits. Three thousand miles of bad highway are more easily traversed than the distance between their social classes, but eventually Claire loses all her snobbery through exposure to the great heart of America, and she leads Milt along the road to understanding and a happy marriage. As Coleman points out,[48] the book presents a variation on the Pygmalion theme: Claire discovers valuable qualities in Milt and tells her father that she is "going to carve him, and paint him, and possibly spoil him. The creation of a man—of one who knows how to handle life—is so much more wonderful than creating absurd pictures or statues or stories." In his halting way, Milt states how he thinks life ought to be handled, and, as Martin Light observes, expresses an idea which might supply the theme for most of Lewis's novels: "Wonder if a fellow could be a big engineer, you know, build bridges and so on, and still talk about, oh, beautiful things?"[49] This is the question which Lewis's Dodsworth, among others, is going to try to solve. If the pioneer and then the pioneering industrialist have had to put utility ahead of beauty, has the time not come to try to unite them?

A particularly interesting chapter of *Free Air* is set in Gopher Prairie, the scene of *Main Street*. When the Boltwoods arrive late one evening, it strikes them as rude, dirty, uninviting, and depressing:

> In the hotel Claire was conscious of the ugliness of the poison-green walls and brass cuspidors and insurance

[48] Coleman, "Genesis," p. 43.
[49] Light, "Characterization," p. 147

calendars and bare floor of the office; conscious of the
interesting fact that all air had been replaced by the
essence of cigar smoke and cooking cabbage; of the stares
of the traveling men lounging in bored lines; and of the
lack of welcome on the part of the night clerk, an oldish,
bleached man with whiskers instead of a collar [38].[50]

But in the morning everything looks changed. The sun is
shining, people are pleasant, and Claire realizes that the
questions which the evening before had seemed trite and
perfunctory derive from an interest in her as a human
being:

"Why!" Claire gasped, "why, they aren't rude. They
care—about people they never saw before. That's why
they ask questions! I never thought—I never thought!
There's people in the world who want to know us without having looked us up in the Social Register! I'm so
ashamed! Not that the sunshine changes my impression
of this coffee. It's frightful! But that will improve. And
the people—they were being friendly, all the time" [46].

The first glance which saw material for satire in the
prairie town was a superficial one; further observation
brings understanding. Though the Middle West seems
raw and hideous to a cultured easterner, he ought to
reflect on its present problems and its potential greatness.
Its first work is that of subduing nature, its second that
of assimilating newcomers to America, and only after
these problems have been solved can it turn to its third—
the development of culture. This is the apology which
Lewis makes for his native region; in effect, he cancels
out *Main Street* before he writes it.

While we may think of these early works as potboilers,
Lewis himself did not do so. He was very much annoyed
when Carl Van Doren, in an article published in the
Nation on October 12, 1921, described the early Lewis as

[50] *Free Air* (New York: Harcourt, Brace and Howe, 1919).

a writer of "bright, colloquial, amusing chatter to be read by those who travel through books at the brisk pace of vaudeville." [51] In a long reply Lewis admitted that he had written much "amusing chatter," but maintained that he had produced three novels which did not fit that description and declared that even in his magazine stories he had constantly sought to do as honest work as possible. [52] The requirements of magazine serialization may account for the contrived happy endings of several of the novels and the shifts in characterization necessary to bring about these endings, but there is no reason to think that the choice of themes was dictated by the intended market; Lewis wrote about what was congenial to him.

In the pamphlet on Lewis which he wrote in 1922, Stuart Sherman asserted that Lewis's much discussed opportunism was the result of his studying himself and his age until he understood the needs and the aspirations of both. [53] Schorer, on the other hand, contends that Lewis never really understood himself at all; but at least we have seen Lewis from the first endeavoring to understand his age, to do what Mark Twain said the American novelist could never do because of the vastness of his country—generalize the nation. [54] Looking outward rather than inward, he attempted to analyze the forces which affected the behavior of his fellow citizens in a confusing transitional period; he tried to discover what were the sources of hope and frustration in the lives of typical young women, white-collar workers, engineers, and garage mechanics of his time. He wanted to comprehend the

[51] Carl Van Doren, "Revolt from the Village: 1920," *Nation*, CXI (October 12, 1921), 914–917.

[52] Letter to Carl Van Doren, October, 1921, *The Man from Main Street*, p. 138.

[53] *Significance*, p. 1.

[54] Mark Twain, "What Paul Bourget Thinks of Us," *North American Review*, CLX (January 1895), 50–52.

experience of the ordinary middle-class person; he had small regard for the feelings of the exceptionally sensitive person fleeing from the common herd and taking refuge in an ivory tower or a bohemian sanctuary. The problem he dealt with was that of making one's way in the everyday business world. Furthermore, in spite of his concern for documentation and accuracy, he never wanted to join the ranks of the social, economic, political, and cultural analysts, the tribe of Steffens, Veblen, and their successors such as Mumford, Riesman, and Galbraith. He considered himself primarily a novelist; whatever he was going to do would be done in fictional form, but not in the short story, which for him was only a means to an end. The concept of the Great American Novel, the novel which would express the spirit of the nation in a compelling form, was in his thoughts; concerning *Babbitt*, he wrote, "I want the novel to be the G.A.N. in so far as it crystallizes and makes real the Average Capable American."[55]

In *Mr. Wrenn* Sherman saw already in evidence "a point of view, detached, critical, illumined by the coming spirit . . . ."[56] Yet Lewis was not detached, but curiously involved, identified in turn with each of two conflicting sides. Like the Galsworthy of *The Man of Property* and *Strife*, he could be very convincing in his presentation of one side and then very convincing in his presentation of the other. What we miss most is a settled perspective or viewpoint, the stance of a mature mind which does not change with every new bit of evidence. If Lewis is strongly oriented toward the future, the goals he would like to see achieved and the principles he would like to see embodied in society remain nebulous; it is more difficult to discover them than it is to trace the values handed down to him from the

[55] Letter to Harcourt, December 28, 1920, *From Main Street to Stockholm*, p. 59.
[56] *Significance*, p. 3.

American past and even from his childhood reading of the tales of Robin Hood and the Knights of the Round Table. If he is critical, he is not critical of the myth that every American can be president or at least rise to the top of the firm through good honest effort. If at times he suggests that there are other things in life besides the building of better mousetraps, he has a businessman's affection for rugged enterprise and material progress. The road to true felicity seems to be the open road you take in your Ford touring car.

According to H. L. Mencken's graphic description, Lewis was a "fugitive, his face blanched by years in the hulks," who in 1920 came "bursting suddenly into the light" with "the foul liquors of the depths still streaming from him . . . ." [57] That this view of Lewis's career is over-dramatic and inaccurate is proved by William Couch in his study of the rise of Lewis's reputation; he provides copious evidence that during this early period from 1914 to 1919 Lewis's sincerity of purpose and promise as a novelist won recognition. [58] In addition to routine newspaper notices, *Our Mr. Wrenn* received a number of important reviews; *The Trail of the Hawk* was reviewed in more than a hundred papers and magazines and brought a letter of praise from William Dean Howells; *The Job* received more than four hundred reviews and was further publicized by a major critical debate over its realism. As an optimistic rebel, avoiding the excesses of sentimental idealism on the one hand and the pessimistic naturalism of Dreiser on the other, Lewis won approval from persons of moderate opinion for his "sane-eyed realism." At the same time,

[57] "Consolation," *Smart Set*, January 1921; reprinted in *Sinclair Lewis: A Collection of Critical Essays*, ed. Mark Schorer (Englewood Cliffs: Prentice-Hall, 1962), p. 18.

[58] William Couch, Jr., "The Emergence, Rise and Decline of the Reputation of Sinclair Lewis" (Ph.D. dissertation, University of Chicago, 1954). Couch discusses Mencken's abrupt dismissal of Lewis's early novels on p. 2.

serious estimates of his work were published in advanced high-brow journals, notably *The Nation*, the *New Republic*, and *The Masses*. Another misconception demolished by Couch is that created by Lewis's sophisticated contemporaries in the 1920's—and one to which he himself contributed by his occasional slighting references to his earlier work—of an errant youth who repents and is absolved, and whose later honest work brings him a just reward. Lewis's later novels probably exhibit no more honesty than his earlier ones; they give an impression of greater intellectual, moral, and artistic assurance, but on close examination they reveal many of the same ambiguities and uncertainties apparent in their forerunners.

3. The Revolt Against Main Street

THOUGH LEWIS was not exactly an errant youth who suddenly repented of wasting his talents and decided to tell the truth in his writing, it is undeniably true that he made his name by attacking, in ways he had not done before, the popular conceptions of the small town and the up-and-coming city. That he altered these conceptions is a matter of history. It has often been pointed out that, in spite of a fairly lengthy tradition of realistic portrayal before *Main Street*, the village still persisted in American lore either as the abode of rustics who used expressions like "I swan" or as the home of honest virtue, simplicity, and friendliness. Indeed the classic statement by Meredith Nicholson about everything being comfortable and cheerful in Indiana, with lots of old-fashioned human kindness flowing round, had been made as recently as 1912.[1] While the opposing tradition received important contributions within the next few years—the poems of

[1] Meredith Nicholson, *A Hoosier Chronicle* (Boston: Houghton Mifflin, 1912), p. 606.

Masters and the stories of Sherwood Anderson, for example
—the conventional view held its sway; John T. Flanagan
writes, "There can be no question that Lewis's novel
[*Main Street*] was the first factual treatment of the American rural community to attract large public response."[2]
But even while destroying the stereotype of the small
town and later of the medium-sized city, Lewis remained
as inconsistent and paradoxical an iconoclast as he had
been in his previous novels. The illusions he destroyed
are no more interesting than the illusions he kept.

Carl Van Doren, in an article entitled "Revolt from
the Village: 1920" which appeared in the *Nation* in the
fall of 1921, described the author of *Main Street* as following in the footsteps of Edgar Lee Masters. In a long and
indignant reply, Lewis said that he had not really read
Masters' poems,[3] and that he had begun to plan *Main
Street* just after his second year in college. On another
occasion he recalled that he had written about twenty
thousand words of the projected novel during the summer
of 1905, that the title then was *The Village Virus*, and that
the central character was not Carol Kennicott but Guy
Pollock. Mark Schorer provides good reason for doubting
that this manuscript, which Lewis said was "clean gone
and vanished away," ever existed; yet he does support
Lewis's statement that he was thinking of the subject as
early as 1905, for a journal entry from that time mentions
"the village virus" and indicates a desire to write a book
about "how it getteth into the veins of a good man and
true."[4] In other words, long before the revolt from the

[2] John T. Flanagan, "A Long Way to Gopher Prairie: Sinclair Lewis'
Apprenticeship," *Southwest Review*, XXXII (1947), 403.

[3] Nevertheless, two years before he had listed Masters among his favorite
authors. See George Gordon [Charles Crittenden Baldwin], *The Men Who
Make Our Novels* (New York: Moffat, Yard, 1919), p. 227.

[4] Mark Schorer, *Sinclair Lewis: An American Life* (New York: McGraw-
Hill, 1961), p. 102.

village became a literary fashion Lewis had concluded
that village life was not all sweet neighborliness and that
here might be the theme for a novel. Not Masters, but
Hamlin Garland, if Lewis's Nobel Prize speech is to be
trusted, taught him that the village was suitable material
for literature; from *Main-Travelled Roads* and *Rose of
Dutcher's Coolly*, which he read as a boy, he learned that it
was possible to discard the conventional view of village life
and to write of midwestern people as one saw them.

The book in which he was going to show the American
small town as something different from "the one sure
abode of friendship, honesty, and clean sweet marriage-
able girls" [5] loomed in Lewis's mind as far more serious
and important than anything he had previously done.
His letters to Harcourt make this clear. In mid-December,
1919, he wrote, "I'll NEVER do a novel more carefully
planned and thought out and more eagerly written than
Main Street, and I hope to see it go for years, as *Jean-
Christophe* goes"; and on Christmas Eve, ". . . all my
thoughts are centered in *Main Street*—which may, perhaps,
be the real beginning of my career as a writer." [6] The
previous summer he had visited James Branch Cabell at
Rockbridge Alum Springs, Virginia, and had shown
him 30,000 words of manuscript; within a few months
he had become completely dissatisfied with what he had
written and destroyed almost all of it. In Washington
that fall and winter, he worked so industriously that by
the end of February he had finished a 738-page first
draft. He completed the final draft of 200,000 words
"on a particularly hot afternoon in early summer of
1920, and that night took the script up to Alfred

[5] The expression is used by Charles L. Sanford in *The Quest for Paradise*
(Urbana: University of Illinois Press, 1961), p. 264.

[6] Letters to Harcourt, December 15 and 24, 1919, *From Main Street to
Stockholm: Letters of Sinclair Lewis 1919–1930*, ed. with an intro. by Harrison
Smith (New York: Harcourt, Brace, 1952), pp. 20, 21.

Harcourt." [7] Harcourt read it that week end, pronounced it the truest book he had ever read, complimented Lewis on doing for America what Arnold Bennett had done for England, and predicted sales of at least twenty thousand copies.

In this novel Lewis was returning to the scenes of his youth. He was fond of stressing that the scene or background "is as much a part of the protagonist's character and development as his heart" and that "one can express adequately only a scene which one knows by the ten thousand unconscious experiences which come from living in it." [8] Of course, in *Main Street* he was hardly the novelist of nostalgic memory, but he refused to criticize Main Street from the standpoint of eastern or urban or aesthetic sophistication. Telling the truth about the village evidently did not mean presenting it in an altogether ridiculous light. If this was Lewis's feeling, it might explain the otherwise surprising statement by Grace Hegger Lewis that *Main Street* was not a satire until the reviewers began calling it one. It would also explain why the résumé which husband and wife prepared for the Harcourt, Brace catalog described the theme of the novel as reconciliation with one's environment: "only in the end does [Carol Kennicott] learn the great secret of life in being content with a real world in which it is never possible to create an ideal setting." [9]

Yet *Main Street* is usually thought of as a devastating satire on the small town. The tone of the headnote supports this preconception.

[7] Introduction to *Main Street* for the Limited Editions Club, 1937; reprinted in *The Man from Main Street: Collected Essays and Other Writings, 1904–1950*, ed. Harry E. Maule and Melville H. Cane (New York: Random House, 1953), p. 216.

[8] "The American Scene in Fiction," New York *Herald Tribune Books*, April 14, 1929; reprinted in *The Man from Main Street*, p. 142.

[9] Grace Hegger Lewis, *With Love from Gracie: Sinclair Lewis: 1912–1925* (New York: Harcourt, Brace, 1955), pp. 190, 147.

Main Street is the climax of civilization. That this Ford car might stand in front of the Bon Ton store, Hannibal invaded Rome and Erasmus wrote in Oxford cloisters. What Ole Jenson the grocer says to Ezra Stowbody the banker is the new law for London, Prague, and the unprofitable isles of the sea; whatsoever Ezra does not know and sanction, that thing is heresy, worthless for knowing and wicked to consider.

Our railway station is the final aspiration of architecture. Sam Clark's annual hardware turnover is the envy of the four counties which constitute God's Country. In the sensitive art of the Rosebud Movie Palace there is a Message, and humor strictly moral.

Such is our comfortable tradition and sure faith. Would he not betray himself an alien cynic who should otherwise portray Main Street, or distress the citizens by speculating whether there may not be other faiths ? [10]

With this opening, the reader expects a thorough-going satire of village life. The book seems to bear out this expectation: its theme is the uniformity and negativism spread by the "village virus":

It is an unimaginatively standardized background, a sluggishness of speech and manners, a rigid ruling of the spirit by the desire to appear respectable. It is contentment ... the contentment of the quiet dead, who are scornful of the living for their restless walking. It is negation canonized as the one positive virtue. It is slavery self-sought and self-defended. It is dullness made God.

A savorless people, gulping tasteless food, and sitting afterward, coatless and thoughtless, in rocking chairs prickly with inane decorations, listening to mechanical music, saying mechanical things about the excellence of Ford automobiles, and viewing themselves as the greatest race in the world [265].

[10] *Main Street* (New York: Harcourt, Brace, 1920).

Lewis knows that such smugness, inhibitions, and prejudices are to be found in small towns in France or Tibet just as easily as in Wyoming or Indiana. The frightening thing about the midwest mentality, however, is that it is pawing at world dominion: "a village in a country which is taking pains to become altogether standardized and pure, which aspires to succeed Victorian England as the chief mediocrity of the world," is not something quaint and restful but "a force seeking to dominate the earth ...." When Lewis speaks out directly as in the passages just quoted, from Chapter XXII, he is as trenchant in denunciation of American mediocrity as Tocqueville or Matthew Arnold.

But usually the criticism of Gopher Prairie is made through the central character, Carol Kennicott. With her, we travel from one end of Main Street to the other, finding almost nothing to please the eye. With her, we meet "the entire aristocracy of Gopher Prairie: all persons engaged in a profession, or possessed of grandparents born in America." With her we discover the village nothingness, "a negative thing; an intellectual squalor; a swamp of prejudices and fears." And with her we feel how horrible it is to be shut in the "ghetto-like confinement" of the small town and to know that any chance of life's being a great adventure is over, finished, past.[11]

Does his heroine, then, represent Lewis's point of view, and are her criticisms his? Usually, but not always. In a review of *Main Street*, H. W. Boynton characterized Carol as "a skittish emanation of Mr. Lewis's fancy, a trivial and pretentious little Phantom with no dignity of mind or soul—a caricature ... of the advanced young female of our kind and time."[12] There is considerable justi-

[11] Lewis uses the expression "ghetto-like confinement" in his Introduction to *Main Street* (see note 7, above).

[12] Review of *Main Street*, *Weekly Review*, III (1920), 623.

fication for this view. In college, Carol was a capricious, illogical reformer: "She wanted, just now, to have a cell in a settlement-house, like a nun without the bother of the black robe, and be kind, and read Bernard Shaw, and enormously improve a horde of grateful poor" (5). When she comes to Gopher Prairie, she wants to plant seeds of beauty and intelligence without knowing very much about either; moreover, she is impulsive, undiplomatic, and ignorant of complications. Sometimes, as when she plays the Princess Winky Poo at a party or when she asks the town millionaire to make Gopher Prairie over completely, she is childishly naive. Boynton seems to have a point: Carol is in part a caricature of a reformer, a take-off on the advanced young woman.

In his introduction to a 1937 edition of *Main Street*, Lewis referred to an article "which confided to the world that it was a tremendous joke on me that Carol wasn't of as good stuff as her husband," and commented drily that since he "had most painstakingly planned that she shouldn't be—that she should be just bright enough to sniff a little but not bright enough to do anything about it," he was delighted to see that the author of the article had read the book before passing judgment on it.[13] He also told Allen Austin that he had meant to make Carol silly—"For example, I deliberately had her decorate a room in bad taste." [14] But these would appear to be second thoughts, reconsiderations after Lewis had read the critics. According to Grace Hegger Lewis, "If Flaubert said, '*Bovary, c'est moi*,' Lewis could well have said, '*Carol, that's me*,' for he was more than approving of what Carol was trying to do to better Gopher Prairie, whereas Emma Bovary only wanted to better life for

[13] See note 7, above.
[14] Allen Austin, "An Interview with Sinclair Lewis," *University of Kansas City Review*, XXIV (1958), 204.

herself; and he thought Carol's Chinese party a very fine party indeed and one he would have enjoyed attending." [15] Still, in view of Lewis's statement that Carol "is dull about all the male world that interests Kennicott," [16] it would seem hazardous to identify his point of view with hers: sometimes the viewpoints coincide, and sometimes they do not. Toward the end of the novel we are told that we have seen only one side of the picture: "It had not occurred to her that there was also a story of Will Kennicott, into which she entered only so much as he entered into hers; that he had bewilderments and concealments as intricate as her own, and soft treacherous desires for sympathy" (439).

Consequently, although satiric exposure is undoubtedly Lewis's principal concern, *Main Street* is not really the merciless and undeviating satire which it was taken to be in the 1920's. Lewis suggests that we must be careful to make a balanced assessment of the small town, and even goes to the trouble of introducing the contrasting point of view of another stranger to Gopher Prairie, Bea Sorenson, Carol's Scandinavian maid. James Branch Cabell wrote that he had to dissuade Lewis from using her to give a continuing rebuttal to Carol:

> ... I still cherish a peculiar leniency for these Kennicotts whom I first met in manuscript; and I read their family history with a double sense of guilt .... Here, murdered by me, I am afraid, in the middle of another man's book, is the unoffending Scandinavian girl, Bea Sorgenson [*sic*], who, but for my lethal intervention, might perhaps have thrived and have utilized the re-

[15] *With Love from Gracie*, p. 190. Lewis did admit to Charles Breasted, who made the identification, that Carol was a self-portrait. See Breasted's "The 'Sauk-Centricities' of Sinclair Lewis," *Saturday Review*, XXXVII (August 15, 1955), 8.

[16] Letter to Carl Van Doren, October, 1921, *The Man from Main Street*, p. 141.

sources, and have educed the covert virtues and nobili-
ties of Gopher Prairie, overlooked by the less practical
heroine in chief; for this was to have been coincidently
the story of Bea's success and of Carol's failure as an
exponent of general social uplift: and would so have
converted the whole affair into a feminized and unreasonable down-to-date version of the Idle and Industrious
Apprentices.[17]

A trace of Lewis's original conception appears near the
beginning of the book. Carol's first walk down Main
Street is followed by Bea's, and the bitterness of one
newcomer is set against the enthusiasm of the other.
The chapter offers a clear indication of Lewis's intention
to make his readers understand the problem of the
Midwestern village in all its aspects.

If we were to regard *Main Street* as entirely satiric, the
ending would offer a special difficulty, for in the last
chapter Carol conforms to the village mores: "It was the
first time she had called Mrs. Clark by her given name;
the first time she had willingly sat back, a woman of
Main Street." Shortly before this she has decided to
forgive the villagers; though they have been shown as
ignorant at best and vicious at worst, she now decides
that they are not to blame:

> And why, she began to ask, did she rage at individuals?
> Not individuals but institutions are the enemies, and
> they most afflict the disciples who the most generously
> serve them. They insinuate their tyranny under a
> hundred guises and pompous names, such as Polite
> Society, the Family, the Church, Sound Business, the
> Party, the Country, the Superior White Race; and the
> only defense against them, Carol beheld, is unembittered
> laughter [430].

[17] James Branch Cabell, *Straws and Prayer-Books* (New York: McBride,
1924), pp. 50–51.

This resolution makes us feel that the comic or satiric spirit is behaving with giddy capriciousness in the novel. The villagers, once called "soulless inhabitants," apparently do not deserve such a harsh description; at any rate, the initial satiric view of them, like that in *Free Air*, is declared one-sided and inadequate. Yet a collectivity, no matter how pompous its name, is composed of individuals, and it is not made clear why the individuals in this book should be relieved of responsibility for the things we have seem them saying and doing. As Martin Light observes, Lewis seems unwilling to exploit the moral context which he himself has set up.[18] With a wave of his hand, he gives the inhabitants of Gopher Prairie a general pardon.

The difference between the title and the subtitle suggests that Lewis had a twofold intention: "Main Street" has an ironic double meaning, but "The Story of Carol Kennicott" promises a simple narrative. If he had wanted to write only a satire, Lewis could have omitted the last two hundred pages: by page 250 nearly all of the principal criticisms have been made. Actually, the book breaks in two at Chapter XIX, where we are told that three years of Carol's life passed like one curt paragraph. The first part deals with the faults of Main Street; it is also the story of a marriage, especially in Chapters XIV to XVII, but the satire is more important. In the second part, when Carol meets the local-boy-made-good, Perce Bresnahan, he does not receive the satiric treatment we might expect; instead, Carol's awareness of his charm is emphasized. Nor does her affair with Erik Valborg add to the satiric picture of the town. A woman approaching middle age, foreseeing a drab future and wanting to hold on to as much of romantic youth as she still possesses, is

[18] Martin Light, "A Study of Characterization in Sinclair Lewis's Fiction" (Ph.D. dissertation, University of Illinois, 1960), pp. 165–166.

attracted to a young bohemian who talks about art instead of practicing it, who is obviously never going to do anything substantial to reform Gopher Prairie, and who eventually sells his soul to Hollywood. The situation focuses our attention on personal, not social, problems; moreover, if Main Street is prudish, gossiping, and censorious, Carol is indiscreet, as Will eventually makes her realize. The latter half of the book is mainly the story of a marriage; in it the novelist, not the satirist, predominates.

But it is the satire which is memorable. The first part of the book is an anatomy of provincialism, an examination, subject by subject, of what makes up life in America's Gopher Prairies: small-town streets, small-town parties, small-town gossip, small-town greed, pitifully small-town cultural endeavors. It is a stripping away of all pretensions to civilized life which leaves Main Street a naked symbol of dullness, conventionality, and sterility. In Carol's Seeing Main Street tour (Chapter IV), Lewis tries to give an impression of impartial observation— he even mentions the cleanliness of Haydock's store and the metallic enterprise of Clark's Hardware—but the cumulative effect (reinforced by Lewis's own comments: he will not allow the description to speak for itself) is of faded, disagreeable colors, planlessness, and impermanence. In the context, even objects which are not unpleasant, such as the agricultural implements in a warehouse, take on an ugly and sinister quality. We are made to see the village as Carol sees it: "The broad, straight, unenticing gashes of the streets let in the grasping prairie on every side." Our normal perspective has been altered; this environment is not merely unattractive, but threatening.

The characters are depicted from the same grotesque point of view. Many of them are types—the town doctor,

the town gossip, the town atheist, the frustrated schoolteacher, the rebellious young artist; they are two-dimen-
sional figures, painted in primary colors. They have no
minds, only voices; loudmouthed, breezy pioneers, they
speak with a "barbaric yawp." Even Miles Bjornstam,
who scoffs at Gopher Prairie's standards, roars at rather
than talks to Carol. The women ordinarily are Juanita
Haydocks, vociferous and insensitive:

> "They're ungrateful, all that class of people. I do
> think the domestic problem is becoming simply awful.
> I don't know what the country's coming to, with these
> Scandahoofian clodhoppers demanding every cent you
> can save, and so ignorant and impertinent, and on my
> word, demanding bath-tubs and everything—as if they
> weren't might good and lucky at home if they got a bath
> in the wash-tub" [89–90].

As the quotation shows, the villager's principles and
behavior are as grotesque as their speech. Sometimes
the effect aimed at is principally one of amusement, as
when the Thanatopsis Club disposes of the English Poets
in one of its meetings and gamely prepares to cover all
of English Fiction and Essays in the next. Similarly,
Lewis sees material for comedy in the opinions of people
like Aunt Bessie and Uncle Whittier, who are staggered
to learn that a real live person in their own Minnesota
can believe that capitalism and the Baptist wedding
ceremony were not known in the Garden of Eden. The
wonderful old pioneers, the Perrys, hold equally out-
landish opinions—for example, they think that all so-
cialists ought to be hanged—but they too are a source of
harmless amusement. On the other hand, the majority
of the townspeople, gathered into packs for defense
against the alien and the unfamiliar, are formidable,
even monstrous. At the first party Carol attends, they
terrify her. "They will be cordial to me," she says,

"because my man belongs to their tribe. God help me if I were an outsider!" (52) Miles and Bea Bjornstam *are* outsiders, and to them no quarter is extended; at their marriage there are only nine guests, at the funeral of Bea and her son, Miles is the only mourner. When Mrs. Bogart accuses Fern Mullins, the schoolteacher, of corrupting her son Cy, the townspeople appear as hateful ogres demanding a sacrifice. Even their children, Carol sees, offer no hope of improvement: "there was no youth in all the town, she agonized. They were born old, grim and old and spying and censorious" (102).

But with his typical inconsistency Lewis sometimes hides the monstrousness of his figures and portrays them as ordinary likable human beings. As in Rabelais, the characters shift in size, seeming to become now larger and now smaller, now more threatening and now less; a characteristic will be stressed and possibly exaggerated by Lewis when it suits his purpose. Will Kennicott, for instance, subdues his local patriotism sufficiently to woo Carol with a challenge: "Come on. Come to Gopher Prairie. Show us" (17). Later he appears crude, loudmouthed, and hidebound: "Next thing, I suppose you'll be yapping about free speech. Free speech! There's too much free speech and free beer and free love and all the rest of your damned mouthy freedom, and if I had my way I'd make you folks live up to the established rules of decency . . ." (420). A few pages after this, he is once more presented as a sensitive and considerate person, possessing some independence from his environment instead of merely voicing its narrow bigotry.

Thus we are faced with the paradox that in the novel in which he gave such a forceful indictment of village life that he made Main Street a generally accepted symbol for constricting provincialism, Lewis revealed his own indecisiveness concerning the prairie village and its inhabitants. He is certainly not criticizing the Midwest from an eastern or a European perspective; the standards of Main Street may be crude, but he is not sure that those of New York, London, or Paris are any more satisfactory. Furthermore, at the same time as he diagnoses Main Street's ills, he provides an excuse for them. It is suggested by the very first sentence of Chapter I: "On a hill by the Mississippi where Chippewas camped two generations ago, a girl stood in relief against the cornflower blue of Northern sky." The excuse is simply that the Midwest is not old enough to know any better. Early in Chapter II, Carol thinks of the northern Middle West as the newest empire of the world and wonders what its future will be: "The ancient stale inequalities, or something different in history, unlike the tedious maturity of other empires?" In Chapter IV, the growth in democracy is emphasized when old Ezra Stowbody, a "distinguished bird of prey" who established a bank in Gopher Prairie in 1865, deplores the fact that the town is no longer run by him, together with the doctor, the lawyer, and the clergyman, but has become "as heterogeneous as Chicago." Shortly before Carol returns to Gopher Prairie, she reflects on it as "a toiling new settlement" whose inhabitants, as Will once told her, are "a lot of pretty good folks, working hard and trying to bring up their families the best they can" (442). Finally, "She looked across the silent fields to the west. She was conscious of an unbroken sweep of land to the Rockies, to Alaska; a dominion which will rise to unexampled greatness when other empires have grown senile" (450). In the Midwest lies the hope of Carol—and of Lewis—for a richer and fuller type of life than has ever before existed.

The fundamental criticism of *Main Street*, according to Walter Fuller Taylor, is that the book is not realistic fiction but "a satirical problem novel, in which the ridiculous is heightened for purposes of caricature, and in which the characters, far from being made true to life, are so created and disposed as to drive home the author's controlling thesis."[19] Thus Carol is created to voice Lewis's own criticisms of Main Street, while Guy Pollock illustrates the enervation of spirit caused by the village virus, Jim Blausser the banality of boosting, and Vida Sherwin the futility of uplift. Taylor's discussion exemplifies the view that writing a satiric novel instead of a realistic one is an indictable offense. He may be correct in his judgment that Lewis's people are "too obviously created to point a moral," but he fails to consider that the satirist's aims, and the means he uses to achieve them, are different from those of the realistic novelist. Humbert Wolfe develops this point with regard to characterization:

> Nor ... is it the business of the satirist to make his creatures men and women, but rather types of their failure. The novelist, who uses his story for the purpose of the satirist, will fail as both, or certainly as one. Thus, if Swift had sought to interest us in the love-affairs of Gulliver, we had had more of a man and less of a satire.[20]

The point is overstressed by Wolfe—obviously such a thing as a satiric novel *is* possible—but he does establish that there is a conflict of allegiances, a conflict to which Lewis fell victim. He should be criticized, not for making his men and women types of their failure, but for insinuating at the end of the book that they possess redeeming qualities which he has denied them throughout.

Perhaps Taylor's contention that Lewis drives home his thesis too insistently is another question. William Lyon Phelps once wrote that each of Lewis's major novels except *Dodsworth* resembles an explosion: "It is like a

[19] *A History of American Letters* (Boston: American Book Co., 1936), p. 384.
[20] Humbert Wolfe, *Notes on English Verse Satire* (London: Hogarth Press, 1929), p. 12.

steady barrage; it is like anything outrageously, persistently, brainsplittingly noisy."[21] Schorer says that Lewis's stylistic method was fixed by his writing of magazine stories; the audience he was addressing demanded the broad, the obvious, the overdrawn; and any potentialities for impressionistic nuance and suggestiveness either vanished entirely or were diverted into purple patches.[22] In *Main Street*, not much is left to the reader's imagination. Frequently the dialogue illustrates a point just previously established in a descriptive passage: Lewis follows a mechanical procedure of saying something first and then giving an example of it. But against the accusation of blatancy and over-obviousness he has two defenses. One is that he was dealing with blatant and obvious conditions, conditions which according to his thesis were obviously, plainly, palpably ludicrous. He was adopting a manner fitted to the portrayal of Boosterland. Second, he probably felt that subtle methods would not be effective. As Herbert J. Seligmann put it in a review of *Main Street*: "Having fed the voracious maw of the *Saturday Evening Post*, he knew that for its millions of readers—the very people who might read his book—it would not be enough to allude satirically to the threadbare qualities of their lives; the case against them and their kind, against this nation of small-towns, must be stated, proved, documented, hammered mercilessly into their consciousness."[23]

Still Lewis is open to the charges that he does not have enough satiric techniques at his disposal, that he over-uses a few favorite devices, and that he lacks variety and ingenuity. He was impatient of discussions of style; in his Nobel Prize address (1930), he made a sardonic reference to the subject: "I am not exactly sure what this mystic

[21] Review of Lewis's *Ann Vickers*, *Scribner's*, XCIII (1933), 256.

[22] *Sinclair Lewis*, p. 241.

[23] Review of *Main Street*, *Freeman*, II (1920), 237.

quality 'style' may be, but I find the word so often in the writings of minor critics that I suppose it must exist ...." [24] In "A Letter on Style" which he wrote for a collection of essays on the art of writing, he declared that no competent writer ever uses the term "style" in regard to his own work after his apprenticeship, that the generic concept of style as something apart from matter or thought does not enter the writer's mind, and that the whole topic is outmoded and as abstract as metaphysics. [25] Grace Lewis calls him a skillful editor rather than a self-conscious stylist: "the use of the leitmotif in language, or regarding a novel as a symphony, a work in counterpoint, a thematic fabric—this was precious entertainment in which Lewis did not indulge." [26] His ideal was to say the thing plainly; he disliked the experimental, the *avant-garde*, the obscure.

In feigning such a lofty unconcern with style, Lewis was, of course, adopting a defensive posture, trying to minimize the critics' attacks on his habitual infelicities. It is worth observing that the success of *Main Street* and *Babbitt* did not rest on a new-found competence by their author in the writing of English prose. He still relied heavily on un-subtle types of verbal irony and irony of manner. Malcolm Cowley complains that if Lewis wants to say that a speech is dull and insipid, he has to call it "the culminating glory of the dinner" and say that it was delivered by a Mrs. Adelaide Tarr Gimmitch. [27] The irony is often used with a coy false naivete, as in the Nobel Prize speech, in which he referred to Hemingway as "a bitter youth" and Wolfe as "a child of, I believe, thirty or younger," and said that

[24] *The Man from Main Street*, p. 8.

[25] The "Letter" was written in 1932; see *The Man from Main Street*, pp. 188–190.

[26] *With Love from Gracie*, p. 191

[27] Malcolm Cowley, "A Natural History of American Naturalism," in *Critiques and Essays on Modern Fiction, 1920–1951*, ed. John W. Aldridge (New York: Ronald Press, 1952), p. 385.

O'Neill "has done nothing much in American drama save to transform it utterly . . . ." Often the attempt at irony is signaled by an adjective chosen for its startling inappropriateness, as when Lewis writes in *Main Street*, "Then in a shy avalanche arrived the entire aristocracy of Gopher Prairie . . . " (74). The use of an unexpected word is one of Lewis's favorite tricks of style; he likes nothing better than to yoke heterogeneous opposites violently together, as when he writes that "England has . . . done quite as much pioneering—and done it as bravely and as cruelly and as unscrupulously as have we . . . ."[28] In *Main Street* we are informed that Mrs. Bogart "had so painfully reared three sons to be Christian gentlemen that one of them had become an Omaha bartender, one a professor of Greek, and one . . . the most brazen member of the toughest gang in Boytown" (69). The juxtaposition of incongruities is, as in the preceding, often too contrived; the bartender and the youthful gangster are conceivable, but not the professor of Greek, so that the sentence strikes the reader as a cheap attempt at humor. The irony is better when it is more restrained, when without comment it suggests the difference between expectation and reality or the contrast in viewpoints; Carol sees the Pacific Flyer go by, "an arrow of golden flame," and then Kennicott gives his version of that fire and wonder: "No. 19. Must be 'bout ten minutes late." The satire is best when it is closest to bald description or when the villagers give themselves away in their speech, either uttering the banalities of Main Street or, as in Jim Blausser's oration on Boosting Gopher Prairie, exuberantly singing its praises.

Main Street was the first example of Sinclair Lewis's astonishing ability to impress and convince the public. "For the first time," Lewis Mumford wrote, "all the nebulous criticism and dissatisfaction, which had been

[28] "Unpublished Introduction to *Babbitt*," *The Man from Main Street*, p. 26.

accumulating over a long period, had found a voice, and what is more important, had been embodied in creatures of flesh and blood."[29] Stuart Sherman described the advent of Sinclair Lewis in similar terms; for years there had been no writer of realistic prose fiction except Dreiser, "a barbarian who has never learned to write English," and then in the fall of 1920 Lewis arrived "to deliver the beleaguered citadel of our hope and sanity . . . ."[30] The literati praised *Main Street* almost in chorus; even when there were reservations about Lewis's plotting, style, or methods of characterization, there was almost unqualified gratitude for so complete a casebook of stupidities, so massive a club with which to beat the philistines. The nature of the book's reception is suggested by a letter which Lewis received from the distinguished English novelist John Galsworthy: "so wholesome and faithful a satiric attitude of mind has been rather conspicuously absent from American thought and literature. . . . Every country, of course, has its Main Streets, all richly deserving of diagnosis, but America is lucky to have found in you so poignant and just and stimulating a diagnostician."[31] Many observers thought that Lewis had written of American herd life with the intellectual rigor and critical detachment previously employed only by alien commentators on American culture such as Matthew Arnold. Sherman declared that *Main Street* had shaken American complacency more thoroughly than any other novel since *Uncle Tom's Cabin*. He also stated that it had broken the tradition that a novel had to be sentimental in order to be read, and asserted that the new form of the American novel depended on its author.

[29] Lewis Mumford, "The America of Sinclair Lewis," *Current History*, XXXIII (1931), 529.

[30] Stuart Sherman, *The Significance of Sinclair Lewis* (New York: Harcourt, Brace, 1922), p. 2.

[31] *From Main Street to Stockholm*, pp. 47–48.

Not all the reactions were favorable; indeed, Couch says that there was a civil war over the book.[32] Lewis Gannett, rereading the novel in 1949, found it an affectionate story, "a fact that wasn't at all obvious in 1920. We were so smug then that any criticism seemed a hostile act."[33] There is some justification for his opinion that America in 1920 was a wife who could not stand having her faults pointed out, for many Americans misunderstood, resented, and denounced the book. Its tone was often described as vitriolic; even a favorable reviewer said that it was leavened with hydrocyanic acid. Hamlin Garland, though he had once tried to write of the Midwest in an unsentimental way, complained that Lewis had belittled the descendants of the old frontier.[34] Catherine Beach Ely called the book "a mud puddle of sordid tattle" and hoped that the inherent wholesomeness of the American system would prevent this pap from being absorbed too deeply.[35] The Episcopal Bishop of Western New York termed *Main Street* a pagan book and declared that novels of this kind were "little more than sodden depression."[36] The abuse, like the praise, poured forth in torrents. Demonstrating the division of feeling, the trustees of Columbia University overruled the jury which had selected Lewis's book for the Pulitzer Prize in fiction and instead gave the award to Edith Warton for *The Age of Innocence*.

With the success of *Main Street*, Lewis was popularly viewed as one of the leaders of a generation in revolt.

[32] William Couch, Jr., "The Emergence, Rise and Decline of the Reputation of Sinclair Lewis" (Ph.D. dissertation, University of Chicago, 1954), p. 67.

[33] Lewis Gannett, "Sinclair Lewis: Main Street," in a series entitled "Looking Backwards," *Saturday Review of Literature*, XXXII (August 6, 1949), 31.

[34] Schorer, *Sinclair Lewis*, p. 269.

[35] Catherine Beach Ely, "A Belated Promenade on Main Street," New York *Times Book Review*, May 8, 1921, p. 16.

[36] Reported in the New York *Times*, July 14, 1921, p. 17.

The disillusioned young intellectuals were then the subject of considerable discussion; usually listed among them, according to Helen Bullitt Lowry, were Sherwood Anderson, Waldo Frank, Floyd Dell, Lewis, and F. Scott Fitzgerald as a specimen of the "flapper-intellectual." She thought that it was very hard to find the basis of their disillusionment; in fact, the only common ground she could discover was that they praised each other's works. In illustration, she quoted a characteristic passage from an essay on Floyd Dell by Lewis which had just appeared in the *Bookman*—"A valiant gentleness, a robust sensitiveness, a faun at the barricades"; wondering at the absence of any sign of disillusionment or bitter realism, she observed that the essay ran on like a purling brook.[37] Interviewing Lewis at about the same time, W. G. Wagstaffe tried to get him to explain the revolutionary ideas of the younger writers. The so-called revolt seemed to Wagstaffe only the old story of the younger generation rebelling against its fathers. Under persistent questioning as to why this particular revolt was unique, Lewis could only respond with trite and well-worn sentiments: the keynote of these writers was experiment, he said, and there was a new note in America's national literature, an attempt to capture truth. He was unable to convince Wagstaffe that the experiment was anything but a tepid one, especially since the dominant impression he conveyed was not of vigorous protest but the self-satisfaction of a man who had just written a best seller.[38]

Lewis was scarcely typical of the writers in revolt. He was not one of those who found America soul-destroying and fled to Paris—though he fled from his native land

[37] Helen Bullitt Lowry, "Mutual Admiration Society of Young Intellectuals," New York *Times Book Review*, May 8, 1921, pp. 6, 25.
[38] W. G. Wagstaffe, "As Sinclair Lewis Sees the Rest of Them," New York *Times Book Review*, May 29, 1921, p. 10.

many times. Nor was he a perfect Greenwich Villager like his "faun at the barricades," Floyd Dell. Such a record of the rebellious mind of the twenties as Dell's *Intellectual Vagabondage*—"A Spiritual Autobiography of My Own Generation in Its Literary and Social Aspects"—did not epitomize the story of Lewis's development. Though he too delighted in vagabondage, took Wells and Shaw as his prophets, and discovered a "Glorious Playfellow," the new woman, he did not run through the variety of intellectual positions and modes of life which Dell describes— and which were described in many another "spiritual autobiography" from the 1920's. Indeed, Henry F. May notes that *Main Street* contains one of the few hostile sketches of the Chicago Bohemia in which Dell lived for five years: Carol "almost gave up library work to become one of the young women who dance in cheese-cloth in the moonlight," but this phase of her life soon passed, and Lewis implies that it was a very good thing it did so.[39]

Yet Lewis was bound to be affected by the spirit of the twenties, a decade in which restraints were abandoned and hedonism tried on an unprecedented scale. In keeping with his times, Lewis sometimes wrote and acted as if marriage were an outmoded institution; but the correlative idea that a free and uninhibited love would provide the key to perfect happiness received little support from him. When he compared *Main Street* with *Madame Bovary*, Stuart Sherman considered that Lewis differed strikingly from Flaubert in not making the erotic passion the center of his theme. Lewis did not appear to think that this was the dominant concern of the American middle class, and Carol's revolt had little to do with the demand for sexual freedom. The aspect of freedom which Lewis probably emphasized most strongly was that singled out by Carl

[39] Henry F. May, *The End of American Innocence* (New York: Knopf, 1959), p. 254.

Van Doren in a comparison of Lewis to Sherwood Anderson. He described them as being enlisted in essentially the same cause—the war against one hundred per cent Americanism and fundamentalism, against the doctrine that "an American to be a good American must agree with every prevailing orthodoxy in theology, politics, economics, and taste, and must school his manners accordingly until he would be interchangeable with any other American . . . ."[40] Van Doren recognized that this narrowness was very much at odds with the American tradition, in which the stock hero has always been the independent pioneer, the venturesome rather than the obedient figure. In Lewis's mind, the urge for freedom from conformity was linked with a return to the spirit of an earlier and simpler era; his constant demand was for change, but to him change meant a reversion to the values of a frontier society.

Freedom was an obsession with Lewis, and money gave him the key to it. Could he live up to his success? The remarkable thing is that, following freedom wherever it led—to flight from entanglements, to unreasonable demands on his friends, to dissipation—he managed to do so for a decade. He was by no means written out when he had finished the novel that had occupied his thoughts for so many years.

One of Lewis's major criticisms of Gopher Prairie is that, although it compares itself to Rome and Vienna, it will not acquire the scientific spirit and the international mind which would make it great. Lewis's own cosmopolitanism was more a matter of words than of spirit. This became apparent when, under very different circumstances from his cattle-boat trip of fourteen years before, he sailed for England with his family in May, 1921. *Main Street*

[40] Carl Van Doren, "Sinclair Lewis and Sherwood Anderson: A Study of Two Moralists," *Century*, CX (1925), 362–369.

had not had a large sale in England, partly because of an unenterprising publisher; yet there was considerable curiosity about the American who had dared to attack his homeland. "We're to meet H. G. Wells and Rebecca West this week, and to dine with Hugh Walpole, Frank Swinnerton, Rose Macaulay," Lewis reported in one letter. But the English intellectuals who expected him to respond favorably to their condescension toward Americans were in for a shock; as one of his friends put it, he charged them like Pancho Villa's irregular cavalry. He had not shown up the weakness and intolerance of his own country for the benefit of foreigners. His letters to Harcourt show him quickly becoming chauvinistic: England is a dying land and he would never like to live there. The younger American writers give a greater impression of energy than the English, who seem to be settling down to "a great smug contentment with their clever selves." The reminiscences of Grace Hegger Lewis, Dorothy Thompson, and his various friends and acquaintances emphasize that Lewis was never in the least Europeanized. In spite of the frequency with which he visited Europe, he did very little sight-seeing, he knew very little about European literature, and he associated with Americans by preference. Perry Miller described him as "about the most unperceptive and blundering of all the myriads of tourists this country annually exports." Thus despite his frequent references to the desirability of assimilating the best of European culture, Lewis assimilated very little of it himself. Abroad, he was defiant and defensive; in his last novel he had his hero say, "Sitting in San Miniato, looking at the altar screen, I caught myself humming *Casey Jones*." [41]

[41] See Lewis's letters to Harcourt, June 15, July 1, and August 3, 1921, *From Main Street to Stockholm*, pp. 73, 76, 81; *With Love from Gracie*, pp. 168–169, 261, 274; Dorothy Thompson, "The Boy and Man from Sauk Centre,"

From the Cornish coast, where the family vacationed in July, Lewis wrote that he had started *Babbitt* and that it was going to be a corker. For this book he needed to do some research; his publisher got requests for up-to-date information on the real estate business. At a sixteenth-century farmhouse in Kent which he rented for two months he finished his planning and began writing a first draft of the new novel. A brief interruption came when he received a visit from Harold Stearns, soon to establish a reputation with the symposium he edited on *Civilization in the United States*. An expert on Paris, Stearns offered to introduce Lewis to the City of Light. As yet, according to Grace Lewis, excessive drinking was not a problem for Lewis; however, this became a highly alcoholic excursion, perhaps a forewarning of things to come. Lewis was in Paris again in October, on the way to Italy with his family. He found a congenial bar frequented by newspapermen, but the literary expatriates did not give him a cordial welcome—Grace Lewis recalls that the crowds of young Americans, "all of whom knew each other and all of whom were playing at being French artists," were extremely hostile to Lewis and said the most insulting things about that commercial best seller, *Main Street*.[42]

The Lewises spent a delightful month at Pallanza—delightful except to Mrs. Lewis, who noticed her husband's interest in a pretty American girl. When the girl left for Rome, so did Lewis, ostensibly to find his family a home for the winter. His wife's suspicions were confirmed when she herself went to Rome, and the first of many estrangements took place. No doubt some of the

Atlantic Monthly, CCVI (November 1960), 45–46; Perry Miller, "The Incorruptible Sinclair Lewis," 30; Mark Schorer, *Sinclair Lewis*, pp. 310–311, 328–329; Vincent Sheean, *Dorothy and Red* (Boston: Houghton Mifflin, 1963), p. 211; Sinclair Lewis, *World So Wide* (New York: Random House, 1951), p. 229.

[42] *With Love from Gracie*, p. 184.

blame was hers, but there seems to be some justification for her complaint that Lewis was trying to turn love on and off like a faucet and was annoyed when the faucet did not work. The affair did not last long, but Rome proved too distracting; and early in January, 1922, Lewis returned to England alone. Established comfortably in London, he worked hard at *Babbitt*, so that he had finished a complete draft by mid-February and had the revised version ready for his wife to read when he met her at the dock at Southampton early in May. Three weeks later they sailed for New York on the *Aquitania*; to the newsmen who met the ship on its arrival, he delivered a lengthy lecture on England's shortcomings and on the chief discovery he had made during his trip abroad— that provincialism existed everywhere. *Babbitt* was published that fall.

In November, 1920, Lewis had written a letter to Carl Van Doren explaining what he intended to do in his next book:

> Already I am planning a second novel of the same general sort as *Main Street*, though utterly different in detail. It is, this time, the story not of a Carol but of an Average Business Man, a Tired Business Man, not in Gopher Prairie but in a city of three or four hundred thousand people (equally Minneapolis or Seattle or Rochester or Atlanta) with its enormous industrial power, its Little Theater and Master of the Fox Hounds and lively country club, and its overwhelming, menacing heresy hunt . . . . I hope to keep as far as may be from "propaganda"; I hope to make that man live.[43]

About a month later, he wrote to Alfred Harcourt that he wanted the book to be the "Great American Novel" "in so far as it crystallizes and makes real the Average Capable American. . . . [Babbitt] is all of us Americans

---

[43] Carl Van Doren, *Three Worlds* (New York: Harper, 1936), p. 146.

at 46, prosperous but worried, wanting—passionately—to seize something more than motor cars and a house *before it's too late*." [44] Although he told Harcourt that *Babbitt* was inherently more satiric than *Main Street*, in an early introduction not published in the book he had called the central character "too tragic a tyrant for the puerilities of deliberate satire." [45] Since the introduction was a carefully formulated statement rather than some preliminary musings on a theme, the uncertainty it reveals concerning whether Babbitt's tyranny or his tragedy ought to be given greater emphasis and whether he could properly be satirized is significant.

The first hundred pages of *Babbitt* describe, almost in mock-heroic fashion, a day in the life of the Average Business Man. The Substantial Citizen is taken at his own valuation; each event of his day is of world-shaking importance, and must be captured in photographic detail: Business Man shaving, Business Man changing suits, Business Man starting car, Business Man completing deal, and so on. The effect would be highly ironic if the author maintained his detachment. But instead of allowing us to infer the limitations of his hero, Lewis himself points them out: he stresses that in a city which seems built for giants George F. Babbitt is really a pygmy.

Babbitt is portrayed as the archetype of the Booster, loudmouthed, unthinking, and insensitive. His speech, compounded of the clichés and prejudices of his group, is not the expression of a sentient, rational human being. His symbols of truth and beauty are the mechanical devices which surround him, even though he understands nothing of their workings. Success for him means conformity to the pattern of living delineated by the one

[44] Letter to Harcourt, December 28, 1920, *From Main Street to Stockholm*, p. 59.
[45] The introduction is published in *The Man from Main Street*, pp. 21–29; the quotation is from p. 22.

true American art, advertising:

> Just as he was an Elk, a Booster, and a member of the
> Chamber of Commerce, just as the priests of the Presby-
> terian Church determined his every religious belief, and
> the senators who controlled the Republican Party decided
> in little smoky rooms in Washington what he should
> think about disarmament, tariff, and Germany, so did
> the large national advertisers fix the surface of his life,
> fix what he believed to be his individuality. These
> standard advertised wares—toothpastes, socks, tires,
> cameras, instantaneous hot-water heaters—were his
> symbols of excellence; at first the signs, then the substi-
> tutes, for joy and passion and wisdom [95].[46]

Though he loves "to speak sonorously of Unselfish
Public Service, the Broker's Obligation to Keep Invio-
late the Trust of His Clients, and a thing called Ethics,
whose nature was confusing," the value of his work to
society is exactly nothing. Beyond this, Seneca Doane, the
middle-of-the-road liberal who seems to represent Lewis's
point of view, maintains that he exercises a fearful
despotism:

> "What I fight in Zenith is standardization of thought, and,
> of course, the traditions of competition. The real villains
> of the piece are the clean, kind, industrious Family Men
> who use every known brand of trickery and cruelty to
> insure the prosperity of their cubs. The worst thing about
> these fellows is that they're so good and, in their work at
> least, so intelligent. You can't hate them properly, and
> yet their standardized minds are the enemy"[101].

Doane's assessment is in keeping with the unpublished
introduction—written when Lewis had not yet made his
final decision concerning his hero's name and was calling
him Pumphrey—which begins, "THIS IS THE STORY OF
THE RULER OF AMERICA" and ironically refers to "Our

[46] *Babbitt* (New York: Harcourt, Brace, 1922).

conqueror, dictator over our commerce, education, labor, art, politics, morals, and lack of conversation." [47] Lewis declares that the thirty million men of this type have an unparalleled autocratic control, for no rulers in past history have ever interfered so completely in their subject's activities:

> Though English morals and French politics and German industry have been determined by the Sound Middle-Class, the Bourgeoisie, the Pumphreysie, have never dared also to announce standards in sculpture and table-manners. For in those lands there are outcasts and aristocrats who smile at the impertinence of the unimaginative. But in America we have created the superman complete, and the mellifluous name of the archangelic monster is Pumphrey, good old G. T. Pumphrey, the plain citizen and omnipotent power. [48]

But Lewis does not sustain this view of his central character. He often shows Babbitt as a caricature of a real person, ironically prevented from becoming fully human by the restrictions which all the people of his class impose upon their society. However, Babbitt does possess an inner life, a yearning for the exotic and a native decency which separate him from his back-slapping associates—the Vergil Gunches and Chum Frinks—and link him with a misfit, Paul Riesling. Babbitt can be regarded as a buffoon: his name has entered the dictionaries as a synonym for blatancy; but that is not the whole of him.

Nor is he an "archangelic monster," a "superman complete." The more subtle conception of a character who, though sympathetic, is still the villain of the piece gives way to the more melodramatic conception of an *homme moyen sensuel* struggling helplessly against powerful ogres. Babbitt's moral failure is partly excusable: he tries to

[47] *The Man from Main Street*, p. 21
[48] *Ibid.*, p. 22.

revolt against conformity, but finds that it is impossible to do so and still survive. The Babbitts are only pawns in the hands of the real villains, the racketeers like Colonel Snow, Jake Offutt, and Henry Thompson. Lewis has fallen back upon a commonly held opinion concerning the source of evil in the American Garden of Eden; Henry F. May writes,

> When the muckrakers brought them to light, cruelty and misery seemed a disgrace to America and the twentieth century. They were the product, not of any innate evil either in human nature or modern society, but of the corrupt power of a few .... Powerful and corrupt individuals had perverted the country's institutions and dammed for their own benefit the rivers of progress.[49]

Lewis accepts the middle-class myth that the Babbitts are not to blame. Though we can convict Babbitt of hypocrisy and affectation—and one main thread of the book is the comic exposure of these—he is the victim of a tragic irony: he acts as though he had some control over his own affairs, becoming almost heroic in a struggle which he has no chance of winning.

Curiously, however, Lewis allows him to sink back from defiant hero to Average Business Man again. Eventually he swears allegiance to the Good Citizen's League:

> Within two weeks no one in the League was more violent regarding the wickedness of Seneca Doane, the crimes of labor unions, the perils of immigration, and the delights of gold, morality, and bank-accounts than was George F. Babbitt [390].

Although he has seen how ugly is the behavior of the Booster's Club and how empty are its oracles, he is happy to be welcomed back into it. And with an incredible disregard of his own bitter experiences, he tells his son, "Go ahead, old man! The world is yours!"

[49] May, *The End of American Innocence*, p. 23.

Just as there are two Babbitts, there are two themes. Lewis is partly concerned with sociological analysis, with an anatomy of the businessman's world. He employs the satirist's techniques of selection and distortion; the day in Babbitt's life which takes up the first quarter of the book shows us a caricature of a businessman engaged in a parody of business activity. After that, there is a series of satirical episodes connected only by the fact that Babbitt has something to do with them. The Real Estate Boards convention shows us hysterical local patriotism and males in a happy state of nature. Lunches at the "Roughnecks' Table" at the Athletic Club, a college reunion, a civic election, and various other events round out the picture of group behavior and exhibit the full range of group opinion and prejudice. The universality of Babbittry is made apparent when Babbitt discovers that his sales techniques are just the thing which religion needs. Lewis's method thus permits a general satiric attack, beginning with a single point, the main character, and tracing around him the whole circle of society.[50]

In his desire to be as comprehensive as possible, Lewis connects some of the satire only very loosely with Babbitt. When young Ted receives some correspondence-school circulars, Lewis is given an opportunity to ridicule them. Since Babbitt knows a real, live, A-one poet, Chum Frink, Lewis can parody the verse and satirize the outlook of an Edgar Guest. When Mrs. Babbitt conducts a revolt of her own in the direction of Higher Thought—presumably suggested by New Thought—Lewis forces his hero to sit through a lecture by Mrs. Opal Emerson Mudge on "Cultivating the Sun Spirit." In a survey of what is going

[50] Arthur B. Coleman in "The Genesis of Social Ideas in Sinclair Lewis" (Ph.D. dissertation, New York University, 1954), pp. 62–64, writes that *Babbitt* is strikingly based on viewpoints expressed in Veblen's *Theory of the Leisure Class* and gives a long list of examples of conspicuous consumption which indicate that the Babbitts are in the best Floral Heights society.

on in Zenith when Babbitt goes to bed, Lewis brings in Mike Monday (Billy Sunday) and lets him evangelize for the length of a page. The loose form of the novel allows Lewis plenty of scope for take-offs on people familiar to the citizens of all the Zeniths.

"Form letters, advertisements, six-page conversations about prohibition, evangelical sermons by Mike Monday, all are put in, head first. And out of this, about two-thirds way through the book, Mr. Lewis gets down to the business of writing a novel with created characters and very nearly pulls it off"—So wrote the *Dial* reviewer.[51] But in the melodramatic story of how Babbitt, now a hero, battles his former friends, now villains, the characters are simple and unreal, the plot is full of improbabilities, and Lewis does not come close to pulling it off. A possible criticism is that, whereas Lewis can amuse us with his Boosters' Club, he cannot frighten us with his Good Citizens' League. The qualities of the characters are as heightened and exaggerated as they were before; previously the exaggeration led to laughter, and it is very difficult for the reader to change his reponse just because Lewis tells him to do so: these fairy-tales giants and ogres cannot hurt us. But perhaps there is something particularly monstrous about these hearty, laughing, mechanical men beginning to torture someone; at any rate, their Vigilante Committee is horrifying, and the growth of Babbitt's fear after their ostracism of him is made very real. Yet it is hard to accept the turns of the plot, especially the new awareness with which Babbitt is endowed and then his loss of it and relapse into his former state.

Edward Wagenknecht contends that the change in Babbitt is prepared for or nonexistent, since Lewis skillfully prevents his hero from ever declining into a mere stalking-horse—in college, for example, he was "an unusually liberal, sensitive chap" who wanted to be a lawyer and take the cases of the poor for nothing.[52] Virginia Woolf, however, seems nearer the mark when she describes Lewis's attempts to convey Babbitt's sensitivity as awkward and unconvincing. Commenting on the dream of a fairy child—"Her dear and tranquil hand caressed his cheek. He was gallant and wise and well-beloved; warm ivory were her arms; and beyond perilous moors the brave sea glittered"—she observes that this is not a dream at all but "the protest of a man who has never dreamed in his life, but is determined to prove that dreaming is as easy as shelling peas."[53] Babbitt's inwardness, of course, is just what Lewis did not want to show if he were to hold to his original conception of a man who lived by externals, by things which could be bought and sold and advertised. He could have shown the uncertainty which mocked the confident exterior, the fear in a handful of dust; instead, he tried to convince his readers that Babbitt's naive questionings and affirmations represented something deep and true and unperverted.

What Frederick J. Hoffman calls the parody Babbitt,[54] therefore, is the vivid and memorable one. The most frequent tributes to the book were that Babbitt was characterized with gusto and that Lewis had succeeded in presenting the commonplace in lively terms; he had caught the American businessman in all his vulgarity and "vile gregariousness," as H. G. Wells put it in a letter of congratulation.[55] He had, in fact, created a whole herd of Babbitts, all of them voicing the same crude prejudices and platitudes, all of them employing the same slangy,

[52] Edward Wagenknecht, *Cavalcade of the American Novel* (New York: Holt, 1952), p. 358.

[53] Virginia Woolf, "American Fiction," in *The Moment* (London: Hogarth Press, 1947), pp. 99–100.

[54] Frederick J. Hoffman, *The Twenties: American Writing in the Postwar Decade* (New York: Viking Press, 1955), p. 366.

[55] The letter is quoted in Schorer, *Sinclair Lewis*, p. 349.

repetitious, bombastic utterance, all of them full of hearty boyish humor based on elaborate exaggeration and deliberate misrepresentation. They live in virtue of their talk; if some critics have disputed the opinion that Lewis had a marvelous ear for American speech, he undoubtedly had a knack for making speech sound authentic. In conversation or in satiric monologues delivered in a racy, convincing idiom, the Babbitts give themselves away; Babbitt's speech to the Zenith Real Estate Board provides what Hoffman terms a whole summary of tribal opinions and evaluations, a literary ordering of Mencken's accumulations, in the "Americana" section of his *Mercury*, of what the booboisie thought.[56]

Mencken delightedly wrote that for the first time the type had been captured in fiction: "For the first time a wholly genuine American has got into a book— not the lowly, aspiring, half-pathetic American of the hinterland, but the cocky, bustling, enormously successful American of the big towns—the Booster, the Master of Salesmanship, the Optimist, the 100 per cent Patriot and Right-Thinker."[57] Was this a large enough subject for a novel? Virginia Woolf did not think so. Rather patronizingly, she wrote that if Lewis had been born in England he might have proved himself the equal of Wells and Bennett, but, denied the riches of an old civilization, he had been forced to criticize rather than explore, and the object of his criticism—the life of Zenith—was unfortunately too meager to sustain him.[58] But the complaint of Cooper and Hawthorne and many another American

[56] Coleman, "Genesis," p. 74, points out a number of parallels between *Babbitt* and Mencken and Nathan's *An American Credo* (1921), for example that the type is insatiably ambitious yet incurably fearful, that he is assertive on the one hand but cautious and subservient on the other.

[57] H. L. Mencken, "Sinclair Lewis and 'Babbitt,'" *Now and Then*, October 22, 1922, p. 22.

[58] Virginia Woolf, "American Fiction," *The Moment*, p. 100.

novelist that the American scene offered a paucity of literary material was not and could not be Lewis's complaint. When *Babbitt* delineates his concept of the Ideal, Standardized Citizen and contrasts the new civilization of vital standardized living with the decadence of Europe, Lewis is implying that the whole nation has got into a blind alley of Babbittry.[59] Surely this is a major subject for satire; Lewis found it and exploited it, but unfortunately he was not satisfied with it—he gave rein to his naive romanticism and brought in some entirely alien fairy children, giants, and ogres.

With *Babbitt* Lewis began what was to be his characteristic method of composition, based on an intensive study of a subject. First came a preliminary stage of investigation, often requiring research trips and the services of an expert adviser, and always involving the taking of copious notes. Then came a stage of amazingly detailed planning. "He wrote his novels from precise and copious outlines of the characters, their professions or trades, and their haunts," wrote Dorothy Thompson, "building the structure of the book as an architect designs a house." [60] He had always drawn detailed maps of the more important fictional towns in his books. Charles Breasted, who was shown those for the novels from *Our Mr. Wrenn* on, noted, however, that between Gopher Prairie and Zenith "the detail increased until it was almost like an annotated commercial map ...." [61] In his arguments with George Soule over the importance of scene, Lewis had maintained that the remembered background, the "scene which ones knows by the ten thousand unconscious experiences of living in it," was the only one which a writer could express adequately.[62]

[59] Raymond Palmer stressed this point in his article "The Nobel Jury Judges America," *Christian Century*, XLVII (1930), 1449.

[60] Dorothy Thompson, "The Boy and Man from Sauk Centre," p. 45.

[61] Breasted, "'Sauk-Centricities,'" p. 35.

[62] "The American Scene in Fiction," *The Man from Main Street*, p. 142.

When he had to deal with an environment not lived in and remembered in this way, he apparently felt that he would have to familiarize himself with it to the greatest possible extent. He knew the streets in the business section of Zenith and the residential area of Floral Heights because he had examined their real-life prototypes with the greatest care; he tried to construct them with all the fullness of cities he knew. "By this folder full of maps," Breasted wrote, "Lewis had translated the world of his imagination and experience into something so close to reality that in listening to him one promptly became wholly convinced of their actuality." [63] When to his maps, charts, and notes recording examples of the various types of folly which he was investigating he added full biographies of all the important characters in his projected novel and an outline of the action, he had a formidable mass of material; his complete plan might be as long as an average novel.

From the first, *Babbitt* made its mark; it was quickly acclaimed as a classic burlesque of the businessman and his world. From expected quarters, especially in the Midwest, there came growls of resentment and protest, but Anne O'Hare McCormick reported in the New York *Times* just a month after the book's publication that even the Rotarians were reading it. Some people thought that Lewis filled his books with spleen; many thought that he hated his native land; but very many thought that he had made a brilliant attack on a vulnerable segment of American society. The reception of *Babbitt* abroad was equally favorable. "After *Babbitt* was published in London," writes Harrison Smith, "there was an immense curiosity about the man who had revitalized American literature, so that he was welcomed everywhere." [64] The curiosity

---

[63] Breasted, "'Sauk-Centricities,'" p. 35.
[64] Harrison Smith, Introduction to *From Main Street to Stockholm*, p. xii.

was not entirely attributable to the view that Lewis's fearless criticism had revitalized American literature; his novels seemed to justify the stereotype of the typical American as uncouth, materialistic, and ignorant of the finer things of life. Therefore Europeans generally viewed Babbitt as Mencken did, as a portrait of the wholly genuine American. They took seriously, of course, only the parody Babbitt, not the hesitant and soul-searching one. "To be labeled a 'Babbitt,'" says the article on the novel in the *Encyclopaedia Americana*, "carries with it the packaged stigma of obtuseness, philistinism, blatant optimism, want of humor, and a smug, uncritical acceptance of one's own standards, however narrow, benighted, and unlovely they may seem to others." [65] Whether or not Lewis wanted to attach other connotations to the name, this is what it has come to convey, both in America and in Europe. Sherard Vines wrote, "it was *Babbitt* which so impressed its portraiture on this island as almost to create a myth of America as one vast Babbitt warren; and at least replaced the old popular image of the thin American with a goatee beard, by that of a fat American with spectacles." [66] Similarly George Bernard Shaw declared that "Mr. Sinclair Lewis has knocked Washington off his pedestal and substituted *Babbitt*, who is now a European byword." [67]

One of the myths destroyed by Schorer is that of Lewis's dedication to his work and willingness to make sacrifices for it. Yet when Lewis wrote after the success of *Main Street* that he was going to "go on plugging at the Post," he added, "but I don't believe I shall ever again be the

[65] "Babbitt," *Encyclopaedia Americana*, Canadian edition, 1962.
[66] Sherard Vines, *A Hundred Years of English Literature* (London: Duckworth, 1950), p. 262.
[67] In a written reply to a New York *Times* correspondent who asked his opinion of Lewis's Nobel Prize address; quoted in "Do We Love Shaw's Abuse?" *Literary Digest*, CVIII (January 3, 1931), 17.

facile Post trickster I by God was . . . ." [68] He was willing
to listen to the criticisms of the more serious reviewers;
for example, he took to heart Francis Hackett's analysis
of some of the weaknesses in *Main Street* and vowed that
he would mend these faults in his next novel. Carl Van
Doren's suggestions that he had been influenced by
Masters and that before *Main Street* he had been a writer
of light chatter brought a long reply in which wounded
professional pride was very much in evidence. But the letters in *From Main Street to Stockholm* make it clear that,
having formerly been a huckster of other people's books,
Lewis continued as a huckster of his own. There were few
sales tricks to which he would not stoop; his publisher had
far more scruples than he. When Lewis wrote that he had
received a note from Hugh Walpole and added, "I'm sure
you could get a nice blurb about *Babbitt* from him . . . .
He leaves Saturday, *so nail him quick*," Harcourt replied
that "some unaccountable quirk of reticence" prevented
him from following the suggestion. [69] If the general public
was not aware of Lewis's intense desire for success, it
could not be hidden from New York literary circles. In
the *Bookman* for September, 1922, Lewis took his turn in a
series entitled "The Literary Spotlight"; an anonymous
writer (John Farrar) observed that mentioning "Main
Street" to Lewis was like putting a coin in a slot: "he
begins to pour forth, like a mechanical record, the latest
news about 'Main St.', and who was the last person to
compliment him upon it, and what it means and will
continue to mean for the world." Farrar declared that
Lewis "looks to the dollar barometer as to that by which
fame is most reliably measurable," and said that Lewis
talked about his books as salesmen talk about their cars:

[68] Letter to Harcourt, November 30, 1920, *From Main Street to Stockholm*,
p. 52.

[69] Letters of Lewis to Harcourt, September 28, 1922, and Harcourt to
Lewis, September 29, 1922, *From Main Street to Stockholm*, p. 112.

"I want to tell you that there's nothing like that little twelve cylinder Main Street . . . . Why, my wife and I went all the way to Europe and back on that car. Next year, we're going to have a new one. A Babbitt. I've tried it out . . . . Watch out for that bus. It's a knockout. I'll bet it beats all the records . . . ."

He concluded that Main Street, the insulted and injured, had won out after all, by taking Lewis into its materialistic camp, and making him worship its kind of success.[70]

[70] "The Literary Spotlight: XII. Sinclair Lewis," *Bookman*, LVI (September 1922), 58–59.

4. Aspiration and Enslavement

THE SYSTEMATIC NATURE of Lewis's assault on American life is obvious enough to have been often commented on.[1] Having examined the life of the village and the city, Lewis went on to explore the world of medicine in *Arrowsmith*, of religion in *Elmer Gantry*, of business leadership in *Dodsworth*, and of social work in *Ann Vickers*. Arthur B. Coleman shows that he employed the same social generalizations and the same pattern of plot in the later novels as he had used in the earlier: in each a character standing for a constructive way of life is pitted against representatives of everything restrictive, narrow, hypocritical, wasteful, and stupid in society. But the later protagonists differ from the earlier in being clearer in their ideas, stronger in their beliefs, and more uncompromising in their positions. Employing a term which Lewis used for the title of a late novel, Coleman describes these heroes as "god-seekers."[2] But did their

[1] See especially Robert Cantwell, "Sinclair Lewis," *New Republic*, LXXXVIII (1936), 298–301, and Leo and Miriam Gurko, "The Two Main Streets of Sinclair Lewis," *College English*, IV (1943), 288–292.

[2] Arthur B. Coleman, "The Genesis of Social Ideas in Sinclair Lewis"

creator believe that there were any gods to be found? At the end of his pamphlet on Lewis, published by Harcourt, Brace at about the same time as *Babbitt*, Stuart Sherman wrote that the one serious objection heard against Lewis's writings was that his standards were not sufficiently in evidence. As if in reply to the criticism, Lewis's next two important novels after *Babbitt* gave indications, first, of what he did believe in, and, second, of what he did not. Yet, in spite of their considerable degree of success as novels and as satires, they left his standards still in question.

Sherman had said that *Babbitt* would have been improved by the introduction of one or more characters "capable of reflecting upon the Babbitts oblique rays from a social and personal felicity, more genuine, more inward than any of the summoned witnesses possesses"; he had also declared that eventually, if Lewis did not wish to pass for a hardened pessimist, he would have to produce a hero registering his notion of the desirable.[3] Even before he had seen the pamphlet, Lewis had written Harcourt from Italy to say, "I think I shall make my next novel after *Babbitt* not satiric at all; rebellious as ever, perhaps, but the central character *heroic*. I'm already getting gleams for it; I see it as the biggest thing I've tackled."[4] During the summer of 1922, when he had finished *Babbitt* and was waiting for its publication, he was a novelist in search of a hero. He still had only vague gleams until the day in August when, at Carl Sandburg's home in Chicago, he met Eugene Victor Debs, former railway fireman, labor leader, and

(Ph.D. dissertation, New York University, 1954), p. 80. Martin Light discusses the same point in his "A Study of Characterization in Sinclair Lewis's Fiction" (Ph.D. dissertation, University of Illinois, 1960), p. 80.

[3] Stuart Sherman, *The Significance of Sinclair Lewis* (New York: Harcourt, Brace, 1922), p. 20.

[4] Letter to Harcourt, December 13, 1921, *From Main Street to Stockholm: Letters of Sinclair Lewis 1919–1930*, ed. with an intro. by Harrison Smith (New York: Harcourt, Brace, 1952), p. 90.

Socialist candidate for President, who had been sentenced to prison in 1918 for advocating pacifism and had recently had his sentence commuted by President Harding. Lewis wrote enthusiastically to his wife that he had found his hero; Gene was "really a Christ spirit. He is infinitely wise, kind, forgiving . . . ." [5] He was also, apparently, a good listener: he gave close and sympathetic attention while Lewis quickly sketched a plan for a labor novel, to be entitled *Neighbor* and to contain "something of himself —tho vastly different in details . . . ." [6] Three days later, however, Lewis's enthusiasm for the subject—but not the hero—had waned; he wrote that he was melancholy and felt rather lost because he did not believe that he would be able to write the novel:

> For an hour or a day I can work up a complete conformist sympathy with the union men; then the sight of a group of lolling & ignorant rough necks, addressed by an agitator who is going immediately to supplant the capitalists—& who couldn't run a fruit stand—gets my goat & I compare him with doctors, bankers, editors we know. A Debs lasts; he is pure spirit; he would walk to his crucifixion with firm & quiet joy. But there's so few Debses! [7]

Meanwhile, another subject had caught his fancy. A year previously, he had met Dr. Morris Fishbein, who in the course of a long career as spokesman for the American Medical Association and editor of its journal was to acquire a fame comparable to Lewis's own and an influence far greater. Now Fishbein introduced him to Paul de Kruif, a bacteriologist who had recently had to leave the Rockefeller Institute after writing a book entitled *Our Medicine Men* in which he had mocked the so-called

[5] Grace Hegger Lewis, *With Love from Gracie: Sinclair Lewis: 1912–1925* (New York: Harcourt, Brace, 1955), p. 210

[6] *Ibid.*, p. 211.

[7] *Ibid.*, p. 212.

experimental rigor of some Rockefeller scientists testing a new type of serum. Since the occasion on which Lewis met de Kruif turned into a prolonged, alcoholic, and confusing evening, Lewis's recollections of it are not entirely trust-worthy; yet it seems likely that, as the other two talked about how difficult it was for a young man in America to devote himself to pure research, Lewis realized that he had found the theme for his next book. In an account which appeared in *The Designer and the Woman's Magazine* in June, 1924, he recalled that as he listened to the others he meditated, "Here's my next novel . . . . What protag-onist of fiction could be more interesting, more dramatic, and less hackneyed than a doctor who, starting out as a competent general practitioner, emerges as a real scien-tist, despising ordinary 'success'?"[8] But if Lewis was capable of grasping the significance of this subject, de Kruif's memoir *The Sweeping Wind* indicates that he was also capable of forgetting it. Lewis proposed that they collaborate on the projected novel; he thought that he had found the ideal scientific informant in de Kruif, and de Kruif, jobless and striving to gain a foothold in the literary world, considered this a heaven-sent opportunity. But later on when they met in New York, de Kruif found to his dismay that the novel seemed to have evaporated from Lewis's memory. Instead, Lewis rapidly outlined a plan for a series of short stories, "stories with a new type of hero, a character—bacteriologist, doctor, public health detective—all in one. A kind of scientific Clarence Budington Kelland production." It took the diplomatic intervention of Harcourt, Brace, de Kruif recalls, to keep Lewis from dragging "me with him on a relapse into the George Horace Lorimer school of literature."[9]

[8] *The Designer and the Woman's Magazine*, LX (June 1924), 2.
[9] Paul de Kruif, *The Sweeping Wind* (New York: Harcourt, Brace, 1962), p. 76.

While Lewis had been in Chicago, his wife and son had been enjoying a resort life at Fishers Island, New York. For the winter the family took what Grace referred to as an "amusing" house in Hartford, but their cordial welcome in that city was soon outlived. The Lewises were appalled at the smug commercialism of Hartford, which Lewis called only another Gopher Prairie or Zenith, and Hartford in turn was shocked by the Lewises' social indiscretions. Lewis escaped to New York, then went on a six-week lecture tour, traveled to Quebec with his wife, and finally left on a ship with de Kruif. In December de Kruif and he signed a contract providing for their collaboration on a novel dealing with medicine; Lewis was to receive 75 per cent of the royalties and de Kruif 25. With a very substantial advance to his credit, de Kruif returned to Michigan to marry a former student of his at the University, before rejoining Lewis for an alcoholic leave-taking of America's shores on January 4.

His publishers apparently hoped that Lewis's growing dependence on alcohol would be restrained by de Kruif, who had promised "to keep our genius, Red, this side of delirium tremens." [10] On their voyage to the Virgin Islands and the Barbados aboard the British ship *Guiana* and during their cruise of the Spanish Main aboard the Dutch ship *Crynssen*, there were ample opportunities for conviviality. But despite "ruinous rum swizzles" and other concoctions, they did a great deal of hard work. Much of it consisted of talking and arguing; out of such discussions Lewis got the material for "hundreds of notes, schedules, maps . . . ." De Kruif had known some great men of science, in particular Jacques Loeb at the Rockefeller Institute and Dr. Frederick George Novy at the University of Michigan, and he was able to convey to Lewis exactly what dedication to scientific research really

[10] *Ibid.*, p. 103.

meant. His theoretical instruction was supplemented with practical when they visited research laboratories, first in Panama and later in Paris and London. As the voyage continued, the skeleton of the book became more and more clearly outlined. De Kruif recalled how a large square on Santa Lucia, deserted on a lazy Sunday afternoon, suggested to their minds the tropical city smitten by bubonic plague which was to be an important setting in the novel. Lewis was enthusiastic about his collaborator; he wrote that de Kruif was perfection—he had an astonishing grasp of scientific detail and yet the imagination of a fiction writer. De Kruif, on his part, was equally admiring. In an account of the experience entitled "An Intimate Glimpse of a Great American Novel in the Making," he described his wonder at Lewis's ability to pick his brains and to assimilate scientific information.[11]

On February 18 Lewis wrote his father that the book was going superbly and that he had written twenty-five thousand words of plan. He had already decided that he would not return to New York but would go to England to do the actual writing; and by early March he was established in London once again, working at the manuscript of a novel provisionally entitled *The Barbarian*. Lewis and Harcourt carried on a lengthy correspondence about other possible choices; when he announced "the plan all finished" in early May, he still had a list of ten titles to be considered. Eventually he decided on *Dr. Martin Arrowsmith* for the serialized version and simply *Arrowsmith* for the American edition of the book, noting that *"it's his personal and scientific career that counts much more than his medical career . . . ."*[12]

When his wife arrived in mid-May, Lewis put his work

---

[11] *The Designer and the Woman's Magazine*, LX (June 1924), 64.

[12] Letter to Harcourt, December 3, 1923, *From Main Street to Stockholm*, p. 147.

aside and attempted to make up for some months of neglect by taking her on a walking tour of Devon and engaging her in a gay round of social life in London. For the summer they rented a house near Fontainebleau, just outside of Paris; there Lewis got back in stride, and after three months of the most concentrated effort he was able to show de Kruif, whose response was enthusiastic, a mammoth first draft of 748 pages, or 245,000 words. This accomplished, Lewis and his wife went on a holiday in Switzerland and Italy, depositing Wells in a boarding school in Lausanne on the way. While they were rambling through the towns of northern Italy, Harcourt was doing his best to contact them, and, when he was unable to do so, deciding on his own to sell the first serial rights of *Arrowsmith* to the *Designer* for fifty thousand dollars—"the highest bona fide price for magazine serialization that I've ever heard of." [13]

When the family returned to London, Lewis rented an office in a lawyer's sanctuary, the Inner Temple, and resolutely began the five months' work of rewriting his novel. He had enough spare time, however, to make what the *Daily Express* termed a "strange irruption into British politics"—he canvassed in Chelsea for the Labour candidate in the general election, Bertrand Russell. When the election was over and Labour had won its first victory, Lewis wrote a letter to the *Express*, not so much to defend himself as to praise his friend Brigadier-General C. B. Thomson, who was soon to be given a peerage and put in charge of the Air Ministry. Between his literary friends and his new political acquaintances, Lewis was now, as he reported, seeing "millions of people." He took to the mad round zestfully, but his wife found the English winter very trying. She tried to escape from a succession of colds by going for a holiday

[13] Letter to Lewis, October 30, 1923, *ibid.*, p. 144.

to Torquay, and in March she and Lewis went to Spain in search of the sun. According to her account, it had not been a successful year for their marriage; whatever his side of the story may have been, she felt pained by "his ruthless and quite public abasing of me before others . . . ." [14] Meditating long afterward on what had happened and where she had failed, she stressed the irreconcilable tendencies—her need for roots and security, his restlessness and desire to escape. The winter over, Lewis escaped again without her; he announced that he and his brother Claude were going on a trip to the Canadian north, and pointed out that it would hardly be worth while for her to return to the United States with him.

Claude and he had arranged to leave in early June on a Canadian Government Treaty Trip—an annual expedition made by agents of the Department of Indian Affairs to pay the Indians the bounty due them in exchange for the loss of their lands. Lewis expected to be in complete wilderness in northern Saskatchewan for two months or more, "which will be just the thing to set me up after a year and a half or more of much too sedentary life." [15] His enthusiasm lasted throughout the alcoholic preliminaries— "twelve days of carousal," according to Schorer. When he dispatched a last note to his publishers, "before vanishing quite beyond post-boxes until I emerge at The Pas, Manitoba, some time between Aug. 15 & Sept. 5," he stated that he had not had a drink for eleven days and that the trip was going beautifully. Eleven days later, however, he decided to quit; in spite of Claude's pleadings he had made up his mind to leave the party at the first opportunity. When his wife heard that he was back in civilization, she commented sardonically, "Enough is enough apparently. The wilderness is all right in its

---

[14] *With Love from Gracie*, p. 274.
[15] Letter to Harcourt, March 26, 1924, *From Main Street to Stockholm*, p. 156.

place but not too much of the same place." [16] Schorer reveals that before the "prodigal Thoreau" returned to "the thin parental bosom" in Sauk Centre at the end of July, there had been enough alcoholic indulgence to undo any good which the period of hearty open-air life may have done him.

Out of the experience came the "shorter and more adventurous" novel Lewis had mentioned to Harcourt in a letter of December 3, 1923, as an interlude between *Arrowsmith* and the next long work; but this shorter work, *Mantrap*, was not to be written until about a year after the trip. Meanwhile, Mrs. Lewis, who had not followed her husband's suggestion that she should spend the summer in France, was staying on Nantucket Island, and he joined her there. The proofs of *Arrowsmith* kept him busy, though the *Nation* got him to report, in a series of articles, how Main Street viewed the forthcoming presidential election; curiously, in one article he had a surprisingly mature and sensible Will Kennicott explain why people like him were going to vote for Coolidge, while he only very perfunctorily allowed Guy Pollock to say why people should vote for LaFollette. Election time found him far from America's shores; almost before she knew it, Mrs. Lewis relates, they were back in London, though not to stay. They enrolled Wells in a school in Switzerland, tramped in the Alps, and settled down—for a whole month and a half—in Paris. Then Philip Goodman, a heavy drinker of the Menckenite persuasion, appeared on the scene and convinced Lewis that Munich at carnival time would be an ideal place for the two of them to try writing a play. After two weeks in Munich, however, Lewis declared that the idea would not work— if they ever completed the play, it would be cheap and sensational. He wrote Harcourt and Brace to this

[16] Letter to Donald Brace, July 29, 1924, *ibid.*, p. 162.

effect on March 4, the day before *Arrowsmith* was published.

As in the preceding novels, Lewis has two intentions in *Arrowsmith*: to tell a story and to expose a situation. Here the two aims are closely linked, and the result is a much better plot than either *Main Street* or *Babbitt* possesses. The analysis of American medicine is just as interesting as the anatomy of the village or the city, and the conflict in which Martin Arrowsmith is engaged is far more gripping than the marital difficulties of Carol Kennicott or the rebellion of George F. Babbitt. The story gains enormously by having a central character who is clearly sympathetic to the author, instead of only doubtfully so; the reader can assume the normalcy of his point of view and laugh, weep, or deplore with him when he encounters examples of irrational or vicious behavior.

What way of life does Martin Arrowsmith seek to follow? There is no chance of his becoming an aesthete; Lewis makes him a man of action, suspicious of whatever may be effete and decadent, and clinches matters by giving the spokesman for literature the contemptible name of Brumfit and describing him as a literary playboy. When Martin examines religion as a guiding principle, Lewis's treatment is cavalier. Martin found himself viewing the cadaver he worked on "as a machine, fascinating, complex, beautiful, but a machine. It damaged his already feeble belief in man's divinity and immortality." The model of Christian behavior whom Martin meets at the University of Winnemac is a grotesque figure, the Reverend Ira Hinkley:

> He never ceased trying to stop their profanity. After three years on a backwoods football team he still believed that he could sterilize young men by administering reproofs, with the nickering of a lady Sunday School teacher and the delicacy of a charging elephant [18] [17].

[17] *Arrowsmith* (New York: Harcourt, Brace, 1925).

Having rejected the principles of this moral pest, Martin puts his faith in the scientism of Max Gottlieb, his instructor in bacteriology. There is nothing certain in life, says Gottlieb, except the quantitative method; employing it, he seeks to discover general laws governing natural phenomena in order to extend man's knowledge and develop new concepts of life. Following him, Arrowsmith embarks on "the search for the fundamental laws which the scientist . . . exalts above temporary healing as the religious exalts the nature and terrible glory of God above pleasant daily virtues" (120). Here is a good example of Lewis's prime rule for the handling of ideas: be brisk with them and count on the flow of words to sweep the reader right past their implications. Who could be so callous as to submit such a high-minded statement to analysis, to ask whether contemplatives really consider that the glory of God makes the practice of the virtues of little account, to question the validity of a scientist's belief that the cure of the sick is of small consequence in comparison with the search for the fundamental laws of nature? Lewis gives the impression of having gone deeply into the problem of the rational foundation for devotion to science, but there is more appearance than reality. He gives Martin's position no metaphysical basis, in fact, no sanction outside itself; furthermore, it seems to be undermined by a radical skepticism, not a mere withholding of judgment:

> She had called Martin a "lie-hunter," a "truth-seeker." They decided now, talking it over in their tight little two-and-a-quarter room flat, that most people who call themselves "truth-seekers"—persons who scurry about chattering of Truth as though it were a tangible separable thing, like houses or salt or bread—did not so much desire to find Truth as to cure their mental itch. In novels, these truth-seekers quested the "secret of life" in laboratories which did not seem to be provided with

Bunsen flames or reagents; or they went, at great expense and much discomfort from hot trains and undesirable snakes, to Himalayan monasteries, to learn from unaseptic sages that the Mind can do all sorts of edifying things if one will but spend thirty or forty years in eating rice and gazing on one's navel.

To these high matters Martin responded, "Rot!" He insisted that there is no Truth but only many truths; that Truth is not a colored bird to be chased among the rocks and captured by its tail, but a skeptical attitude toward life. He insisted that no one could expect more than, by stubborness or luck, to have the kind of work he enjoyed and an ability to become better acquainted with the facts of work than the average job-holder [271].

Does this leave Martin with any better reason for acting than the "mental itch" he derides? If truth is nothing more than a skeptical attitude towards life, why not be skeptical about the value of scientific research?

It is interesting to observe that Lewis gains support for Martin's position partly by caricaturing alternatives to it, partly by associating with it moral and intellectual attitudes which the reader is likely to favor (honesty, open-mindedness, a disposition to question received opinions, and so on), and partly by attaching religious overtones to it. He gives it prestige, if not an intellectual defense. The comparison of the scientist to the religious occurs many times. Science is the new religion to supplant outmoded creeds, and Gottlieb is its prophet; Arrowsmith says, "You think Gottlieb isn't religious, Hinkley. Why, his just being in a lab is a prayer" (30). Like the Messiah, Gottlieb has to endure scorn and ignominy:

Not once did he fail to be hated by his colleagues, who were respectful to his face, uncomfortable in feeling his ironic power, but privily joyous to call him Mephisto, Diabolist, Killjoy, Pessimist, Destructive Critic, Flippant

Cynic, Scientific Bounder Lacking in Dignity and Seriousness, Intellectual Snob, Pacifist, Anarchist, Atheist, Jew [124].

Gottlieb himself refers to great scientists as though they were members of a priesthood or a religious order: "Father Koch and Father Pasteur and Brother Jacques Loeb and Brother Arrhenius." In a moment of spiritual rapture, Martin composes a scientist's prayer which concludes with the paradox "God give me strength not to trust to God !" In the manner of Comte, Lewis tries to ennoble science by referring to it in religious terms and to present it as a worthy successor to religion as an object of mankind's devotion.

The novel might be described as an anatomy of the obstacles in the scientist's way. They are put there by the medical profession, by the character of the scientist himself, by various social groups, and by the general outlook of the American people. Almost all the possible attitudes toward research are presented, and each one is supported or illustrated by an impressive amount of detail. The Main Street view is shown when Martin goes to Wheatsylvania, North Dakota; here the doctor is a medicine man and conformity to the tribal code is much more important than medical skill. The view of Babbitt's friends is shown when Martin gets a job in Nautilus, Iowa, another Zenith: "The only difference between Nautilus and Zenith is that in both cases all the streets look alike but in Nautilus they do not look alike for so many miles." Here the Public Health Director must be a Booster and not a conscientious pursuer of germs; in fact, the worst mistake he can make is to try to clean up dirty houses or dirty restaurants owned by influential citizens. Everywhere, it seems, the Boosters overcome the Truth-seekers. Pharmaceutical houses are so unscrupulous that they market preparations even before they have been tested and continue to sell them after they have been proved useless; clinics are mere medical factories which will tolerate no research nonsense; and even genuine research organizations are only the playthings of so-called philanthropists.

All these are valid subjects for satire. But the last great obstacle to scientific asceticism, humanity, is not. Should the quest for scientific knowledge override every other human consideration? In Gottlieb's life, it does. Martin decides in favor of humanitarianism when he abandons his controlled experiment on St. Hubert during an epidemic and administers his serum to everyone, but he regards himself as a traitor to science. At the end, he casts everything else aside for the sake of research. The pursuit of truth to the exclusion of error is clearly something desirable; the pursuit of scientific truth to the exclusion of all human values is something else again. We have moved, therefore, from an area in which satire attacks deviations from a reasonable, normal position to an area in which there is a dramatic tension between two kinds of value. But the transition is not awkward; the central character this time does not make an unpredictable change, and the book does not break in two like *Main Street* and *Babbitt*.

But it does have two types of characters—the realistic and the unrealistic. The latter can be identified by their comic-strip names. Martin works under Dr. Benjamin Holabird in a research institute headed by Dr. A. De Witt Tubbs and financed by Capitola McGurk, the Great White Uplifter. Earlier he has served under Dr. Almus Pickerbaugh, dynamic Director of Public Health in Zenith, Booster extraordinary, and father of the Healthette Octette—eight strapping girls floridly ranging from Orchid to Gladiola. Through this brilliant caricature, Lewis shows that the archetypal qualities of the Booster—brashness, vulgarity, hatred of nonconformity, worship of success—are as conspicuous in the world of medicine as they are in real estate and advertising. Yet Lewis's use of such comic-strip characters would seem to give the lie to those who consider the primary quality of his work its documentary veracity or photographic realism. For the moment, it is perhaps sufficient to observe that Lewis's use of characters with extravagant names and personalities is not necessarily an error in artistic judgment: these parodies or travesties of human beings illustrate his contention that America, in seeking to develop a new kind of person, has only turned out new specimens of the grotesque.

If Lewis's central theme in *Arrowsmith* was the difficulty of avoiding the prostitution of standards in medical science, the theme had wider implications. T. K. Whipple, in an excellent review in the *New Republic*, pointed out that the novel really showed how the American environment affects the creative spirit. In the United States, he said, art and religion are made bondslaves to practical success—and he took Lewis himself as an example. Lewis made greater use of irony as a defensive weapon than any other writer Whipple knew; he always wrote as if he were conscious of a hostile audience, and he took endless pains to make clear that he was more sophisticated than his characters, to ridicule their naive enthusiasms. In other words, he exemplified the morbid self-consciousness and insecurity of his own creations, who were always suspicious that they were the objects of comment and who had no inner standards of their own because they had no integral personalities. Like them, Whipple said, Lewis was a man of multiple personality, though his many attitudes could be resolved into two—the romantic and the philistine. Besides the conventional Tennyson-and-water romanticism, there was also, as in Arnold Bennett, the romance of the commonplace; allied to it was a philistinism which was homey and folksy and strongly opposed to anything "arty" or "superior." Even *Arrowsmith*, Whipple wrote, was the work of a mangled artist. But he conceded that Lewis's romanticism and philistinism and vulgarity of style made him powerful because they made him popular; the attack on practicality needed its shock troops, and perhaps it was worth spoiling an artist to have him take so salutary a revenge. "Lewis is the most successful critic of American society," he concluded, "because he is himself the best proof that his charges are just." [18]

In showing what had happened in one field of endeavor, Lewis was describing the failure of the epic dream: America had aspired to be a nation of free individuals, but the worship of material success by the many had forced the few independent spirits to turn their backs on their fellow men. Carl Van Doren said that readers found in the story a familiar American pattern of behavior. Despairing of medical practice because of its confusions and compromises, Arrowsmith forsook it to do his true work in a wilderness, "almost exactly as Leather-Stocking and Daniel Boone had in the eighteenth century turned away from the corrupted settlements to be themselves beyond the tumult of mankind." [19] Arrowsmith is aware of his resemblance to other types of pioneer; when he explains to Joyce, his wealthy wife, that he is going to escape from the captivity which her way of life imposes on him, he refers to "those of us that are pioneers." In fact, the pioneering theme is established in the opening scene of the novel, which depicts the intrepid determination of Arrowsmith's great-grandmother in the Ohio wilderness.

Arrowsmith's mental make-up is derived from the pioneer ethos at least as much as from Max Gottlieb. Maxwell

[18] T. K. Whipple, "Sinclair Lewis," *New Republic*, XLII (April 15, 1925), 3

[19] Carl Van Doren, *Sinclair Lewis: A Biographical Sketch* (Garden City: Doubleday, Doran, 1933), p. 45.

Geismar is dubious about the scientific skepticism of the novel and would prefer to call it a fashionable cynicism,[20] but actually Martin holds to the tradition of dissent which Geismar describes in his *American Moderns* as perhaps the most vital element in American democracy:[21]

> Gradually Martin's contemplation moved beyond Almus Pickerbaugh to all leaders, of armies or empires, of universities or churches, and he saw that most of them were Pickerbaughs. He preached to himself, as Max Gottlieb had once preached to him, the loyalty of dissent, the faith of being very doubtful, the gospel of not bawling gospels, the wisdom of admitting the probable ignorance of one's self and of everybody else, and the energetic acceleration of a movement for going very slow [228].

We have seen that Lewis is so much of Geismar's mind regarding the tradition of dissent that near the end of *Main Street* he makes institutions rather than individuals responsible for everything he has satirized. The truest American, in his view, is the aloof, independent, egocentric, suspicious pioneer. So strong is his emphasis on isolation that—as Geismar stresses, though Raymond H. Palmer said it long before him[22]—he nowhere gives a picture of a true home or a true church or a true corporate life of any kind; he has taken the tradition of dissent to its logical and ultimate conclusion. As Raymond Williams states in a discussion of Dickens, there is always a system of some kind, and the argument against system per se is usually either fretful or ignorant. This type of anti-institutionalism seems to be the retained position of

[20] *The Last of the Provincials: The American Novel, 1915–1925* (Boston: Houghton Mifflin, 1949), p. 101.

[21] *American Moderns: From Rebellion to Conformity* (London: W. H. Allen, 1958), p. 26.

[22] Raymond H. Palmer, "The Nobel Jury Judges America," *Christian Century*, XLVII (1930), 1448. Geismar develops the point in detail in both *The Last of the Provincials* and *American Moderns*.

the adolescent, the innocence which essentially rejects the adult world.[23] On the evidence of Lewis's life and writings, Palmer is justified in calling him "the great undisciplined American, the apotheosis of American individuality and irresponsibility."[24] *Arrowsmith* is thus a paradoxical combination of an attack on conditions which inhibit scientific progress and a flight from maturity, a plea for a return to a simpler and more uncomplicated way of life than the modern world can offer.[25]

There were, of course, two version of *Arrowsmith*. In his reply to Harcourt's news about the sale of the serial rights, Lewis paid less attention to the amount of money involved than to the possibility of editorial interference; he expressed the hope (in capital letters) that the magazine publisher understood that he would not "change the thing into a sunny sweet tale." When the same magazine made overtures for his next novel, he rejected them, fearing to be deprived of "the freedom without which very few decent novels are written." In a comparison of the two versions of *Arrowsmith*, however, Lyon N. Richardson has shown that the greater freedom which Lewis could employ in the book version was not really helpful to him. "Indeed, it can well be argued," Richardson declares, "that the story really lost little in the serial form and in many ways

[23] Raymond Williams, *Culture and Society, 1780–1950* (London: Chatto and Windus, 1958), pp. 59, 95–96.

[24] "The Nobel Jury Judges America," p. 1448

[25] William Couch, Jr., in "The Emergence, Rise and Decline of the Reputation of Sinclair Lewis" (Ph.D. dissertation, University of Chicago, 1954), points out that Alfred North Whitehead contended in his *Science and the Modern World*, published in the same year as *Babbitt*, that the concept of the self-sufficing, independent man, with his peculiar advantages which concerned no one else, possessed no validity for modern civilization. The same point of view was taken by John Dewey in his *Individualism Old and New* (1930). As Couch says, Dewey would have regarded Arrowsmith as an example of the tragedy of the lost individual, unable to accept modern corporate society and mistakenly viewing science as an isolated and independent activity, a refuge from the modern world.

was improved by deletions of words and sentences which merely belabored the ideas or were blatant Lewisian expletives and obtrusive, derisive remarks."[26] The *Designer* could not tolerate some of his "mere buzzing and stinging" at moral smugness; the changes sometimes indicated squeamishness on the part of the magazine's editors, but on the other hand they imposed a wholesome restraint on such things as Lewis's heavy-handed over-working of references to the Wassermann test. It checked what Richardson calls "the more angular characteristics of his satire"—seeking emphasis by expletives; satirizing hypocrisy, selfishness, mediocrity, and so on "with the petulant impatience of a zealot unarmed by humor"; and manipulating characters too obviously to prove a point. Richardson concludes that most of the many deletions made for serial publication removed irritating blemishes: "Lewis and the editor of the *Designer* improved the story, though the author, in his eagerness to challenge hypocrisy and mediocrity, would not believe it."

Couch notes that *Arrowsmith* has been one of the most highly praised—some would say overpraised—of Lewis's works. To many reviewers it was either a genuine step forward by its author or conclusive proof of his excellence as a novelist.[27] Its weaknesses, however, have become more apparent with the passing of the years. Many male readers seem to have fallen in love with Leora: Harcourt called her "just about the best woman character in American fiction that I know of."[28] But Martin Light

[26] Lyon N. Richardson, "*Arrowsmith*: Genesis, Development, Versions," *American Literature*, XXVII (1955–1956), 230.

[27] See Couch "Reputation," pp. 110 ff. Two examples he cites are Henry Seidel Canby in the *Saturday Review of Literature* and Henry Longan Stuart in the New York *Times*, both of whom said in effect that it was time to stop prating of the limitations of Sinclair Lewis and give him credit for his brilliant studies of his society.

[28] Letter to Lewis, March 11, 1925, *From Main Street to Stockholm*, p. 179.

thinks her quite incredible—chiefly a convenience who
does all the right things, especially in never interfering
with her husband's plans, and who tops it all off by
becoming a martyr to science. He is equally unimpressed
by the character of Arrowsmith; although Lewis says
that he matures, he doesn't show it, and his tone throughout remains that of an exuberant schoolboy.[29] A similar
criticism was made by Warren Beck in a notable attack
on Lewis's reputation. He grudgingly allowed that
Arrowsmith was one of the two consistent characters
Lewis had created—Babbitt was the other—but maintained that Lewis had failed to control him: "He has run
off not only with many a reader but with his author, for
in glorifying Arrowsmith as scientist Lewis seems unaware
of what a crude and lopsided human being he had made
of him."[30] Arrowsmith as doctor has been both criticized
and defended; perhaps the most famous criticism is that
by Hans Zinsser, in *Rats, Lice and History*, to the effect
that if an epidemiologist on a plague study behaved in
the manner of Arrowsmith he would be regarded by his
associates as a yellow ass and a nuisance.[31]

De Kruif, giving a verdict "aged in the wood of my
head over many years," does not criticize Arrowsmith so
much as Gottlieb, whom he considers a muddied mélange

See also Canby's and other rhapsodic eulogies of Leora quoted by Couch,
"Reputation," pp. 111–112.

[29] Light, "Characterization," pp. 252, 263. Sheldon Grebstein, in his
Sinclair Lewis, "United States Authors Series" (New York: Twayne, 1962),
p. 87, argues that in each of the novel's situations Martin learns from his
mistakes.

[30] Warren Beck, "How Good is Sinclair Lewis?" *College English*, IX
(1947–1948), 177.

[31] Hans Zinsser, *Rats, Lice and History* (Boston: Little, Brown, 1935), p. 13.
The medical correspondent of the Chicago *Tribune*, Dr. Evans, examined in
detail Arrowsmith's performance as a doctor and concluded that there
were a number of improbable things. Fishbein replied to this, in an article
signed with his initials, "Dr. Evans and Arrowsmith," *Hygeia*, October,
1925, pp. 588–589. See Couch, "Reputation," p. 113.

of his own scientific mentor and of Jacques Loeb, "who was my master in a philosophy of the mechanistic conception of life, of God a mathematician, of God a Univac, of God a superstition, of God a childish concept, of God nonexistent."[32] This conception, he writes, accorded with Lewis's own philosophy. For Loeb, it was undoubtedly the product of considerable reflection about causality, creation, the existence of matter, and related topics. But when Lewis writes, "Like all ardent agnostics, Martin was a religious man," it is obvious that there is not very much deep reflection behind the remark; it is merely a glib paradox designed to give an appearance of profundity. Light finds the heroic pretensions of the novel embarrassing, in view of the slick-magazine language of many of its passages;[33] when Lewis writes that Martin "was homesick for the laboratory, for the thrill of uncharted discoveries, the quest below the surface and beyond the moment," we feel, as we did about Babbitt's dreams of his fairy child, that the whole thing is overwritten and slickly contrived. In spite of the excellence of much of the satire and the author's success in fusing satire and novel, the book shows that Lewis could not do what Sherman asked him to do—give a satisfactory exposition of values.

With *Arrowsmith* published, Lewis was now thinking a great deal about a novel concerning an American abroad, to be entitled *The Yearner*. This and the excuse that it was his "first real loaf in years" justified his setting off on a "two months hike" through Europe with his wife. He reported that Cannes was charming, Monte Carlo sensationally beautiful, and Vienna superb; but no matter how charming, beautiful, or superb, each was quickly left behind. Early May found them back in Paris, and by the first of June they were again in the United States;

[32] De Kruif, *The Sweeping Wing*, p. 109.
[33] Light, "Characterization," p. 253.

Mrs. Lewis went to a farm at Katonah in Westchester County and Lewis to the Midwest. When he returned to the East, he worked on *Mantrap*, which did not occupy his energies for very long. Although it was written as a serial for *Red Book*, the magazine had the good sense to reject it when it was finished. Then suddenly Lewis had had enough of Katonah and his wife; he packed up and went to a New York hotel. While wife and son were discussing how impossible it was to domesticate father, Lewis was writing letters to her proposing that their marriage be put on a new footing of complete independence—so that if, for example, he fell in love with some girl it would be entirely his business—and proposing that if they met they should merely laugh and be pleasant. This was not a final separation—there were to be reconciliations of a sort and trips together—but the marriage was now so empty of meaning that Mrs. Lewis's account of it stops at this point.

Accompanied by a new secretary, Louis E. Florey, Lewis sailed for Bermuda at the end of October, to begin another of his futile attempts at writing a play in a suitable environment. Meanwhile, *Collier's* had accepted *Red Book's* leavings, and was planning to publish *Mantrap* as a serial beginning in February, 1926. Harcourt was reluctant to have it appear as a book. With astonishing lack of discrimination, Lewis wrote that he saw no reason not to publish it; looking back at it, he could remember nothing shoddy in it, "and as for the critics who insist that I have no right to do anything but social documents, they may all go to hell." [34] Lewis's wishes prevailed, and *Mantrap* was published by Harcourt, Brace in June.

In this "shorter and more adventurous book," there was very little that was not shoddy. As Schorer points out, it was basically a dishonest treatment of Lewis's own

[34] Letter to Harcourt, November 10, 1925, *From Main Street to Stockholm*, p. 188.

experience. He had quit in the middle of the trip; in the book he transposes the actualities so as to vindicate the gentle city man and show him equal to any hardships. In part the book is a satire on "the most blatant of all our American myths: roughing it in the wilds !" (57) [35] The ridicule of the notion that the virile open spaces are good for the soul is packed into the conclusive aphorism that "sleeping on the ground is *rot* !" But this theme is soon disposed of; a more important one is the confrontation of a mild-mannered, liberal lawyer named Ralph Prescott and a Babbitt by the name of E. Wesson Woodbury. They are thrown together in the north woods, with only Cree Indians for company; and in this isolation the Babbitt proves to have few inner resources. His incessant talk turns first to fussiness and then to nagging; Prescott sees him as "a wistful fat boy . . . always longing for some one to bully as he had been bullied." But Prescott—and Lewis—are curiously reluctant to strip away his pretenses and show him for what he is. There is no point in analyzing him, and nobody to blame: "It would be just as silly to try to find out which of a divorced couple was to blame, when they just didn't get along together and that was all." When the inevitable blowup occurs, a patch of shingle by a river becomes the arena for the "clash of incompatible senses of humor." However, Ralph's evaluation of Woodbury is as dispassionate as Una Golden's of Julius Edward Schwirtz: "You're not a bad fellow, essentially. You're merely an ignoramus who's been elevated to prosperity by this amazing modern system of the sanctity of salesmanship . . ." (93).

This conflict resolved, the story declines further into nonsense with the appearance of a self-conscious backwoods philosopher named Joe Easter and his wife Alverna. The triangular romantic situation develops as one might expect, save for the fact that Joe and Ralph remain

[35] *Mantrap* (New York: Grosset and Dunlap, 1926).

friends; in fact, the relationship between them is similar to that of Pip and Joe Gargery in *Great Expectations*: they are friends who belong to different worlds. In the end, each of the three members of the triangle returns to his own environment. As Schorer shows, the reviewers were much kinder to this trivial book than they ought to have been. It was made into a successful movie starring Clara Bow, and with the sale of the novel to a magazine and to Hollywood Lewis had perpetrated a notable swindle.

Lewis had written from London at the end of 1923 that, after a vacation in the wilds to get *Arrowsmith* out of his system, he would be ready to go at the next book, which would be either a detective story or "the big religious novel I've planned so long—paying my compliments to the Methodist cardinals, the Lords Day Alliance, the S.P.V., and all the rest—not slightly and meekly as in *M St* and *Babbitt* but at full length, and very, very lovingly."[36] Not long after this—even before his trip into the Canadian wilds—he wrote for copies of periodicals such as would be used by Baptist and Methodist ministers. He got down to serious research, however, only in 1926: a Harcourt, Brace publicity release of January 13 announced his departure for Kansas City, where he planned to spend ten days with the Reverend William Stidger, whom he had met several years before. Since Stidger apparently expected that Lewis was going to write another *Arrowsmith* instead of a second *Babbitt*, he gave Lewis the fullest cooperation; Lewis stayed two weeks at this time and reported that he had got a lot out of his visit, not only from Stidger but from "at least a dozen other preachers of all denominations who varied from mild sympathy to real friendliness."

Lewis spent most of February on the West Coast, and

[36] Letter to Harcourt, December 27, 1923, *From Main Street to Stockholm*, p. 150.

then was joined by his wife in Tucson for several weeks of touring through Arizona and New Mexico. To Harcourt he described how delightful it was to sleep in the "soft yet rousing desert air" and to awaken to a view of mountains bright in the morning sun; in spite of *Mantrap*, there was still romance to be found in the great outdoors. This time, of course, he was not roughing it: he was accompanied by a luxurious caravan, a Japanese cook, and his wife, "the most delightful and amusing companion conceivable for a motor hike." [37]

At the beginning of April he was back in Kansas City, regretting that the provisional title for the religious book— *Sounding Brass*—had just been used for a novel by Ethel Mannin. As an alternative he suggested *Rev. Bloor*, the central character at that time being called Elmer Bloor. He found a more congenial assistant and informant than Stidger in the Reverend L. M. Birkhead, who could advise Lewis on a variety of religious positions from his own experience: having been born a Baptist, he had been converted to Methodism, changed to Unitarianism, and now professed to be an agnostic. But Lewis did not have to rely on one or two informants; he had a whole "Sunday School Class," a group of fifteen to twenty ministers who lunched with him every Wednesday so that he could ask impertinent questions about their calling. All accounts of the proceedings emphasize that the self-styled Right Reverend Bishop Dr. Lewis was able to impress his class with the breadth of his knowledge and to ask them the most soul-searching questions. "You're a fine bunch," he is reported to have told them. "You get up and preach things that neither you nor your congregations believe. Why don't you be honest in your pulpits?" [38]

[37] Letter to Harcourt, February 24, 1926, *ibid.*, p. 197.
[38] New York *Times*, May 18, 1926, p. 1.

Some of them invited Lewis into their pulpits, and on April 18, in one of these, occurred an incident which made headlines throughout America: Lewis held a watch in his hand and gave the Almighty fifteen minutes to strike him dead. The challenge was not as dramatic as it sounds. Luther Burbank, the great naturalist and proponent of evolution, had recently died, and Lewis read excerpts from a letter to a newspaper expressing the fundamentalist conviction that his death was God's judgment on him. Lewis objected to this conception of a vengeful deity, and said that if there were such a God he would certainly strike him dead within the next fifteen minutes. But if the clergy and the press maximized the irreverence of the occasion, some apologists for Lewis have minimized it. Carl Van Doren writes that Lewis had been engaged in an experiment to disprove a superstition: he had only carried out a realistic test in a natural way. Similarly the first Mrs. Lewis writes that there was nothing defiant or denunciatory about Lewis's speech or his dramatic gesture with the watch. But the terms in which Lewis referred to the episode soon after—"it was in his pulpit that I spoke up to papa God" [39]—hardly suggest that there was nothing inflammatory about his actions. At the last meeting of his class, Lewis announced that he was going to Minnesota to write a novel about them: "I'm going to give you hell, but I love every one of you."

Lewis's challenge-to-God incident was followed by a second spectacular episode in the spring of 1926: he was offered the Pulitzer Prize for *Arrowsmith* and refused it. Carl Van Doren, writing in 1933, was lost in admiration of Lewis's behavior at this time, and observed that Lewis gave serious reasons for his stand, "declaring that he thought little of literary prizes in general and less than little of the Pulitzer prize in particular." The rejection

[39] Letter to Harcourt, May 11, 1926, *From Main Street to Stockholm*, p. 217.

was not simply a publicity stratagem: "His craft was pure nature. He was simply and originally himself . . . ."[40] However, the fact that Lewis had earlier suggested intriguing for the Pulitzer Prize—in a letter to Harcourt he had asked, "Any thoughts on pulling wires for *Martin* for Nobel prize?"[41]—is sufficient commentary on the sincerity of his theoretical objections to literary prizes. Still chafing at "the *Main Street* burglary"—the fact that the selection committee had chosen *Main Street* in 1920, but the trustees of Columbia University, who were responsible for the Pulitzer awards, had overruled the committee and selected Edith Wharton's *Age of Innocence* instead—Lewis, when he heard that the award to *Arrowsmith* was in the air, wrote Harcourt that he had always planned to refuse the prize if it were offered to him. From that time on, the affair proceeded like a military operation, with preliminary preparation of ammunition from the publisher's files, carefully rehearsed maneuvers, carefully worded communiqués ("Joel [Spingarn] and I have just had lunch over the P.P. business, and we have gone over your statement with eagle eyes"), and precision timing ("a summary story released at 4:01 P.M., followed by the complete letter at 4:07").[42]

In his letter of refusal, Lewis objected first of all to the terms of the award: it was for the American novel published during the year "which shall best present the wholesome atmosphere of American life and the highest standards of American manners and manhood." To this the committee replied that it had not insisted on these terms; as an example it pointed to the award to Eugene O'Neill for *Anna Christie*. Lewis objected furthermore to the very idea of an award as such; it meant that writers

[40] Van Doren, *Sinclair Lewis*, pp. 18–19.
[41] Letter to Harcourt, March 26, 1925, *From Main Street to Stockholm*, p. 180.
[42] Letters, *ibid.*, pp. 203–216.

intrigued for approval and wrote to please judges. On this point he received support, in the correspondence columns of the New York *Times*, from the sculptor Gutzon Borglum, who deplored any type of restraint upon the artist; the *Times* gave witty—if ironical—agreement, citing examples of the deplorable influence of prizes to. artists through the ages, all the way back to the time of Aeschylus and Sophocles.

In the controversy which followed, the suspicion could not be stilled that America's best-publicized novelist had found an ingenious way to keep himself in the news. Ralph Pulitzer, son of Joseph, the donor of the awards, said that Lewis had the right to refuse the money, "whether he does so from principle or from self-exploitation." The secretary of Columbia University, when he announced that Lewis had returned the prize check, pointed out that the book had been placed in nomination by Lewis's publishers. Finally, on May 15 Lewis was sent an enormous straw hat, size 207 5/8, by a Kansas City jeweler. For once he was speechless; he had no comeback.

The summer of 1926 found Lewis in Minnesota, hard at work on his satire of religion in America. Charles Breasted, who met him that summer, described Lewis as curiously subdued, no doubt at least in part because his father was in his last illness; old Dr. Lewis died on August 29 at the age of seventy-seven.[43] Lewis told Breasted that his father had never forgiven him for libeling his birthplace in *Main Street*. Breasted was impressed by Lewis's calm self-assessment and humility; though he was only forty-one he spoke of his best work as over, and said that the best of what he would ever have produced would bear only a faint resemblance to true literary achievement. That fall, Breasted says, Lewis and his wife attempted

[43] Charles Breasted, "The 'Sauk-Centricities' of Sinclair Lewis," *Saturday Review*, XXXVII (August 15, 1955), p. 8.

another reconciliation; they took a house in Washington, and Lewis settled down to write *Elmer Gantry*. Both were later to pour the cumulative bitterness which their incompatibility had engendered into novels dealing with their marriage, but Breasted suggests that this bitterness found its way into *Gantry* as well. A final flare-up took place, and when Breasted received a telephone call from Lewis in New York he found that Lewis had fled from Washington with nothing but his manuscript: "The only other personal effects I noted were three brandy bottles, two of them empty."

Lewis entered once more on the familiar round of drink and people, but this did not prevent him from finishing *Elmer Gantry* with incredible speed; he turned it over to Harcourt, as promised, before Christmas. A week later he was taken by Harcourt to a rehabilitation center for alcoholics on the Hudson; he returned to Breasted's New York apartment looking fit—and called a bootlegger before unpacking. Still he might have derived consolation from the fact that his publishers were so enthusiastic about his new novel that they had ordered 140,000 copies, the largest first printing of any book on record to that time. On January 4, Mrs. Lewis wrote Harcourt to say that the Washington venture was her last gesture, and it had failed. Her parting gift to Lewis was silence until the book was out and the controversy over it had died down: "For him to divorce God and wife simultaneously would be bad publicity." In reply, Harcourt hoped that she could achieve serenity in the course of time; he had the same wish for Lewis, "but those hopes are much more faint." [44]

Elmer Gantry was launched with tremendous fanfare on March 10, 1927. The brethren in Kansas City had been

[44] Letters of Grace Hegger Lewis to Harcourt, January 4, 1927, and of Harcourt to her on January 5, *From Main Street to Stockholm*, p. 231.

spluttering with rage even before this. On March 11 the New York *Times* carried an account of the reaction of an old friend of Lewis's, William Allen White:

> "Sinclair Lewis stood in the pulpit of a Kansas City church last Spring and defied God to strike him dead. So far as Sinclair Lewis the artist is concerned, in the book 'Elmer Gantry' God took him at his word. He got so excited making faces at God that he forgot his craftsmanship." [45]

On the same day Harcourt cabled to Lewis, who had prudently left the country and was then in Paris, that news stories were everywhere, the reviews were violent either way, the sales were about a hundred thousand and reorders were already coming in, and everything was lovely. Reporting on developments to the end of March, Harrison Smith, of Harcourt, Brace, said that the book was being advertised "in every conceivable way from here to the Pacific Ocean." He commented that it was very amusing to watch the sales map and to see the novel catch on in one territory after another. But after the initial response the sales slowed down, and the banning of the book in Boston did not help them. By the end of March, 150,000 copies had been sold; it took till the end of May for the 200,000 mark to be reached, and till October for the next 25,000 to be sold. These sales figures are, of course, very high, but they were achieved only with an enormous amount of publicity and advertising. When the General Conference of the Methodist Church met in Kansas City in May, 1928, it found the city plastered with billboards, forty-nine in all, advertising *Elmer Gantry*.

Elmer Gantry is a picaresque novel. Its hero makes his way, with the help of native cunning and oratorical ability, through almost the whole domain of religion in the United

[45] New York *Times*, March 11, 1927, p. 4.

States. One device after another is employed to introduce him to new denominations and round out the picture. However, Lewis does not seem to have had such an intention at first; once again, half the novel is concerned with one theme and half with a related but different one. It begins as a satire of revivalism: Elmer is thrown out of a Baptist seminary, becomes a farm implement salesman, and then finds his niche—or pedestal—as a Billy Sunday partnered with an Aimee Semple McPherson. But though this satire is perhaps the best part of the book, revivalism is not the only target. The Baptist influences to which Elmer is subjected in his youth, particularly at Terwillinger College and Mizpah Theological Seminary, are handled very roughly. And when his hero joins the Methodist Church, Lewis takes full advantage of the opportunity to satirize another sect. Other Protestant groups also get their share of abuse, as do the Jews and the Catholics. Lewis seems determined to avoid religious discrimination: all sects appear in equally bad light.

It is not merely a case of the good priest versus the bad priest. Elmer is, obviously enough, an example of the latter. But the only good ministers of the Gospel seem to be those who, like Dr. Bruno Zechlin, the Old Testament scholar at Mizpah, have given up their religious beliefs. Philip McGarry, Ph.D. in economics and philosophy, is made to show that no educated person can believe in Christianity except in a very vague way: "the only dogma he was known to give out positively was the leadership of Jesus—as to whose divinity he was indefinite" (326).[46] The good pastor, the Reverend Andrew Pengilly, finds God in nature, feels religion rather than reasons about it, and doesn't give a hang for doctrinal differences.

There is a good priest whose career runs counter to that of the bad priest Gantry, but he ceases to be a priest.

[46] *Elmer Gantry* (New York: Harcourt, Brace, 1927).

Frank Shallard has doubts while he is still at the Seminary. They are encouraged by Dr. Zechlin, who tells him that no reasonable person can be a believing Christian; nevertheless, he ought to stay in the church to liberalize it from within—in effect, to destroy it. Eventually pressure from Gantry and his own conscience force Frank to resign from the ministry and turn to social work. But the honest man who dares to live according to his convictions, and to speak about them in public, has no place in a superstitious society; when he gives an antifundamentalist lecture, Frank is beaten and blinded.

Undoubtedly many of the excesses Lewis describes, especially those connected with revivalism, deserve the treatment they get. Nevertheless, it is soon apparent that he has gone too far; to him, Christianity is not only untrue, but inconceivable. All those who profess to be religious in the novel are shown as hypocrites or morons; the best we can expect, apparently, is a nominal profession of belief for the sake of convenience: the good shepherd is the one who sees that his lambs are fed with material food, not stale spiritual claptrap. If a satirist depicts the object of his satire as based on humbug, advocated by humbug, and defended by humbug, he must employ a great deal of wit and fantasy to prevent his attack from seeming cross-grained and peevish. *Elmer Gantry* fails because it is neither a realistic portrayal of the state of religion in America nor a caricature whose manifest unfairness can be forgiven because of the wit and humor which have gone into it.

There is a great deal of fantasy in the novel, but it is weird and crude and goes badly with the realism. An example is the bizarre marriage ceremony which takes place between Elmer and evangelist Sharon Falconer before her grotesque shrine. A more elaborate kind of fantasy arises out of Lewis's belief that formal religion

is based on the self-interest of its leaders. As in *Babbitt*
and *Arrowsmith*, we are made aware that there are
sinister forces combining to strike at the very foundations
of American liberties. Here, they are the sinister forces of
righteousness.

> It was on the steamer home that he met and became
> intimate with J. E. North, the renowned vice-slayer,
> executive secretary of the National Association for the
> Purification of Art and the Press—affectionately known
> through all the evangelical world as "the Napap." Mr.
> North was not a clergyman (though he was a warm
> Presbyterian layman), but no clergyman in the country
> had more furiously pursued wickedness, more craftily
> forced congressmen, through threats in their home dis-
> tricts, to see legislation in the same reasonable manner as
> himself. For several sessions of congress he had backed a
> bill for a federal censorship of all fiction, plays, and
> moving pictures, with a penitentiary sentence for any
> author mentioning adultery even by implication, ridicu-
> ling prohibition, or making light of any Christian sect or
> minister.
>
> The bill had always been defeated, but it was gaining
> more votes in every session . . . [407–408].

It is Elmer's Napoleonic ambition to combine all such
organizations to the greater glory of himself:

> He would combine in one association all the moral
> organizations in America—perhaps, later, in the entire
> world. He would be the executive of that combination; he
> would be the super-president of the United States, and
> some day the dictator of the world [409].

We are back in the land of wizards and ogres once more.

In fact, the question of whether Elmer is a human being
or an ogre in the novel is a relevant one. At times he is
almost satanic, a compendium of all the vices; they are
too many and too flagrant for him to be real. But occasionally Lewis tries to endow him with a soul, as in the incident

of his conversion at Terwillinger College. Elmer is the great man steadily making his way upward in the world—the man of immoderate personal ambition—and the great man hasn't time for scruples. Since he is ordinarily only a caricature, we cannot consider him a believeable human being; and when Lewis tells us that he has a conscience, we refuse to believe it.

After he had become a celebrity, Lewis usually managed to avoid controversy over his books by being out of the United States when they appeared. The publication day of *Elmer Gantry* found him wandering through Europe with Ramon Guthrie; from Dubrovnik, Yugoslavia, he commented in the most innocent tones on the stir he had caused: "The violent Kansas City blokes have been asinine. I'm grateful to them for proving the book."[47] Very few observers, however, thought that he had been as fair and dispassionate as he pretended; one comparatively balanced review of the novel was entitled "'Red' Lewis in a Red Rage," and his former professor William Lyon Phelps declared in an interview that the book must have been written when Lewis was "literally foaming at the mouth . . . ."[48] Edwin Muir was one of the few critics who found some complexity in Lewis's attitude toward his central character; he thought this complexity was due to the division of intentions which was evident in other Lewis novels—Lewis wanted to write both a satire and a novel, to indict his hero and to sympathize with

[47] Letter to Harrison Smith, April 25, 1927, *From Main Street to Stockholm*, p. 241. Couch, "Reputation," pp. 121 ff., and Grebstein, *Sinclair Lewis*, pp. 100 ff., show how timely the book was and mention a number of actual occurrences which are reflected in it, especially the parallels between Lewis's characters and Billy Sunday and Aimee Semple McPherson. Grebstein notes that while Lewis was writing the novel the judgment in the famous Scopes trial over the teaching of evolution in Tennessee was still being deliberated, so that Lewis was writing "in the most hotly charged religious atmosphere in America since the Salem witch burnings."

[48] New York *Times*, March 20, 1927, p. 19.

him at the same time.[49] It might seem that the last thing in the world Lewis wanted was sympathy for Elmer Gantry, whom he regarded, he told Allen Austin years later, as "a hypocrite through and through."[50] Yet he wrote in the *Nation* in 1928, "Actually, I like the Babbitts, the Dr. Pickerbaughs, the Will Kennicotts, and even the Elmer Gantrys rather better than anyone else on earth."[51] Furthermore, he told Betty Stevens that the Babbitts "were my children and I wanted to reform them. Gantry, too. Even Gantry wouldn't have been such a bad fellow if he'd been, say, a salesman."[52] Only a very curious moral outlook could have permitted the creator of such a monster as Elmer Gantry to say that his character's lack of a sense of decency would not have been objectionable if he had changed his profession.

The book was both attacked and defended with considerable acrimony. The *Literary Review* printed two opposing reviews: W. E. Woodward described the book as "the greatest, most vital and most penetrating study of religious hypocrisy that has been written since Voltaire," while the well-known evangelical clergyman John Roach Straton said that he had been allotted two thousand words and needed only one—"bunk." But although many of the reviews concentrated on the issues and forgot the book, there were some excellent discussions of it; and they raised fundamental questions concerning Lewis's artistry and outlook. Muir thought the book an artistic failure for the reason suggested above; undecided whether to be novelist or satirist, Lewis made Elmer essentially a type, but also attempted to particularize him—attempts which did not

---

[49] Edwin Muir, review of *Elmer Gantry*, *Nation and Athenaeum*, XLI (1927), 85.

[50] Allen Austin, "An Interview with Sinclair Lewis," *University of Kansas City Review*, XXIV (1958), 201.

[51] "Mr. Lorimer and Me," *Nation*, CXXVII (1928), 81.

[52] Austin, "Interview," p. 201.

sufficiently define him as a character and yet shook his validity as a type. Yet he thought that a more devastating piece of satire was not to be found in contemporary literature.

Rebecca West, on the other hand, considered it one of the most disappointing books ever produced by a man of genius. Elaborating on this opinion, she reiterated the old demand that Lewis indicate his positives; he had neglected, she said, a necessary prerequisite for the satirist's work: possession at least in imagination of the quality whose lack is satirized. Lewis pilloried Elmer Gantry and others for their misuse of "the force that makes men want to speak and hear religion"; but he had no conception of what a proper use of this force might be, and his attempts at describing it were disconcertingly jejune—on the same mental plane, in fact, as Elmer's. As an example she took the concluding part of Chapter 28, in which Lewis had Frank Shallard declare that Jesus was a person chiefly interested in flattering His vanity; criticize Him for failing to recommend sanitation, which would have saved millions from the plague in years to come; and state that the one thing which stood out in His teaching was a system of economics whereby no one saved money or stored up wheat or did anything but live like a tramp. This clodhopping handling of the biblical narrative, she pointed out, was not exhibited for our pity but for our admiration; Lewis apparently felt that to combat Babbittry it was necessary to enter into argument with Babbitt and reverse his opinions, and he did so in thought and language on the very same level as Babbitt's own.[53]

A similar criticism lies behind the searching reassessment of *Elmer Gantry* which Mark Schorer wrote for *New*

[53] Rebecca West, review of *Elmer Gantry*, New York *Herald Tribune Books*, March 13, 1927, p. 1.

Republic in 1955.[54] *Elmer Gantry*, he said, lacks even the bits of sentimental reverie found in *Main Street* and *Babbitt*; the book shows a world of total death, of monsters without shadow. On reflection, he thought that this was the purest Lewis, this stark image of barbarity, in which "nothing is missing but all religion and all humanity." In *Elmer Gantry* all is corrupt; there are a few indistinct figures of good, but none of them really challenges the demonic hero—a character like Frank Shallard serves chiefly to illustrate Elmer's power and ruthlessness. In fact, the conflict, social or individual, through which most novels operate is entirely missing; there are no dynamics of social action, only a static image, a "melodramatic stereotype" of bare brutality. Elmer has, perhaps, one brief moment of honesty, but he quickly argues himself out of it: "I'm leading an absolutely Christian life, and I'm bringing a whale of a lot more souls into churches than any of these pussy-footing tin-saints . . ." (315).

Elmer is exhibited, Schorer says, as the product of "an important if stultifying American tradition: the protestantism of the hinterland . . . ." Early in the novel Lewis gives a completely devastating account of his hero's religious upbringing:

> The church and Sunday School at Elmer's village . . . had nurtured in him a fear of religious machinery which he could never lose. . . . That small pasty-white Baptist church had been the center of all his emotions, aside from hell-raising, hunger, sleepiness, and love [25].

In the church he heard all the music he ever heard as a boy; from the church came all his philosophy; from the

[54] Mark Schorer, "The Monstrous Self-Deception of Elmer Gantry," *New Republic*, CXXXIII (October 31, 1955), 13–15, expanded and published as "Sinclair Lewis and the Method of Half-Truths," in *Society and Self in the Novel*, ed. Mark Schorer, English Institute Essays, 1955 (New York: Columbia University Press, 1956).

Bible stories, the hymns, and the preachers' anecdotes came all his knowledge of literature. "He had, in fact," Lewis concludes, "got everything from the church and Sunday School, except, perhaps, any longing for decency and kindness and reason" [28]. Possessing none of these qualities, Schorer maintains, Elmer is in no position to evaluate the forces which have made him or the historical situation in which he is involved; Sinclair Lewis is aware of these, but the very nature of his creation prevents it from sharing his knowledge. Furthermore, he has no alternatives: "the poor fool of the hinterland . . . had never been given more by it than the dubious gift of deriding it, and therefore of having finally to love it." [55] He is thus "trapped in his own hallucination of the world as a trap":

> . . . in no novel does Sinclair Lewis more clearly announce his loathing of the social environment with which he is concerned, and in no novel does he make it more mandatory that we remain within the terrifying limits of that environment. Sinclair Lewis is not unlike Elmer Gantry. For the vicious circle in this picture exists, of course, in the fact that Elmer re-makes society in precisely the terms that society has already made him. No one can break out; everyone, including the novelist, spins more madly in the mechanical orbit. [56]

He had to create the image of the thing he loathed, in order to express his loathing. It is useless to argue, Schorer believes, that he did not see enough; he looked and listened, and from his accumulation of evidence he selected only those details that would serve to create the half-truth at which he aimed.

The subject of Lewis's relationship to another widely known malcontent was brought up by Elmer Davis, in

[55] Schorer, "The Monstrous Self-Deception of Elmer Gantry," p. 15.
[56] *Ibid.*

his searching review of *Elmer Gantry* in the New York *Times*. In the novel, said Davis, Lewis had assembled the scattered evidences against Christianity into a single massive indictment, and had set it forth in language which no one could misunderstand. If Christianity was unsatisfactory, as it was to increasing numbers of Americans, most people would require something to take its place. And the substitute was ready. Lewis had dedicated the book, in "profound admiration," to H. L. Mencken. Davis was not surprised to find that the ideas expressed in *Elmer Gantry* were held in common by Mencken and Lewis, but the fact that the style and vocabulary were often Mencken's too had to be taken as a confession of faith. Lewis employed the "ritual language which enables true believers to recognize each other as surely as members of the Loyal Order of Moose." Mencken's ideas, Davis said, compromised a body of doctrine, the doctrine of a new and popular religion: "No doubt Mr. Mencken, like other prophets, set out to teach men the truth with the idea that the truth would make them free; and like other prophets, he sees them line up in a joyful goosestep, proclaiming that his truth is the sole truth, in which alone lies salvation." This he considered the most extraordinary of recent religious phenomena—"the welding together of assorted disgruntlements into a new church, as thoroughly regimented as any Christian body and quite as intolerant." [57]

Just what was Mencken's influence on Lewis? It is hard

[57] Elmer Davis, review of *Elmer Gantry*, New York *Times Book Review*, March 13, 1927, p. 1. Mencken's view of American religion was set forth in the section on "High and Ghostly Matters" in *Prejudices*, Fourth Series (New York: Knopf, 1924). Couch points out that in *Prejudices*, Fifth Series, published the year before *Elmer Gantry*, Mencken had invited novelists to join him in attacking the revival evangelists and had mentioned Lewis by name. Lewis, of course, had begun work on his novel long before this. See Couch, "Reputation," p. 119.

to estimate. Schorer calls it the most influential literary relationship that Lewis experienced. He accepts with reservations George Jean Nathan's account, as given in his *Intimate Notebooks*, of how it all began—of an evening when Mencken and Nathan were subjected to the "self-endorsing uproar" of a "tall, skinny, paprika-headed stranger" who informed them that he had "just finished a book that'll be published in a week or two and it's the gottdamn best book of its kind that this here gottdamn country has had and don't you guys forget it !'", of their joint conclusion that he was the worst idiot they had ever laid eyes on, and of the letter which Nathan received from Mencken three days later: "I've just read the advance sheets of the book of that *Lump* we met at Schmidt's and, by God, he has done the job !" [58] After this, when the Sage of Baltimore visited New York he sometimes found a drinking companion in Lewis; occasionally Mencken regaled bar patrons with quotations from prohibition pamphlets, and Lewis matched his performance with orations on the merits of Rotary. So says William Manchester in his biography of Mencken, *Disturber of the Peace*, but he makes fewer references to Lewis than one would expect. The letters to Harcourt in which Lewis alludes to Mencken do not suggest an easy intimacy between them; instead, Lewis thinks of Mencken as a very touchy individual who requires kid-glove treatment. According to Manchester, however, the friendship continued fairly strong—in spite of a devastating assault which Lewis made on Mencken's fabulous Prohibition cache—until after Mencken's marriage in 1930, when it lapsed because of Mrs. Mencken's dislike of Dorothy Thompson.

In the letters from Lewis to Mencken which Schorer quotes, one can see how easy it was for Lewis to fall into

[58] *The Intimate Notebooks of George Jean Nathan* (New York: Knopf, 1932), pp. 8–10.

Mencken's way of mocking the clergy: from one godly brother in the ministry to another went descriptions of labors in the vineyard, requests for prayers for President Coolidge, even requests for prayers for the Pope. Although he had developed his own attitude toward Main Street and the Babbitts independently, Lewis accepted Mencken's mythology of the businessman, the great American boob. Undoubtedly he shared Mencken's enjoyment in the game of hunting down the boobs and hypocrites; he too knew the pleasure it gave "to nail the hides of a million American absurdities upon an immeasurable barn door." [59] And he could adopt Mencken's standpoint, that of the detached, amused observer who took the follies of democracy for granted but pointed them out to others so that they could share in the amusement. He might almost have answered, as Mencken did when he was asked why he lived in the United States if he found so much to complain about, "Why do men go to zoos?" But his attitude of superiority did not rest on the same philosophic or pseudo-philosophic basis as Mencken's: he did not give his assent to Mencken's version of Nietzscheism. In fact, the cult of the superman was profoundly at variance with his deepest convictions; he sided with the ordinary man against the elite, and he was capable of envisaging a bourgeois utopia—"a world of delightful little houses" [60]—which would have made Mencken retch. The faithless, hopeless Lewis is therefore not really, as Schorer thinks, the purest Lewis; it is the Lewis who has adopted the alien cynicism of Mencken. Fundamentally Lewis was a man of simple belief; as we have seen in *The Job*, he could envisage his fellow citizens as caught in a trap, but he was usually confident that, because of native American ingenuity, American enterprise, or the destiny planned for Americans, in some miraculous way they were going to escape from it.

[59] Van Doren, *Sinclair Lewis*, p. 48.   [60] "Mr. Lorimer and Me," p. 81.

5. An Alien View
of America

Elmer Gantry, Couch shows, brought a pronounced change of attitude towards Lewis.[1] Though the novel had been praised as the greatest blow ever struck in America at religious hypocrisy, the impression grew that its author was insufficiently concerned with truth and fairness. In his assessment of Lewis in *Men of Destiny*, Walter Lippmann called the book "a witch-burning to make an atheist holiday." There was some curiosity, he wrote, about what Lewis would tackle next—the politician, the editor, the lawyer, the professor, the business executive. But he was more interested in

> whether Mr. Lewis will reach maturity, or remain arrested in his adolescent rebellion. After "Arrowsmith" one would have said that he was beginning to be free of that shapeless irritation and yearning which Carol Kennicott typifies. But after "Elmer Gantry" one cannot be so sure. The hatreds are turned inward, as if the effort to escape

[1] William Couch, Jr., "The Emergence, Rise and Decline of the Reputation of Sinclair Lewis" (Ph.D. dissertation, University of Chicago, 1954), p. 134.

had failed and become morbid. There is some sort of crisis in this astonishing career, which is not yet resolved.[2]

But Lewis, who in the spring of 1927 was drifting about Europe in a leisurely way, was still thinking about a labor novel. Impulsive as ever, he had invited Ramon Guthrie—soon to become a Harcourt, Brace author himself—to come with him to Spain, and took him to Venice instead. To Guthrie he described his plans for the book with Debs as hero; it was still sometimes referred to as *Neighbor*, but now he had another title—*The Man Who Sought God*. So far, however, he had found neither the place to work nor the incentive. Then suddenly he had had enough "Europe-trotting." On July 2 he wrote his wife from Munich that he would be back in New York in six weeks' time, and asked her to spend the rest of the summer on Nantucket with him. But from Munich he went to Berlin; and from Berlin on July 24 came a cable to Harcourt: "Staying Europe several months more. Please inform Gracie." In Berlin he had met Dorothy Thompson.

Already a well-known newspaper correspondent, Miss Thompson had just received a divorce from a Hungarian named Josef Bard and was presumably free of entanglements. Eight months later, however, Lewis was to stress his own unavailability in a strongly worded telegram to the Associated Press: "As I am married and as my wife is not suing me nor I her for divorce, any rumor of my engagement is ridiculous and even libellous."[3] But apparently he proposed to Dorothy the first night he met her, and from that time on he engaged in a feverish pursuit. In mid-July she flew to cover the riots

[2] Walter Lippmann, *Men of Destiny* (New York: Macmillan, 1927), pp. 91–92.

[3] New York *Times*, March 17, 1929, p. 15.

in Vienna, and he flew along with her; in August they went on a walking trip through Shropshire and Cornwall; then they toured the Rhineland; and in mid-September Lewis began looking for a flat in Berlin, where Dorothy was chief of a news bureau. When Dorothy left for Moscow at the end of October, Lewis stayed behind in Berlin to do some work; but a month later he followed. The Russians, informed of his coming, greeted him with a delegation of cultural representatives and a brass band, and, expecting some quotable remarks on the class struggle, asked him why he had come; they were somewhat bewildered by his answer: "To see Dorothy."

The meeting with Miss Thompson had spurred him to literary activity. He advised Harcourt on October 25 that, though he was still devoted to German beer and wine, he had not touched a drop of their "delightful but rather destructive little brothers"; furthermore, he warned Harcourt to expect "several nice lil books by Sinclair Lewis, now that he's gone through his apprenticeship and begun to live." [4] At the urging of Guthrie and Miss Thompson, and as a warm-up for his next novel, he wrote a 15,000-word story for Mencken—something he had been promising Mencken for a long time, the account by a Babbitt of how he called on Coolidge at the White House. "Of course I love this sort of drool," he wrote, "and it'll be my swan-song to Babbittism." [5] Mencken and Nathan were enthusiastic about the story, and Harcourt, when he saw the proofs, thought it would make a nice little book to sell at a dollar. When he suggested this, Lewis replied in a lengthy cable that he wanted to add three similar pieces to the first and publish

[4] Letter to Harcourt, October 25, 1927, *From Main Street to Stockholm: Letters of Sinclair Lewis 1919–1930*, ed. with an intro. by Harrison Smith (New York: Harcourt, Brace, 1952), p. 255.

[5] *Ibid.*

the whole as a complete novel. Not without misgivings— "it's much better to have too little than too much of such highly humorous, satirical material"—the publisher deferred to the author.[6] True to his claim that he could "write this stuff incredible speed," Lewis dispatched the additional pages of manuscript only about two weeks after his cable, so that Harcourt, Brace was able to publish the book the following April. Lewis exuberantly suggested that a sale of 200,000 was possible; Harcourt warned him to expect a reaction closer to that of *Mantrap* than to that of *Gantry*.

The Man Who Knew Coolidge is not a novel, but a series of "Babbilogues," as Malcolm Cowley called them. Its interest lies in its use of Lewis's favorite literary and conversational device, the satiric monologue. The reminiscences of Lewis's friends all testify to his fondness for it; Harrison Smith, for example, writes of

> the long satiric monologues in which he imitated with astonishing virtuosity the accents of characters he had not yet brought to birth. Oddly enough he never parodied women; but the voices of long-winded men in smoking cars, of Babbitts and Elmer Gantrys and the men who knew Coolidge were always echoing in his friends' ears.[7]

Such monologues are essential elements of all his satiric novels; a speaker unconsciously exposes his own shortcomings and those of the class or group which he represents. But though he could make effective use of this technique, Lewis could not always control it. Dorothy Thompson, referring to his "hilarious gift for mimicry," adds that he would prolong a monologue until his listeners were exhausted or bored;[8] and Arnold Bennett

[6] Letter to Lewis, December 14, 1927, *ibid.*, p. 261.

[7] Introduction, *ibid.*, p. xi.

[8] "The Boy and Man from Sauk Centre," *Atlantic Monthly*, CCVI (November 1960), 46.

mentioned Lewis's "habit of breaking into a discussion with long pieces of imaginary conversation" which were "goodish, but too long." [9] Similarly, if a Lewis novel managed to avoid becoming simply a satiric survey of various types of extraordinary behavior, it was still in danger of becoming a string of satiric monologues. George F. Whicher asserts that Lewis's method of composition was nothing but the fabrication of such a string: "Given the prescribed title and tone, Lewis simply turned on the faucet of an inexhaustible mimicry, leaving it to his publisher to check the flow when enough had run to make a profitable book." [10] *The Man Who Knew Coolidge* gives evidence that the publisher sometimes found it difficult to check the flow.

The satiric monologue, to succeed as humor, must resemble the speech of some person or type whom the reader can recognize. Once the resemblance has been established, the details need not be perfectly realistic. Listen to the voice of Lowell Schmaltz, the man who knew Coolidge, as he hymns the praises of the filing cabinet:

> "Maybe you think I'm getting kind of woozy about it," I tell 'em, "but to me the beauties of the modern filing systems, which enable a man to instantly and without the least loss of time or effort find a letter on which, perhaps, depends the closing of an important deal, is in its practical way, to say nothing of the physical appearance of modern up-to-date filing-cabinets, no longer mere wooden boxes but whether in steel or fireproofed wood, the finest example of the cabinet-maker's art and imitating perfectly the rarest woods—To me," I often tell them, "these filing-systems are in every way as beautiful as the poet's song, as the flush on the maiden's cheek

[9] Quoted in Grace Hegger Lewis, *With Love from Gracie: Sinclair Lewis: 1912–1925* (New York: Harcourt, Brace, 1955), p. 267.
[10] George F. Whicher, in *The Literature of the American People*, ed. A. H. Quinn (New York: Appleton-Century-Crofts, 1951), p. 854.

when she first hears the first whispered words of love, or
the soft chirp of the mother bird at eveningtide, chirping
to her birdlings. Yes sir, you bet your sweet life they are,
and you can laugh all you want to !" [29] [11]

Obviously, this is not the verbatim account of a sales talk
which Lewis has heard, but a burlesque of such a talk; it
is made ridiculous by verbosity, exaggeration, incongruities, and contradictions.

The ultimate appeal of such a monologue is to ideas,
through the employment of irony; the actual standards of
the speaker are in grotesque opposition to his expressed
ones. Sometimes he contradicts a principle in the very
speech in which he advocates it; Lowell Schmaltz firmly
believes that prohibition, having been made the law of
the land, ought to be rigidly enforced—"But same time,
that don't mean you got to be a fanatic" (20). Sometimes
he draws attention to the faults of others, thereby emphasizing his own culpability on the same score; for example,
Lowell ridicules the speaker who wanders all over the
place and laments the younger generation's maltreatment
of the Queen's English. Sometimes the contradiction
becomes apparent only when one speech is compared
with a previous or subsequent declaration of principle.
At any rate, the satiric monologue provides a stark
revelation of what the speaker would keep hidden if he
could.

The Man Who Knew Coolidge is another of Lewis's
analyses of a social class through presentation of a typical
member of it. The result here is not pleasant: the reader
who examines the values of Lowell Schmaltz has a hard
time thinking of the book as good-humored exposure.
The description in the subtitle—"Being the soul of
Lowell Schmaltz, constructive and Nordic Citizen"—
is, of course, ironic; Lowell Schmaltz hasn't got a soul,

---

[11] *The Man Who Knew Coolidge* (New York: Harcourt, Brace, 1928).

at least not a rational soul. His mind is simply a rever-
berating device for the advertising slogans and chauvinistic propaganda which are his society's substitutes for
cultural expression. The United States is "the greatest
nation in the world, with more autos and radios and
furnaces and suits of clothes and miles of cement pave-
ments and sky-scrapers than the rest of the world put
together . . ." (176). The material and the mechanical are
adequate substitutes for the gods of past ages: "I guess
in the vacuum cleaner America has added to the world *its*
own mystery, that'll last when the columns of the Acropo-
lis have crumbled to mere dust!" (168) "The Basic and
Fundamental Ideals of Christian American Citizenship,"
the subject of the sixth "Babbilogue," turn out to be
merely the salesman's talking points, service and practica-
bility. The New Era of American Civilization, which is
replacing the effete and decadent culture of the Old
World, has no nobler guiding rule than "Read widely,
think scientifically, speak briefly, and sell the goods!"
(275)

If we glimpse a personality beneath the garrulously
repeated slogans, it is an ugly one. Schmaltz is a failure
and a fraud, both in his family life and in business.
In his relations with his wife, he appears as a sadistic
monster who rationalizes his behavior on the basis of his
own convenient misinterpretation of Freudianism. In
his social and political attitudes, he aligns himself eagerly
with the sinister antidemocratic forces which Lewis
exposes in this book as in others; he is capable of insisting
that if the Germans haven't understood our democratic
ideas, they ought to've been *forced* to," and he tells
proudly how the Americanization Committee of the
Zenith Chamber of Commerce manhandled "some dog-
gone sorehead Bolshevik . . . that insisted they keep up
all these ridiculous and uncivilized customs they'd had

back in Hungary (or is it Jugoslovakia?—wherever it is that Hunkies come from) instead of reaching outward and upward and grabbing their chance to become real Americans" (121). There is sufficient emphasis on Lowell Schmaltz's sinister qualities to make him completely unsympathetic. Babbitt is redeemable; Schmaltz isn't.

Discussing this character as a Babbitt gone nasty, Maxwell Geismar points out that, where Babbitt was naive and complacent, Schmaltz is arrogant and assertive. Consequently Geismar sees *Coolidge* as an important case history of an epoch: he is the epitome of the complacency of the Boom Market, when God Himself became a junior partner. (Schmaltz talks eloquently about the Purposes of God as shown in American History and calls attention to God's wisdom in creating a California for the midwestern farmer to retire to.) But in Geismar's view Schmaltz is an ignoble and inadequate portrait of human nature; Lewis has mistaken a set of cultural reflexes obvious at the time for the whole circle of human experience. Furthermore, he has not really come to grips with his projection or tried to understand its underlying causes.[12] Frederick J. Hoffman also puts special emphasis on *Coolidge* in his discussion of Lewis; he sees the book as "pure" Lewis, an unadulterated review of the materials upon which he exercised his comic imagination.[13] But the Lewis character who gives the impression of being "tasteless, mirthless, savorless"[14] and who is so isolated from reality that even his business exists in his consciousness almost entirely in the terms of standardized publicity is not typical. Moreover, although the book gives a review of Lewis's satirical materials, it is not an

[12] Maxwell Geismar, *The Last of the Provincials: The American Novel, 1915–1925* (Boston: Houghton Mifflin, 1949), pp. 105–111.

[13] Frederick J. Hoffman, *The Modern Novel in America, 1900–1950* (Chicago: Regnery, 1951), p. 113.

[14] Henry Longan Stuart, "Mr. Lewis Goes Back to Babbitt," New York *Times Book Review*, April 8, 1928, p. 1.

unadulterated review, nor is it a compendium of all Lewis's opinions about the American middle class. In its assessment of the novel, the *Independent* complained that Lewis's zeal for reform was running away with his judgment as a novelist; [15] and Malcolm Cowley described the book as a punitive expedition after the average American and declared that Lewis was "inspired by a hatred of Babbitt which is changing from a passion into an obsession." [16] Yet only a few months later, in his contribution to a series in the *Nation* in which various writers described the world in which they would like to live, Lewis maintained that he was no more of a reformer than George Horace Lorimer of the *Saturday Evening Post* and proclaimed his affection for the Babbitts:

> I am frequently credited with being the worst crab, next to Father Mencken and Father Nathan, in our Beloved States. I am informed by innumerous preachers and editorial writers that I'm all for anarchism and bombing and general hell to pay. Actually, I like the Babbitts, the Dr. Pickerbaughs, the Will Kennicotts, and even the Elmer Gantrys rather better than anyone else on earth. They are good fellows. They laugh—really laugh. [17]

The "real" or "pure" Lewis could both love and hate the Babbitts and Gantrys, depending on his mood. He was not always as patronizing and superior to the average American as he was in *The Man Who Knew Coolidge*; that book was begun with *Mercury* readers in mind, and Lewis was describing the cultural reflexes which these readers had been trained by Mencken to recognize and ridicule.

Lewis's farewell to Babbittry and to Menckenism did

[15] *Independent*, CXX (1928), 461.
[16] Malcolm Cowley, "Babbilogues," *New Republic*, LIV (April 25, 1928), 302.
[17] "Mr. Lorimer and Me," *Nation*, CXXVII (1928), 81.

not sell as satisfactorily as he had expected. Harcourt's judgment was vindicated; he observed some time later that it was astonishing how few copies the public bought, that it was almost as if an unfavorable impression of the book had spread from one end of the country to the other within twenty-four hours.

Lewis wrote Harcourt in October, 1927, that he had "settled down to the quietest kind of life, seeing very few people while I work on the new novel," [18] his long-projected story of an American abroad, tentatively entitled *Exile*. Lewis had finished fifty thousand words of the first draft before his trip to Moscow. It is understandable that the writing of the book and the wooing of Dorothy should have proceeded simultaneously, for Lewis was telling the story of his first marriage and exorcising the spirit of his first wife, as it were, before marrying a second time. Long before he was sure that Dorothy would agree to marry him, he had made inquiries as to whether a German or a French divorce would be recognized in the United States. Eventually Mrs. Lewis, who now had her own reasons for a divorce, consented to go to Reno early in the new year; and on April 16, 1928, a Nevada court declared their fourteen-year-old marriage to be at an end. A fifty-thousand-dollar trust fund was set up for Wells, and Mrs. Lewis was given alimony of one thousand dollars a month as long as Lewis's income remained above forty-eight thousand dollars a year. A week later Lewis announced his engagement to Dorothy Thompson.

Miss Thompson's first impression of Lewis was like our first view of Ahab in *Moby Dick*: "a narrow, ravaged face, roughened, red, and scarred by repeated radium and electric needle burnings . . . . The face of a man who had walked through flame throwers." [19] Her response to this

[18] Letter to Harcourt, October 27, 1927, *From Main Street to Stockholm*, p. 256.

[19] "The Boy and Man from Sauk Centre," p. 46.

apparition and its "strange, shy, imploring look" was partly one of pity: "My instantaneous reaction was, God, what a lonely, unhappy, helpless man! Somebody *must* love and take care of him!" Yet with him he brought a "disturbing atmospheric tension," "an immediate aura of greatness"; soon she was identifying herself with Leora:

> ... I doubt if even her creator realizes how truly her life fulfills the longing of the real woman. One is willing to be swallowed up by a man, if in his brain and heart one is transmuted into something "rich and strange," something better than one could be of one's self.[20]

Although such journal entries show how and why Lewis became important to her, others make it seem almost inconceivable that she should have taken on the burden of looking after a man whose condition was nearly hopeless. There were many disillusioning incidents; perhaps one of the worst was the occasion when she waited in a Lanvin gown and sumptuous evening cloak for him to take her to a dance and finally went to his apartment, to find him sodden drunk, staring at her "with fishy, dead eyes."[21] Yet she continued to hope for a stability and security—represented in her mind by the vision of a home in New England—which she knew were impossible to achieve. Lewis and she were married in London on May 14, 1928, with a civil ceremony at a registry office, followed by a religious ceremony in the Savoy Chapel. As Vincent Sheean says, there was something rather touching about Lewis's desire to make this marriage as solid and enduring as possible by going through all the formalities which had been omitted from his first wedding. Yet a ludicrous element entered into the luncheon at the Savoy; Lewis could not resist the temptation to deliver

[20] Vincent Sheean, *Dorothy and Red* (Boston: Houghton Mifflin, 1963), p. 33.
[21] *Ibid.*, pp. 41 ff.

one of his monologues—addressing the assembled wedding guests as though they were all jute merchants, he reviewed the state of the jute business in the whole of the British Empire.

For their honeymoon the Lewises set out on an extended trip through England, in a caravan so luxurious that it resembled a Pullman car. Lewis wrote a series of articles for the New York *Herald Tribune* on the way, many of them making comparisons between English customs and American. He also worked at his new book, now given the title of *Dodsworth*. It took on larger proportions than he had envisaged, so that by the end of the caravan trip he had to cable Harcourt that it would take him four more months to finish it. The cable was sent from Paris on August 17, and a few days later the Lewises sailed for the United States; he was returning after an absence of eighteen months, and she was bringing back the accumulation of eight years in Europe.

Before long they bought what Lewis called "my first authentic home—a farm in the pastoral state of Vermont." He showed such enthusiasm at moving to this three-hundred-acre property—which they called Twin Farms—near Barnard and having guests come to stay that the question of whether he could be domesticated seemed to demand re-examination. When winter approached, the Lewises moved to a New York apartment; and in February they went to Florida for six weeks. Meanwhile, Lewis found himself giving advice to an aspiring writer, somewhat younger than himself, whose expertise in international affairs was proving to be a marketable commodity. While he revised *Dodsworth*, his wife was working on the articles she had written on her trip to Moscow. They were published in book form under the title *The New Russia*, and, with Lewis skillfully assisting her to exploit the possibilities created by her authorship of a successful book, she was soon in considerable demand as a speaker and writer. In March, Lewis interrupted his promotional activities long enough to write an article for the *Nation* on "Publicity Gone Mad"; he complained that in the greatest nation the world had ever known, all individuality had been subordinated to a machine-ruled industrialism and the most secret thoughts of any human being had been made the property of any swine who cared to read about them. He took almost the opposite approach, however, in an article "The American Scene in Fiction" which appeared in the New York *Herald Tribune Books* in mid-April. Here he observed that it was astonishing how many American scenes were as yet untouched by literature and discounted "the common plaint that Americans are so much alike, divided into so few classes, that there is no chance for the portrayer of the American scene to find fresh aspects." Emphasizing that the Babbitt of Boston and the Babbitt of Seattle have differences beneath the similarities, he paid tribute to writers like Willa Cather who rendered their environments discriminatingly and faithfully.[22]

In the meantime, *Dodsworth*, Lewis's longest discussion of what it means to be an American, had appeared: it was published in March, 1929. In *The Complex Fate*, Marius Bewley argues that the largest problem confronting the American artist of the nineteenth century and a continuing problem for his twentieth-century successor has been the nature of his separateness from and connection with European culture.[23] The problem of Hawthorne and Howells and James was also the problem of Sinclair Lewis, who had reviled Main Street and sought refuge in Europe, had publicly expressed the wish that the Babbitts would lose their insularity and suspicion of

[22] Reprinted in *The Man from Main Street: Collected Essays and Other Writings, 1904–1950*, ed. Harry E. Maule and Melville H. Cane (New York: Random House, 1953), pp. 142–147.

[23] Marius Bewley, *The Complex Fate* (London: Chatto and Windus, 1952).

foreigners, and yet had defended Main Street against the English equivalent, High Street, from the most chauvinistic point of view. [24] As a novel on the international theme, *Dodsworth* is an investigation and an analysis done with the usual Lewis thoroughness. Basically, it is an inquiry rather than a satire; Lewis does not take either American or European culture as a standard, but tries to discover what is most valuable in each. He does, of course, satirize obviously ridiculous positions, such as that of the American expatriates who disparage their native land as hopelessly crude and vulgar, and that of Europeans who describe America as past all redemption without ever having seen it. But he presents so many aspects of the question with sympathy and understanding that many of the critics— those who were not disappointed at finding him lowering the banner of rebellion—considered that the novel gave evidence of broader spiritual perception than they had previously found in his writing.

As in his earlier books, the inquiry is pursued in terms of personal relationships; *Dodsworth* is, in fact, both the anatomy of a situation and the story of a marriage. One side of that story is presented sympathetically, the other satirically; one main character exemplifies loyalty in marriage, the other disloyalty, just as one shows us how to see Europe, the other how not to see it. Sam Dodsworth goes abroad aware of his own provincialism and open to new influences, but still tenacious of his own individuality and his own heritage. He perceives what is really worth while in European culture, takes what he can of it, and blends it with his own native endowments to emerge a fuller person. For his wife, Fran, culture is interesting "only as it adorned her socially"; going abroad for selfish and snobbish reasons, she mingles with a frothy international set, gains the ephemeral admiration of a succes-

[24] In a debate with the British writer Ian Hay in May, 1923.

sion of gigolos, and destroys the relationship with Sam which is her only possible basis for happiness.

The characterization of Sam Dodsworth is proof, if proof were needed, that the Sinclair Lewis of the 1920's was no more dedicated to the overthrow of capitalism than the Sinclair Lewis of a decade earlier. Sam is introduced as "the American Captain of Industry, believing in the Republican Party, high tariffs and, so long as they did not annoy him personally, in prohibition and the Episcopal Church." Any one of his Republicanism, prohibitionism or Episcopalianism ought to be enough to condemn him in Lewis's eyes; but, though he sometimes talks like one, he is not by any means a Schmaltz or a Babbitt:

> To define what Sam Dodsworth was, at fifty, it is easiest to state what he was not. He was none of the things which most Europeans and Americans expect in a leader of American industry. He was not a Babbitt, not a Rotarian, not an Elk, not a deacon. He rarely shouted, never slapped people on the back, and he had attended only six baseball games since 1900. . . .
>
> While he was bored by free verse and cubism, he thought rather well of Dreiser, Cabell, and so much of Proust as he had rather laboriously mastered. . . . He was common sense apotheosized, he had the energy and reliability of a dynamo, he liked whisky and poker and pâté de foie gras, and all the while he dreamed of motors like thunderbolts, as poets less modern than himself might dream of stars and roses and nymphs by a pool [11].[25]

The dynamo held no terrors or occult significance for Lewis, as it did for Henry Adams; as in his early novels, he could still sing the praises of the engineer and see poetry in the automobile. Sam Dodsworth, inventor,

[25] *Dodsworth* (New York: Harcourt, Brace, 1929).

entrepreneur, technologist, is the capitalist hero; and Lewis is still writing the epic of American progress— progress through material advancement.

At the beginning, however, the suggestion is made that Sam's type of rugged individualism is passing away. His Revelation Automobile Company is being absorbed by the billion-dollar Unit Automotive Company, whose president, Alec Kynance, is a stereotyped businessman. When Sam hesitates to accept a vice-presidency, saying that he wants to take a four-months' rest in Europe, Kynance explodes, "My God, man, what do you think is the purpose of life?" He himself has "done" Europe, and found that it has nothing to offer—which is not surprising, since he prefers assembly lines to cathedrals. Significantly, he loves advertising slogans—Sam hates them—and is not interested in excellence: he is planning to turn out a tinnier model of the car which is Sam's pride and joy. We can see here a Veblenesque opposition between the engineer and the captain of finance; here and elsewhere Lewis establishes a contrast between the heroic maker and doer and the ignoble manipulator of stocks and bonds and balance sheets.[26] The question is thus raised whether America is going to provide scope for its Sam Dodsworths, or whether they are going to be put on the shelf by the Alec Kynances; whether America is going to strive for excellence, or settle for mediocrity—and pass uncomplainingly into decadence without ever having achieved civilization.

The "queer cold bewilderment" which Dodsworth feels on his first contact with Europe emphasizes that, despite his liking for Proust and pâté, he is "the child

[26] Arthur B. Coleman, "The Genesis of Social Ideas in Sinclair Lewis" (Ph.D. dissertation, New York University, 1954), pp. 103–105 and 169–170, shows how the conflict between industrial and pecuniary elements in society appears in *Dodsworth*, and especially how Fran is portrayed as the spoiled leisure-class woman.

of nature brought into the world of civilization." [27] The theme is the familiar one of American innocence contrasted with European sophistication. The fact that his wife is much more competent than he does nothing to lessen Dodsworth's feeling of inadequacy. Nevertheless, while she is with her social butterflies—she prefers butterflies to ants, she tells him, and makes it clear that she considers him one of the ants—he sneaks off to enjoy Notre Dame; he can appreciate its beauty, recognize it as the masterwork of a culture, and feel a kinship with the "anonymous and vulgar" artists who created it. Dodsworth is both responsive and inquiring. He is particularly bothered by one question: What does America lack? There are many to give him answers, such as the businessman who won't go back to the United States because one-third of its population are meddlesome morality hounds, and the foreign correspondent who does go back and can't stand it; in fact, Lewis himself is always ready to give a short lecture on America's shortcomings, without bothering to invent a character to analyze them for him. But in the main we see things through Dodsworth's eyes, learn through his experiences, and watch him undergo a process of development and maturation.

The distance he has come becomes apparent when he returns to the United States for a short visit. The noise and insanity of New York provoke a diatribe against it and its lesser imitators. And now that he has succumbed to the disease of analysis, Sam finds his home town, Zenith, a very depressing city:

> He saw, slowly, that none of his prosperous industrialized friends in Zenith were very much interested in anything whatever. They had cultivated caution until they had lost the power to be interested. . . . The things over

[27] Carl Van Doren, "Zenith Meets Europe," *Nation*, CXXVIII (1929), 400.

which they were most exclamatory—money, golf, drinking—. . . were to the lords of Zenith not pleasures but ways of keeping so busy that they would not admit how bored they were, how empty their ambitions . . . .

They did things, they rushed, they supervised, they contended—but they were not interested [192–193].

Here the image of the midwestern city is much as it was in *Babbitt*—a vision of pygmies in a land made for giants. Dodsworth is bigger than these people when the novel begins, and he vastly outgrows them. Still, he does not reject his society, and he does not become despondent about it. As in *Free Air*, *Main Street*, and *Babbitt*, Lewis provides the partial excuse that this is a young country, still raw and crude because it has had to fight for survival; he suggests, however, through Dodsworth's experiences, that it must now look abroad for the materials of culture. Yet it possesses a vitality which the effete eastern states and the Old World cannot match; it is still a frontier where great things can be accomplished, and the novel concludes with the hero returning to do them.[28]

Dodsworth is the sort of man who is restless if he is not making something. Earlier, when he had puzzled over what was missing in the United States, he thought of it as an inward thing; but the emphasis on making and doing stays with him. Lewis picks for his central character a man who will reproduce in the practical sphere something of what he has assimilated in Europe; the illusion of the undiscriminating multiplication of material possibil-

[28] Martin Light, "A Study of Characterization in Sinclair Lewis's Fiction" (Ph.D. dissertation, University of Illinois, 1960), pp. 20 ff., has a very interesting discussion of the theme of the novel, particularly of the idea that America offers but one cluster of immediate and dramatic definitions of life—success, wealth, position. It is a pleasant surprise, he observes, to see the skill with which Lewis cuts across Sam's awakening contentment by means of Fran's shrill letters; he also thinks that the conclusion of *Dodsworth*, since its tone is much more successfully controlled than in Lewis's other novels, is the best Lewis ever wrote.

ities which Bewley describes as being at the heart of the American dream is still apparently Lewis's illusion.[29] Dodsworth returns with renewed vigor to embark on another industrial venture—involving not motor cars this time but garden suburbs, with nothing sham or pretentious about them, which will be his contribution to the building of a city finer than any which America now can boast. In Europe he sees a past but not a future; he returns to participate in the American adventure, which he views as the greatest in the world.

Although American manhood can resolve its perplexities, American womanhood has not yet reached the stage of self-criticism. As Leo and Miriam Gurko point out,[30] Fran Dodsworth is a kind of Carol Kennicott in her forties, chafing under the dullness of life in Zenith; but in this novel the rebel is a lost and empty soul. The epithet "childish" is used for her again and again—she is a spoiled child who indulges in tantrums, thinks of nobody but herself, and demands attention from everybody. Nevertheless, she is a child who can pose awkward questions; and she voices two criticisms of America which Lewis wants seriously considered. The first is that it is possible to exhaust everything which a city like Zenith can offer and become like a horse on a treadmill, endlessly repeating a monotonous and meaningless routine; escape from Zenith is necessary for survival as a person, and the salvation of the Zeniths, if it is to come, must come from without. The second is that woman in America is sacrificed to the industrial system; her so-called freedom results from the American man's preoccupation with the industrial mill. "Any real woman," she says, "is quite willing . . . to give up her own chances of fame for her

[29] Marius Bewley, *The Eccentric Design* (London: Chatto and Windus, 1959), p. 266.
[30] "The Two Main Streets of Sinclair Lewis," *College English*, IV (1943), 290.

husband, *providing* he is doing something she can admire
. . . . but she isn't willing to give up all her own capabilities
for the ideal of industrial America—which is to manu-
facture more vacuum-cleaners this year than we did last!"
(255) When she complains about the soullessness in
American life, Fran is making exactly the same kind of
criticism as Lewis has made in half a dozen other books.

Nevertheless, she is presented ironically; she complains
that the American male fails to treat his wife as a person,
yet it is she who tramples on her husband's personality.
When she accuses Sam of being a slave to industrialism,
Fran is treating him as though he were an Alec Kynance.
She does so partly because it provides her with an excuse,
for she goes to Europe in search of romantic encounters—
of a type not readily available to a Zenith matron soon
to be a grandmother. Sam wryly sees that he is expected
to take her to Europe to provide her with playmates; he
can understand, and pity, what is essentially a pathetic
attempt by Fran to recapture her lost youth. But any
compassion the reader may feel for her soon disappears,
as she tries to reduce her husband to a state of infantile
subjection to her will. As one reviewer saw,[31] it is a
Samson-and-Delilah situation, with the strong man in
bondage to a woman with the soul of a harlot. But the
seductress goes too far when she casts off her faithful
strong man for a German count—Sam has the "incredible
jar" of being dismissed by his wife. But she in turn is
rejected by the count, whose mother refuses to let him
marry. Since one of the reasons is that Fran would be
too old to bear a son, the illusion of recaptured youth is
shattered, along with the hope of social distinction.
Samson, seemingly ever faithful, comes back when called.
But Delilah behaves as though nothing had happened;
she is as flirtatious and inconsiderate as ever; and this

[31] Francis Lamont Robbins, "Samson Agonistes," *Outlook*, CLI (1929),
466.

time it is she who is abandoned, for good. There is unconscious irony in her final cry, "You haven't learned anything, not one single thing, out of all our sorrows!" For the outstanding thing about her is that she has not learned a single thing herself, and has not seen how much her husband has learned.

Dodsworth is ready to leave her now because he has found a more congenial companion, Edith Cortright. Significantly, she is an American who has achieved maturity and gained serenity through long acquaintance with Europe. It is made clear that she will be able to rebuild Sam's self-confidence and inspire him to create something authentic and uniquely American. So Lewis tells the story of his own transfer of affections from Grace to Dorothy Thompson. He even conveys some of his pride in his new home, when Sam, taught by Edith that the Europeans remain close to the earth while the Americans try to insulate themselves from it, begins to long for a piece of land which will not be a gentleman's show place but an authentic farm.

Perhaps Lewis's closeness to the story spoils it. As a representative of American womanhood, Fran lacks typicality and verisimilitude; she is too much like Grace Lewis, and the author's animus against her destroys the detachment necessary for good satire. At times her screeching voice hardly seems that of a human being at all; dislike has destroyed the author's ability to portray her convincingly. On the other hand, Lewis goes to great lengths to show us how kind and indulgent American husbands—such as he—are to their wives; as a result, Sam is so patient and forbearing that he becomes wishy-washy. Besides making Fran so unlovable and Sam so idiotically devoted, Lewis fails in other ways to make this a satisfactory novel. His desire to include as many attitudes toward America as possible leads him to introduce, in a rather mechanical way, London businessmen,

French socialites, German professors, and so on. Some of these characters have the double function of criticizing America and carrying on the story of the breakup of the marriage; but frequently they serve only the former purpose and the second is forgotten for pages at a stretch, with the result that *Dodsworth* is not a successful fusion of novel and satire.[32]

The year of the publication of *Dodsworth* saw Lewis casting about for a new subject, and unable to settle upon one; or perhaps it is more accurate to say that he returned to an old subject, labor, and found that he could do nothing with it. He turned again to shorter works and sold a number of short stories to *Cosmopolitan*— the beginning of what was to be a long connection with that magazine. For the *Pictorial Review* he engaged in a debate with Dorothy on the question "Is America a Paradise for Women?" This piece is reprinted in *The Man From Main Street*, and Maule and Cane, introducing it, describe it as an example of Lewis's adopting a position for the moment and arguing it with astonishing facility. Lewis is probably not indulging in hyperbole, however, when he argues that "for the woman with imagination and eagerness this country presents problems and opportunities, presents a conceivable future, which are more stimulating than the beautiful peace of any other land." He sees America as woman's paradise, not because of modern conveniences, but because it offers her a chance to help create a "new world of industry, education, family life," to take part in "the world's greatest revolution . . . ."[33]

But he continued to be concerned primarily with the

[32] See Couch, "Reputation," pp. 137–140, for a discussion of the reactions to the novel. In the *American Mercury*, Mencken called it a "somewhat sombre work" whose obvious faults would give comfort to Lewis's enemies. This was an unusually adverse opinion, however.

[33] *The Man from Main Street*, p. 300.

labor novel. He had written in March, 1924: "Ah, but when I get to Neighbor! That's going to be THE book. And in less than five years I shall get to it." [34] The five years were up, and Lewis entered upon the necessary spadework with industry, surrounding himself with innumerable books and pamphlets. At one time he would describe the task as so enormous and discouraging that he might never finish the book; at another he would announce a tentative date for completion: "I hope to have the novel (which will be longer than the new edition of the Encyc Britannica) finished a year from now, ready for publication (naturally, as The Big Book of the Season) in early spring 1931 . . . ." [35] A trip to Marion, North Carolina, to report on a cotton mill strike for the United Features Syndicate gave him some useful experience for his novel and, of course, whetted his enthusiasm. He wrote a series of articles on the Marion situation which appeared in the Scripps-Howard newspapers and later as a pamphlet; entitled *Cheap and Contented Labor: The Picture of a Southern Mill Town in 1929*, his account was a slashing attack on industrial slavery. Shortly after this, Lewis and his wife went to Toronto to attend an American Federation of Labor convention. Though the convention did not come up to his expectations, it provided him with what he needed—an expert informant:

> After seeing the Marion strike, and spending a few days at the American Federation of Labor convention, I'm keener about this novel than anything since *Arrowsmith*. And at the A F of L convention I met exactly the right man for the De Kruif-Birkhead of my novel—Carl Haessler of the Federated Press; college man, Rhodes scholar at Oxford, imprisoned as conscientious obj during

[34] Letter to Harcourt and Donald Brace, March 4, 1924, *From Main Street to Stockholm*, p. 155.

[35] Letter to Harcourt, October 26, 1929, *ibid.*, p. 284.

the war, ever since up to his ears in the labor movement....[36]

As his novel about a Captain of Industry passed the
hundred-thousand mark in sales, Lewis, with his new
hired helper, was learning all he could about the labor
movement, by personal investigation of steel towns,
mining towns, and textile towns, and by mingling with
workers, organizers, strikers, and the unemployed.

Yet, after all this, the novel was never written. Some of
the reasons are given in a letter that Lewis wrote to
Haessler early in January, 1930, ending their collaboration: Lewis considered the present plan for the novel "too
thin, sketchy, journalistic." He said that he needed perhaps a year of "fasting and prayer" before he could even
begin, he found the complexity of the topic overwhelming,
and he was uncertain how to approach it.[37] Ben Stolberg,
a labor journalist and one of the experts Lewis consulted,
later gave a possible reason for Lewis's uncertainty—that
Lewis was intellectually and temperamentally unfitted
for writing a labor novel. Lewis had found in the course
of his research that a labor leader's career involves treatment of social and economic theories, and an ideological
as well as a literary enterprise, and Lewis was no intellectual—he knew the details of American Life as no one
else did, but he could not tell what they added up to.[38]
One must agree with Schorer, however, that Stolberg was
demanding an approach to the novel which did not suit
Lewis's talent; he was in effect condemning Lewis for not
writing the sort of book he himself would have liked to
write, and he was denying the possibility of an imaginative
rendering of the labor situation which was not in terms
of Marxian dialectic. Moreover, he ridiculed Lewis's

[36] *Ibid.*, p. 283.

[37] Mark Schorer, *Sinclair Lewis: An American Life* (New York: McGraw-
Hill, 1961), pp. 527–528.

[38] Ben Stolberg, "Sinclair Lewis," *American Mercury*, LIII (1941), 455–456.

plan of building the story around Debs, and thereby deprived Lewis of the central figure whom he needed. Ramon Guthrie suggests, on the other hand, that the labor novel would have been Lewis's most direct attack on everything his father had represented, and that Lewis could not bring himself to write it.[39] Many additional reasons have been advanced, but surely a good one is suggested by the rapidity with which Lewis's enthusiasm waned when he first seized hold of the subject in 1924. For an hour or a day, he wrote, he could be in complete sympathy with union men, but he soon came to realize that a large percentage of them—just like the capitalists—were just plain boobs; the working class had no special speech which he could identify, he could not get interested in union news, and the labor people he had met were "either crooks or a bunch of Babbitts—Babbitts in overalls."[40] Even though the plight of the working man could move him strongly, as it did when he went to Marion, he did not find in the labor movement an idealism, a sense of dedication, a heroic sense of purpose which could command his sustained admiration. Dorothy Thompson wrote that she accompanied him to the A.F. of L. convention in Toronto, and that "he railed at its leaders all the way back."[41] Over a number of years, she said, he tried to write the novel, "and finally threw the manuscript away with the dictum that few labor leaders were really concerned with helping the rank and file . . . ."

[39] Ramon Guthrie, "The Labor Novel Sinclair Lewis Never Wrote," New York *Herald Tribune Books*, February 10, 1952, pp. 1, 6.

[40] *With Love from Gracie*, pp. 212–215.

[41] "The Boy and Man from Sauk Centre," p. 42. There is a good discussion of this subject in Sheldon Grebstein's article "Sinclair Lewis's Unwritten Novel," *Philological Quarterly*, XXXVII (1958), 399–409. Asking why Lewis lost his distinctive energy and genius, Grebstein suggests that his inability to complete his labor novel may have been a pivotal point in his career.

When the great boom of the twenties came to an end with the stock market crash of October, 1929, the man who had tried to ruffle the businessman's smugness and mock the Babbittry of his "selling efficiency and whooping it up for ... prosperity" [42] was no better prepared for the collapse than anyone else. He could not even recognize that an era had come to an end. Writing to Donald Brace on November 5, he thanked him for making some investments for him—"otherwise I would never have got in on the bargain stocks—as I hope they will prove to be!" [43] Several months before this, he had been agitating for an expensive illustrated edition of *Babbitt* to sell at five dollars. It was not entirely a matter of money, but of prestige as well; Grosset and Dunlap were selling reprints of his books on a lowbrow basis, he thought, just as they did the novels of Zane Grey. Harcourt had his own ideas regarding cheap editions, but before he could do anything about them the crash came. Yet in August, 1930, months after the crash, Lewis was demanding a "really fine edition" of his works, to sell at three or three and a half dollars a volume, with introductions by distinguished European writers; Harcourt, on the other hand, was calling Lewis's attention to the depressed state of the publishing business, the collapse of some venerable publishing houses, and the mergers of others. Lewis had a growing sense of injustice, a feeling that he had been badly treated by his publisher, and nothing that Harcourt could say could counteract that impression.

Lewis's quarrelsomeness with Harcourt was only one aspect of his renewed instability, but this time it was in tune with the times—with the swirling madness of

---

[42] From Babbitt's speech at the dinner of the Zenith Real Estate Board, *Babbitt* (New York: Harcourt, Brace, 1922), p. 188.

[43] *From Main Street to Stockholm*, p. 284.

literary New York in 1930 which Schorer refers to and which Malcolm Cowley describes at the end of *Exile's Return*. He had taken to drink again; in August, 1929, Harcourt had written, "More power to your elbow, which I hope had enough pleasant exercise to justify your visit to our metropolis during this hot term." [44] And his old restlessness had returned. In January, 1930, he impulsively decided to go to California, taking Dorothy with him, though she was pregnant and did not want to go; when she became anxious to return, he allowed her to do so by herself. She was to write later of the difficulty of never knowing whether he cared about anybody or anything besides his work; a new home, a new wife, and a new son—Michael Lewis was born on June 20, 1930— were not enough for a novelist who had a shrinking bank balance and who appeared to have written himself out.

It was at this low point in his fortunes, when he was unable to settle down to serious work and was approaching what for him was a state of chill penury, that Lewis won the Nobel Prize. As Schorer tells the story, the first of many ironies occurred when a Swedish newspaperman called from New York to tell him that he had been awarded the one prize which he really coveted: Lewis would not believe him. There was irony too in the statement which he prepared for a press conference later that day. In reply to a question about what he was going to do with the money, he said that he was going to use it "to support a well-known young American author and his family"—a specimen of American tongue-in-cheek humor which some Europeans misinterpreted. There was a different sort of irony in his reply to a second question: why was he going to accept the Nobel Prize when he had refused the Pulitzer? Lewis struggled as best he could to show that they were different kinds of

[44] Harcourt to Lewis, August 12, 1929, *ibid.*, p. 278.

prizes, that even though Nobel's will specified that the award was to be given for "the most distinguished work of an idealistic tendency" the Swedish Academy had ignored this clause in practice. This was in fact no truer of the Nobel Prize than of the Pulitzer, which carried a similar qualification; furthermore in refusing the Pulitzer Lewis had denounced the very concept of a literary prize. Still another irony, as far as many observers were concerned, lay in the fact that the first Nobel Prize for Literature to be awarded to an American was going to a second-rate novelist. In a congratulatory editorial, the New York *Times* guardedly supposed that the European judges had wanted something distinctively American and had found it in Lewis's work, and that undoubtedly he had earned distinction by the mass and quality of his achievement. But the paper indicated that there was another side to the story, and that there were Americans who would question the award. Many Americans immediately did so; and what should have been the supreme accolade for Lewis became the occasion for a most searching and unfavorable review of his career.

Carl L. Anderson's account of the circumstances surrounding the award makes it clear that there was a further irony: the prize was awarded to Lewis for reasons which he would have considered mistaken.[45] As Anderson shows, the Scandinavian conception of the United States was formed by the bitter attack—its title in translation is *The Cultural Life of Modern America*—which the Norwegian novelist Knut Hamsun wrote in 1889. Hamsun pictured America as too much preoccupied with making money to be interested in art; he said that literature had no force in its life, and declared that its cultural redemption could not begin until some doubters arose to question

[45] Carl L. Anderson, *The Swedish Acceptance of American Literature* (Philadelphia: University of Pennsylvania Press, 1957), p. 91.

its complacency. In the forty-year period from 1890 to 1930, not one important voice in Swedish writing was raised in dissent from the view that in a country which had received not the culture but the dregs of Europe, and had mingled with these the barbarism of Africa, a country which moreover was excessively proud of its material advantages, the life of the imagination and the spirit was obviously impossible. During the 1920's, Lewis became interesting to the Swedes because he looked at his country through critical eyes; he attacked and condemned just those aspects of American life and culture which they regarded with greatest disfavor. Similarly Dreiser's theme of tragedy found ready acceptance, and he and Lewis were regarded as the great figures of contemporary American literature. Dreiser, no less than Lewis, with whom he was invariably coupled in reviews, was acclaimed as a pioneer in the heroic struggle to speak a word of truth in a land of hypocrisy and materialism.

Anderson points out that, though the proceedings of the Nobel selection committee are kept from public view, very often enough is known about the candidacies—and about the opinions of the committee members—to arouse speculation. In 1930 it was common knowledge that an American author was to be chosen, and eventually the field narrowed down to Dreiser and Lewis. Their respective qualifications were discussed shortly before the announcement in a series of articles in a Stockholm newspaper by Tosten Fogelqvist, an intimate friend of Erik Axel Karlfeldt, permanent secretary of the Swedish Academy, distinguished poet, and member of the selection committee. The first article established the point of view: if America now has a literature worthy of the name, it is almost in spite of itself, and the literature indeed reveals the low state of culture in an industrialized and materialistic society. In the speech which Karlfeldt made at the presentation of the award, Anderson shows, the prevailing opinion was expressed: Lewis was the first to use the satiric powers of an artist against the middle-class complacency and hypocrisy which are common to our civilization but take their worst form under the name "Americanism." Lewis's novels were seen as documents of social protest, and his point of view was identified, without question, with that of a European elite.

Thus there was some justification for Americans to feel that the first Nobel Prize in Literature to be awarded to one of their countrymen had been given to him for abusing his native land. The Reverend Dr. Henry van Dyke, Princeton professor, author, and well-known Presbyterian minister, expressed this opinion in a speech to the Germantown Business Men's Luncheon Club on November 28. He was reported as saying that the choice of the author of *Main Street* and other books which scoffed at America and its traditions was an insult to the United States. "It shows the Swedish Academy knows nothing of the English language," he said. "They handed Lewis a bouquet, but they gave America a very back-handed compliment." [46] Van Dyke, an old man of seventy-eight, was a member of the American Academy of Arts and Letters, the inner circle or upper chamber of the National Institute of Arts and Letters. Charles Fenton has wittily described the melancholy crusade which the Academy kept up during the twenties in behalf of the genteel tradition and in opposition to disturbing innovations. [47] The success of Lewis's novels had been a heavy cross for it to bear; it had been attacking him for ten years, without his answering back. Van Dyke's speech, in the

[46] New York *Times*, November 29, 1930, p. 1.

[47] Charles Fenton, "The American Academy of Arts and Letters Versus All Comers: Literary Rags and Riches in the 1920's," *South Atlantic Quarterly*, LVIII (1959), 572–586.

perspective in which Fenton puts it, was merely a casual broadside, a set-piece lament that the national literary heritage was being ignored and books based on alien principles being acclaimed. But it was delivered the day before Lewis sailed for Sweden on the *Drottningholm*, and it gave him something to brood on aboard ship.

Stormed at by reporters and photographers on his arrival at Gothenburg, Lewis disarmed and delighted them with his modesty and accessibility. He was pictured in the Swedish press as a representative of the American temperament at its best and of American literature at its most mature; just as the Nobel award, whether presented for the right reasons or not, meant the recognition by Europeans that American literature existed and would have to be taken cognizance of, so the personal impression which Lewis made did a great deal to destroy the prejudiced view of Americans as greedy, uncultured, and materialistic.[48]

On the afternoon of December 10, the official presentation took place at the Stockholm Concert House; from the hands of King Gustav, Lewis received an embossed diploma and a specially engraved check for $46,350.[49] He was described as being as nervous as a schoolboy. The official citation read: "The 1930 Nobel Prize in Literature is awarded to Sinclair Lewis for his powerful and vivid art of description and his ability to use wit and humor in the creation of original characters." Dr. Karlfeldt, who sponsored and introduced Lewis, made an effective and amusing survey of his works, placing special emphasis on *Babbitt*, which Sweden generally considered Lewis's masterpiece. Emphasizing the positive achievements of Lewis's art, he called *Main Street* one of the best descriptions

[48] Anderson emphasizes this fact in his *Swedish Acceptance of American Literature*, p. 91.

[49] This was the amount reported in the New York *Times*.

of small-town life ever written and stated that *Babbitt* probably approached the ideal of an American popular hero of the middle class. Behind Lewis's depiction of Babbitt, he said, there was love; Lewis was not attacking people but values, and was asking his readers to view his country as not yet finished or melted down but still in the turbulent years of adolescence. The great new American literature, he asserted, had started with self-criticism, and this indeed was a sign of health.

On the afternoon of December 12, Lewis delivered his epoch-marking Nobel Prize address on the state of American letters. Early in the speech he drew a satiric portrait of "a learned and most amiable old gentleman who has been a pastor, a university professor, and a diplomat," who was a member of the American Academy of Arts and Letters, and who as a writer was "chiefly known for his pleasant little essays on the joy of fishing." Thus he began—referring specifically to van Dyke's attack on him, though not naming van Dyke—his devastating attack on the standard-bearers of gentility. Fenton describes it as "the entrance of a master of invective into a swarm of apprentices":

> The speech was Lewis at his very best, calm, orderly, frequently humble, occasionally boyish, then momentarily savage with cruel sarcasm and icy authenticity. He played his tune in a variety of pitches; his range included satire, irony, the belly laugh, gentle patience, outrageous burlesque. . . .[50]

In fine, he handled his victim with the loving care of a satirist into whose hands the good Lord had delivered his opponent, and who was so strong and so sure of himself that he had no need for anger. In fact, he expressed his gratitude for being attacked by a member of the Academy, for now he had the right to speak frankly of it.

[50] "The American Academy of Arts and Letters," pp. 584–585.

The same groans of protest would have been heard, he said, if the Swedish Academy had selected Theodore Dreiser or Eugene O'Neill or any other of the possible candidates, for the American people were afraid of literature which did not glorify everything American; they still revered writers who pretended that the United States had gone through the revolutionary change from rustic colony to world empire without altering its bucolic simplicity. The American artist was oppressed by the fact that he was not taken seriously; he was expected to be a decorator or a clownish entertainer. And instead of finding standards and institutions to support him, he found an American Academy which included several first-rate writers, excluded a formidable list of writers and critics—Lewis named twenty-one of them, including Dreiser, O'Neill, Anderson, and Hemingway—and found room for "three extraordinarily bad poets, two very melo-dramatic and insignificant playwrights," and other mediocrities or nonentities. An Academy which was so cut off from what was living and vigorous and original in American letters did not represent contemporary American literature; it represented only Henry Wadsworth Longfellow.

Still, Lewis said, he was not attacking the Academy itself; he was taking it as an example of the divorce of intellectual life in America from all authentic standards of importance and reality. The universities were equally cloistered from reality; American professors liked their literature "clear and cold and very dead." Out of the universities, in fact, had recently come the astonishing phenomenon of the New Humanism, "a doctrine of the blackest reaction introduced into a stirringly revolutionary world." Although Lewis's satire on the universities was effective, however, it was rather unfair. They had no need to apologize for such versatile and erudite men as George Lyman Kittredge, John M. Manly, and John Livingston Lowes; and if they were sometimes still so genteel as to exclude ruffians like Dreiser from their anthologies, out of one of them had recently come a monumental study of the critical realism for which Lewis was a spokesman, the third volume of Parrington's *Main Currents in American Thought*, published, indeed, by Harcourt, Brace. In his attack on New Humanism, Lewis ceased to argue from a standpoint of confidence and strength; he pictured himself as bewildered by the movement's subtleties—and in his discussion of it demonstrated his inability to comprehend it. Earlier he had satirized the American view of the artist as insignificant in a land of eighty-story buildings and motors by the million; now he satirized the Humanists by showing them as insignificant against the same background, a background "brilliant with Zeppelins." Continuing, he overstated his case by asserting that Emerson and his circle were sentimental reflections of Europe, and that when something approaching a native standard of excellence finally came into being with William Dean Howells, it was "the code of a pious old maid whose greatest delight was to have tea at the vicarage." He closed, however, on a note of optimism: without standards or institutions to support it, American literature was nevertheless emerging from provincialism; and in such younger writers as Hemingway, Wolfe, and Faulkner he saw a determination to give America a literature worthy of her vastness.

The speech aroused a great deal of controversy in the United States. Some, like Carl Van Doren, saw it as an example of Lewis's passionate, frank courage, as the outburst of a man who insisted on telling the truth. Others, more cynically, deplored the fact that Lewis had chosen an international stage for the paying off of old scores, or regretted that even on an occasion like this Lewis could not forego an opportunity for sensational publicity. The speech, like the award, heralded a major victory for the realists over the idealists; since Santayana's famous attack on "The Genteel Tradition in American Philosophy" in 1911, one outpost after another had succumbed to realism, but the speech was a triumphant announcement that the main bastion had fallen and that the literary innovators were sweeping all before them.[51] Perhaps in his attack on the septuagenarian van Dyke and his moribund fellow Academicians Lewis was uncharitable, but Fenton points out that the Academy had weathered the storms of the twenties better than might have been predicted—in fact, its public position was increasingly secure—so that a blockbuster such as Lewis delivered was indeed in order. But excellent as was his account of the perennial plight of the artist in America, he became involved in paradoxes and contradictions. He had said that the artist was, first of all, prosperous, and second, not listened to; and questioners wondered how the writer became prosperous if no one read his books. He implied, if he did not state outright, that a novel would not sell unless it abided by the American credo; but, as Brooks Atkinson sarcastically commented, "If Mr. Lewis stops talking long enough to balance his bank book he must know that honoring the American credo in the breach is quite as profitable as honoring it in the observance."[52] Atkinson noted that Lewis's "incurable romanticism" was in the saddle, and indeed the speech bore out his point: as prototype of the artist he took the "vagabond and

[51] Malcolm Cowley's *After the Genteel Tradition* (New York: W. W. Norton, 1937) begins with a discussion of Lewis's speech and thereby stresses its importance; at the same time, however, Cowley states that the speech was ten years out of date in some of its assertions and that the main battles had taken place before 1920.

[52] J. Brooks Atkinson, "Mr. Lewis Mentions the Drama," *New York Times*, December 21, 1930, section 8, p. 1.

criminal François Villon," who "had for his lot the gutter and the hardened crust"; he referred to "Midwestern peasants" who were "sometimes bewildered and hungry and vile—and heroic"; he described America as a "new and vital and experimental land." The issues were overdramatized, oversimplified, and overromanticized. Yet the speech did reveal something about the position of the creative artist in the United States, and did assert the claim of American literature to serious consideration.

At any rate, it must be taken as the high point of his career, the point of achievement and recognition beyond which Lewis would not go. Or perhaps the high point was reached the night before, at the state dinner at the beautiful Italian Renaissance palace in Stockholm, when the man from Sauk Centre, Minnesota, dined in the company of King Gustav, from dishes of gold and silver, at a table almost buried in roses.

6. Defending the
Republican Virtues

OVER AND AGAINST W. E. Woodward's opinion that the
Nobel Prize cured Lewis of his inferiority complex[1]—a
contention with which Sheldon Grebstein seems to agree[2]
—Mark Schorer indicates that Lewis, even though he had
won the prize he wanted, was not a triumphant man.
Certainly the award brought no new confidence to his
writing; instead, something seemed to go out of it, though
this may have been attributable to the changed conditions in his world rather than to changes in Lewis himself.
Grebstein believes that Lewis was a timely and important
writer only when he was rebelling against convention;
and in the 1930's, when the American Dream seemed about
to explode entirely, when it became pointless to attack
smugness and complacency, he was temporarily lost, a
rebel without a cause. When he turned to an exposure of
evils in American prisons and to a defense of ethical

[1] W. E. Woodward, "The World and Sauk Centre," *New Yorker*, IX
(January 27, 1934), 24.
[2] Sheldon Grebstein, "Sinclair Lewis and the Nobel Prize," *Western
Humanities Review*, XIII (1959), 163–171.

hotelkeeping, he was dealing with subjects which may have been valid but were hardly crucial to people who wanted to know the meaning of closing banks and lengthening breadlines. However, Lewis was not only a rebel without a cause, but a rebel who was not sure of the merit of rebelliousness; in Berlin on December 23, 1930, he said: "Reform in general is all right. Individual reformers are all hell. The world is suffering from too many reformers. . . . Sometimes people have accused me of being a reformer, but they would have a hard time proving that against me." [3] In the novels of the thirties, one can often see him expostulating, sometimes petulantly, that the proposals of radical groups will do nothing to solve America's problems, that there is still room in America for the man of energy and ambition, and that more emphasis should be placed upon homely American virtues, even Republican virtues, such as conscientiousness in doing one's job. As in his previous novels, he attacked certain conventions only to defend others. Furthermore, if his intense sensitivity to the climate of opinion deteriorated after 1930, he still continued to find and exploit topical themes, though his writing was not so central to the experience of the decade as it had been in the 1920's.

Among the many revaluations of Lewis's career which the Nobel award provoked, Lewis Mumford's in *Current History* for January, 1931, shows how his reputation appeared to a discerning contemporary. Mumford begrudgingly allowed that Lewis should have been considered along with ten or twelve others for the prize; he suggested, however, that Robert Frost more nearly represented what was most significant in contemporary American literature, and he considered the award a subtle disparagement of America. Yet his survey of Lewis's novels was not simply an exposure of their inadequacies.

[3] New York *Times*, December 23, 1930, p. 3.

The novels, he said, survive better than expected. Declaring that Lewis was the most effective satirist that America had produced, that his achievement was no small one and that it merited closer examination, he described the merits of *Main Street, Babbitt,* and *Arrowsmith,* dismissed *Elmer Gantry* as almost a caricature of Lewis's method of caricature, and gave special praise to *Dodsworth* for portraying the dilemmas of the untutored American in Europe better than had been done since Henry James. Mumford balanced against Lewis's great merits his refusal to dig beneath the appearance of things in America, "to clarify its essence, its soul." But if Mumford showed that Lewis was overrated and forecast the impending decline in his reputation, his estimate of Lewis's importance was a higher one than has been given by many critics since.

From Stockholm the Lewises went to Berlin, where Dorothy suddenly became ill and had to undergo an emergency appendectomy. While she was in hospital, Lewis indicated in a radio interview how he felt about the United States—at least when he was abroad: "Intellectually I know America is no better than any other country. Emotionally I know she is better than every other country." [4] He concluded by saying that he was going back to his farm in Vermont and try for once to write a beautiful book.

It was not going to be published by Harcourt, Brace, however. Dorothy's convalescence provided Lewis with an opportunity for quiet reflection; and on January 21 he addressed a long letter to Harcourt severing relations with the publishing firm with which his career had been linked. He reminded Harcourt of an outburst the previous spring, caused by his impression that the company felt it had just about done enough for him. After the Nobel

[4] *Ibid.*, December 30, 1930, p. 9.

award, he thought, the firm had let him down by not reviving the sale of his books as it might have done (actually, the Nobel Prize edition of his novels appeared only a week after he wrote the letter) and by not counteracting the attacks on the award in America by making it clear how favorably the rest of the world had responded to it. In the letter Lewis conveyed a twofold impression of himself: first as a public figure subjected to ignominious assaults because he had not received the support due him, and second as an author who was hindered in starting work on a new novel because of lack of confidence in his publisher. In his own view, he was doubly wronged.

In a brief, dignified, and sympathetic reply, Harcourt made no attempt to argue with Lewis over the points of dispute, generously returned the canceled contracts for the "next book" and for *Neighbor*, and expressed his regret that events had taken this turn. Thus ended an association which had been immensely profitable for both publisher and author. The letters in *From Main Street to Stockholm* show that Harcourt could sometimes control the excesses and exuberances of his impetuous author; deprived of his wise guidance, Lewis was going to be the worse off in future.

On February 20, Lewis was an unexpected guest at a luncheon of American newspaper correspondents in London, and in the course of a witty speech recalling his own newspaper days, he declared that, like Dodsworth, he had pangs of homesickness; he said that he was unable to do any writing while abroad, and that therefore he was sailing for home the following week. But again he was to discover in his homeland not solitude, but quarrels and controversies. Even before he was off the ship, he was angrily fending off inquiries about the rumors that he was leaving his publishers, and was being asked to comment on some disparaging remarks made about him by

J. B. Priestley, then on a lecture tour of the United States. He was able to turn the Priestley episode to good account soon after when he gave a lecture on "American Literature Comes of Age": uncomplimentary as their comments on the United States were, visiting English lecturers such as Priestley were really a boon, he said, because they would encourage Americans to sever the strings that still bound their literature to the older English tradition. This address was delivered in the Town Hall in New York on March 19; he had been scheduled to repeat it in Constitution Hall in Washington on March 24, but the Daughters of the American Revolution made clear what they thought of him as a spokesman for American literature by refusing to allow him to use their hall. Instead he had to speak in a high school auditorium. As if these incidents did not provide sufficient copy for the newspaper reporters, in the month of his return Lewis became involved in another episode which made the headlines—he was slapped by Theodore Dreiser.

The occasion was a dinner at the Metropolitan Club in honor of a visiting Russian author, on March 19. When the chairman invited Lewis to say a few words, he replied that he did not care to speak in the presence of a man who had plagiarized three thousand words from his wife's book on Russia. The quarrel was a three-year-old one dating from the publication of Dorothy Thompson's *The New Russia* in October, 1928, and Dreiser's *Dreiser Looks at Russia* soon after. There were striking verbal similarities between the two books; and though there were charges and counter charges, the explanation seems to have been that both of them relied heavily upon a common source—that in fact they sometimes transcribed without change material which had been provided by the Soviet government. Dreiser did not reply to Lewis's insult at the dinner. But afterwards Lewis called him a liar and a thief not once but several times, and each time Dreiser slapped him. After several resounding slaps, William C. Lengel, assistant editor of *Cosmopolitan*, pulled Dreiser away, only to receive from Lewis an astonishing rebuke: "Bill, hereafter—when Theodore is slapping me—I'll ask you not to interfere." [5]

Two months after this widely publicized disturbance, another of the more notorious episodes in Lewis's career took place when he and Harrison Smith, "their faces glowing at the idea of doing something fine for their alma mater," [6] marched up the steps of the new Sterling Library at Yale to make a presentation of the Nobel medal to the librarian. Since the librarian was away, they were introduced to the assistant librarian; and their condition was such as to make him very doubtful of who they were and what they wanted. At any rate, he felt justified in explaining to the newspapers later that Lewis had "failed to make his wishes known." Lewis, of course, was enraged at the fact that his spontaneous gesture of affection for Yale had met such a rebuff.

Once again Lewis turned to his labor novel, and again he turned away from it, this time to write another novel dealing with the position of women. In the fall of 1931 Dorothy Thompson went to Europe; it was on this trip that she had her famous interview with Hitler. She returned to the United States, spent a busy winter lecturing, and went back to Europe again. Lewis followed her in April, and brought her back on the *Europa* at the end of May, finishing his 170,000-word novel—or at least a draft of it—at sea. Announcing this to reporters, he also told them that he intended to return to Europe for the winter, and to walk from Innsbruck to Vienna—

[5] This is the account given by Rupert Hughes, as reported in the "Trade Winds" department of the *Saturday Review*, XXXIX (February 25, 1956), p. 7. There are various versions.

[6] New York *Times*, May 20, 1931, p. 27.

Mencken had once tried it, he said, but had got only as far as a tavern on the edge of Innsbruck. He arranged for publication of his new novel by Doubleday and its serialization in *Redbook*, and then left for Europe with Dorothy and their two-year-old son on the twenty-fourth of August. On departure he made perhaps the most inept comment on politics of which he was ever guilty: the forthcoming Presidential election—which put Franklin Delano Roosevelt in the White House for the first time— he declared, would be one in which no principles would be involved, and "either the fat-head who is in now will be re-elected, or another fat-head will be elected in his place." [7]

When the Lewises went to Europe now, the famous novelist went along almost as excess baggage—certainly as the silent partner in a concern whose success was not due to his efforts and in whose affairs he had neither competence nor interest. If Lewis's career was waning, Dorothy Thompson's was waxing; and if Europe was a refuge to him, it was a *métier* to her. Theirs was an extraordinary alliance, between a woman who was in her element when she was discussing the fate of Austria or Czechoslovakia or Hungary with a political leader, an ambassador, or another foreign correspondent, and a man whom she could describe as "basically apolitical." It was no wonder that on one occasion Lewis, out of place in his own New York apartment—thronging with refugees and other people interested in the international situation but not in him—was heard to mutter, "I wrote a book once." And in Europe he became an aimless and lonely wanderer, while his wife conferred with heads of states.

While the Lewises were in Austria, his first novel since 1929, *Ann Vickers*, was published on January 25, 1933. He had the satisfaction of knowing that his new publishers were doing everything possible to advertise and promote

[7] *Ibid.*, August 24, 1932, p. 17.

it: it was published simultaneously in thirteen languages and sixteen countries. His biographer shows that the book sold remarkably well for a depression year. Yet it represents a falling-off; in particular, it shows loss of the detachment necessary for the comic creation—especially of character—which was the handmaid of his satire. The theme becomes uppermost, and Lewis fussily makes sure that his readers take a correct view of it.

Ann Vickers both tells the story of a woman and describes a situation. Desiring, like her elder sisters Ann Veronica (in Wells's novel by the same name) and Una Golden (in Lewis's *The Job*), both a career and love, she enters upon a series of occupations—suffragette, social worker, investigator of prison conditions, and finally director of a model prison. Having achieved this useful and honored place in society, she falls in love with a Tammany judge; and after he has served a jail sentence for accepting bribes, she gives up everything to go away with him. Out the window goes her career, and all her previous work becomes insignificant.

As Malcolm Cowley pointed out in his review,[8] the novel is mostly an undistinguished medley of incidents. But after the first 150 pages, the book's central concern is with prison conditions, showing first how prisons should not be run, and then how they should. The problem is investigated with the usual Lewis thoroughness, and, especially in the portrayal of conditions in a southern penitentiary, the writing is vivid, the inhumanity disgusting, the brutality terrifying. The tone, however, is that of an exposé, not a satire. The author describes a situation and dictates the reader's response to it; he does not, as in *Babbitt* or even in *Elmer Gantry*, embody an attitude or a position in a character whom the reader can

[8] Malcolm Cowley, "Tired Feminist," *New Republic*, LXXIV (February 12, 1933), 22.

recognize as warped in mind or outlook. In this novel Lewis is directing us to take a serious view of vice; the characters, badly constructed puppets, are not to be laughed at but hissed. They are secondary to the situation, which is presented as a documentary study rather than a satire.

But there is a good deal of satire both in the attack on prisons and in the rest of the book. In fact, the satire is so widespread as to embrace almost all normal activities of average Americans. Ann, like Carol Kennicott, wants to get her hands on the world and make it over: "'It's like what you get in this new novel by H. G. Wells, this *Tono-Bungay*. I'd like to contribute, oh, one-millionth of a degree to helping make this race of fat-heads and grouches something more like the angels'" (49).[9] The question, of course, is how to do it. At one point she credits the human race with the ability to get along satisfactorily, but she views it as both hindered by tradition and undergoing changes which are almost always of no benefit. As Burton Rascoe pointed out in his review,

> In hundreds of places throughout the novel, Mr. Lewis records by implication his unhappy conviction that any humane movement for the betterment of society . . . is always stalemated by egotism and stupidity, cruelty and selfishness among the members of the movement itself. . . .[10]

But it is not just a question of human failure preventing intelligent improvement; though the novel shows the urgent need for reform and describes reforms which succeed, the ideological foundation for reform is missing. Like Arrowsmith, Ann is basically skeptical: "Was she

[9] *Ann Vickers* (New York: Doubleday, Doran, 1933).
[10] Burton Rascoe, "The Old Sinclair Lewis with his Great Gifts," New York *Herald Tribune Books*, January 29, 1933, p. 1.

certain only that she could not be so certain of anything as in the good old days; that in the grammar of social science, all the triumphant Therefore's had been replaced by But's?" (217) This attitude of uncertainty deprives Ann's zealous crusade for positive changes in society of any real motive. At the same time, it could have served as the rational basis for satire of conventionalism; in the novel, however, rational criticism is less evident than petulant dissatisfaction.

The ribald, skeptical tone which Lewis adopts in *Ann Vickers* is accompanied by an extraordinary degree of intellectual and ethical confusion. It seems as if Lewis has cultivated perversity for its own sake. Imprisonment has nothing to do with justice; it is only sadism on a society-wide basis. In a prison, there is a clear division of good and bad: the jailers are villains, the prisoners heroes. In fact, prisoners are nobler than most people, including social workers. Social work, come to think of it, has nothing worth while about it at all—except the fact that it isn't charity. Love is grand; it is a law unto itself; but for it to be really satisfactory it is essential that the lover be somebody else's husband or wife. The conventional attitude toward abortion is unjustifiable, but abortion is justified by the conventional attitude toward it. The beatitudes have a message for us only when they are travestied: "Blessed are the rich in spirit, for they shall not *need* the Kingdom of Heaven! Blessed are the fearless in heart, for God shall see them!" (101)

Such paradoxes and perversities might be defensible, but they are not really provided with defenses, either in the form of arguments in their favor or through dramatic illustration of the conflicts between received opinions and basic human values. Lewis sets down his opinions as obvious and axiomatic; what defense he does make is embarrassingly naive and oversimplified. He tilts at society for its perverseness, and thereby convinces us of his own.

Michael Williams' review of the book in *Commonweal* was severe, but his basic criticism is a valid one—that as a sentimental fairy tale of love triumphant, this book belongs in "that great school of popular fiction which goes on forever, telling its one and only story—the story of the Heroine and her Fairy Prince . . . simply changing its language and its incidents to suit the times. . . ."[11] Williams draws attention particularly to the last scene, which shows Ann riding away with her shining white knight, Barney Dolphin—just out of prison. (Since his wife Mona is a Good Woman if there ever was one, Barney is provided with considerable justification for running away.) They face the world in the true spirit of romance. Barney says that he will "get busy and make a million dollars in real estate"; America, even in the midst of depression, is still a land of glowing business opportunity. But Barney is worried about the effect of scandal upon Ann and suggests that she should resign from her prison job. Brave Ann, of course, has no thought of resigning, in fact, sees no reason to resign, because "it's so *right*, to be with you." In the land of Vickery, Williams comments, what you wish to be right automatically becomes so. Barney still is afraid of the effect of scandal on their illegitimate son Mat, but again Ann consoles him: "Listen! This is a new age. By the time Mat is sixteen he'll have to look in a dictionary to find out what the word 'scandal' means." Thus the two of them escape from the actual and metaphorical prisons in which they have been incarcerated and ride away to an ideal world where a million dollars is an easy matter for the man with determination, where a man's abandonment of his

[11] Michael Williams, "Babbittry into Vickery," *Commonweal*, XVII (1933), 567.

wife does not require a second thought, and where there is no such thing as gossip. Truly, love conquers all in this book by Sinclair Lewis.

Returning to the United States as inconspicuously as possible, Lewis avoided the regular passenger steamers and sailed from London on February 24 aboard the *American Farmer*, which carried only seventeen passengers. Nevertheless, the news of his departure leaked out, and the reporters were on hand to greet him when he landed in New York. Told that *Ann Vickers* was heading the best-seller lists, he replied, "Please, don't be so commercial minded. After all, you are talking to a creative artist and money is a secondary matter." Then in the next breath he asked, "Does anyone know how many of the books have sold?" [12]

He also told the reporters about his working habits— about the maps he drew and the elaborate plans he dictated and the fact that he never dictated the novels but typed them out himself. The New York *Times* considered the topic sufficiently newsworthy for it to secure further details from Lewis's secretary, Louis Florey, and an interview with him appeared in the paper on March 9. Sometimes, Florey said, he had to sleep in his clothes for long periods, when Lewis wanted to work; he might dictate for five minutes or five hours at a stretch, then go into his bedroom and fall asleep immediately, and awaken after minutes or hours to resume dictation once more. Florey said that he had worked thirty hours straight the previous summer typing Sidney Howard's stage version of *Dodsworth*, while Lewis and Howard sat going over the typescript as it came from the machine.

Previously Lewis had made several attempts at writing plays; but the experience of working with Howard during the summer of 1932 whetted his appetite for the theater and launched him on a theatrical career—as playwright,

[12] New York *Times*, March 7, 1933, p. 18.

actor, producer, and director. Into these activities he entered with zest and thoroughness, even if he always remained something of an outsider and never accepted the routine of the stage as a professional would. He seemed to enjoy the theater partly because it was a communal activity; and he was fond of contrasting the lonely task of novel writing with the pleasure of working with others in the process of bringing a play into production.

When the dramatic version of *Dodsworth* was published in 1933, he wrote an introduction for it which showed considerable understanding of the differences between the problems confronting a novelist and those facing a dramatist.[13] Instead of appearing as the sensitive novelist annoyed that his precious creation had been tampered with, he very reasonably saw that the parts of a play may possess value "precisely as they *depart* from the detail of the original fiction." In illustration, he quoted thirty-eight pages of the novel and showed how they were adequately represented by nine pages of the play. He saw that a drama could not be a "mere dramatization" of a novel but had to be "as much an act of creation as any play based entirely upon the dramatist's own design."

Dodsworth as a play, starring Walter Huston and Fay Bainter, was a great success. As such it offered a remarkable contrast to another play in which Lewis collaborated at this time—*Jayhawker*, which he wrote with Lloyd Lewis, drama critic of the Chicago *Daily News*. *Jayhawker* dealt with the post-Civil War period, on which Lloyd Lewis had written a number of books. After writings and rewritings, it opened in Washington in October, 1934; and in November it went to New York, where it soon met the fate which its lifeless characters

[13] Reprinted in *The Man from Main Street: Collected Essays and Other Writings, 1904–1950*, ed. Harry E. Maule and Melville H. Cane (New York: Random House, 1953), pp. 219–227.

and mawkish dialogue deserved to bring it. (Still it was published as a book by Doubleday, with a facetious introduction by Lewis.) Lewis was able to swallow his disappointment and rise above resentment at the critics; Elmer Rice had recently been denouncing them, and in reply Lewis published his own comments in a black-edged box which appeared in the New York *Times* on Sunday, November 18. He had no complaints; he hoped that the critics would go on getting rid of rubbish in the theater, "whether it's my rubbish, or Mr. Elmer Rice's rubbish, or anybody else's rubbish"; and, in answer to Rice's complaint that the theater was commercial, he replied that he did not see how a man could put fifty thousand dollars into a play and not want to get it back.

Meanwhile, he had concocted and published another novel—his first "serious" novel since *Main Street*, Schorer observes, to be completely without distinction. Entitled *Work of Art*, it was published in January, 1934. In this retelling of a familiar tale, the idle apprentice uses the poetical works of Shelley as his bible and the industrious apprentice uses a manual of hotelkeeping—and Lewis shows himself incapable of telling the difference between the two books. Hotelkeeping, as Babbitt would say, is really an art. In his notebook, which Lewis calls "the Notebook of a Poet," Myron Weagle makes the following entry:

> What is an art, what is a profession, what is a business, what is a job? Is a man who runs a great grocery store like Park & Tilford, Acker, Charles, or the gr. department of Macy's just a business man, while anybody who makes smart pictures of girls is artist, and doc or lawyer who thinks about nothing but making money a profession and cranky old prof who goes on handing out same lectures yr after yr a scholar and not just on a white collar job? (254) [14]

[14] *Work of Art* (New York: Doubleday, Doran, 1934).

The whole book reflects this refusal to believe in a separation of artistic and practical concerns. Ora Weagle, who considers himself a winged genius soaring above the dull plodding throng of people like his brother Myron, succumbs to materialism and forgets his ambition of being an American Dickens or Keats, while Myron, who is consistently referred to as a poet, remains true to his vision of building a Perfect Epic Hotel.

Praise of the practical man is nothing new for Lewis, but praise of dullness is. Ora, the rebel against the narrowness of Main Street, is made to appear selfish and unprepossessing; Myron, the conformist, is eulogized. His limitations do not matter: "'I'm a smug, complacent, mechanical, ordinary food merchant. But I enjoy it!' he lamented, touched at the spectacle of a man who couldn't be modern and melancholy" (204). In other books Lewis had attempted to shake the bourgeois out of their complacency; here he defends it: "Probably, like other 'successes,' Myron was priggish. Nor is it certain that the enjoyment of priggishness is not one of the most innocent and wholesome of pleasures . . ." (32). Lauding "the Forgotten Man who gets the necessary work of the world done," Lewis ridicules those who, like Carol Kennicott, yearn for something beyond the dull round of practical day-to-day affairs. He appears as a high-pressure publicity agent so absorbed in selling the hotel business that he forgets his previous attacks on dullness made God.

Lewis had once told Harcourt that he did not think much of his short stories and that it would be a mistake to collect them; in 1935 he made that mistake. His *Selected Short Stories* included contributions to *Redbook* as early as 1917 and to the *Saturday Evening Post* and *Cosmopolitan* in 1931. He had never practiced the short story as an art form—it was a frankly commercial product; and it is easy to agree with the view of Peter Monro Jack that his stories persistently exploit his lesser qualities— facetiousness, whimsicality, caricature, and sentimentality. In fact Jack, in a searching review of the volume, quarreled even with the introduction.[15] Here Lewis said that he had not realized that the earlier stories were so optimistic and laudatory, "so certain that large, bulky Americans are going ͻ do something and do it quickly and help the whole world by doing it"; still he wondered whether this "American optimism, this hope and courage, so submerged now in 1935" were not authentic parts of American life. Jack pointed out that only two of ten stories written before 1930 were optimistic or laudatory, and that the remainder cut through whatever optimism there was on the surface to show the cankering discontent beneath. Furthermore, contrary to what Lewis believed, the optimism had not been submerged in his later stories—for example, in "Go East, Young Man," where a young man returns from Paris set on a career in the real estate business in Zenith, and in "Land," where a love of the Vermont countryside finds expression. Thus he showed that Lewis was curiously imperceptive to what was in his own stories. That lack of perception was in fact clearly demonstrated by Lewis's special recommendation of the most recently written story, "Let's Play King," a naive and silly fantasy about a boy from Hollywood trading places with a Balkan boy king. Long practice in writing short stories had not made him perfect in the art; the strain of sentimentality and ingenuous romanticism was often allowed to go unchecked; and he could not tell good from bad.

While Lewis was preparing for the rehearsals of *Jayhawker* in August, 1934, he received the news—apparently

---

[15] Peter Monro Jack, review of Lewis's *Selected Short Stories*, New York *Times Book Review*, June 30, 1935, p. 3.

without very much perturbation—of his wife's expulsion from Germany by the Nazis. Spending much of her time abroad and absorbed in learning, lecturing, and writing about the international situation when in the United States, she was following her own career—indeed, taking refuge in it. Her letters, as quoted by Schorer, testify to her conscious decision to make herself independent; since she could find no inner security in her marriage, she would have to create it for herself. Lewis's second marriage was going the same way as his first, and again his own instability was very much to blame.

Nevertheless, in 1935 Lewis secured a huge success with a novel on a topic close to his wife's heart—the spread of fascism in Europe and American indifference to its menace. Schorer describes the circumstances of its composition; even more than most Lewis novels, it was the product of a great flood of enthusiasm and was written with remarkable concentration in a very short space of time. Begun in May, it was finished in July and completely revised by the early part of August. Realizing they had a success on their hands, the publishers rushed it into print, and it appeared in October, not six months after it had been started.

It Can't Happen Here is a horror story. It is meant as a warning: the tyranny which has driven others from their homelands can strike the United States as well. Artistic detachment—the detachment essential for the satirist—is forgotten; the message is made to appear of overwhelming importance, and the feelings of the author are violently conveyed by every page.

Though it is an attack on the enemies of the American system, the novel defends the system in a strangely uncommitted way. "Blessed be they not Patriots and Idealists," says Doremus Jessup, the Vermont editor who is the leading character. He holds to a liberalism which dislikes attachments; he has become convinced "that everything that is worthwhile in the world has been accomplished by the free, inquiring, critical spirit, and that the preservation of this spirit is far more important than any social system whatsoever" (433).[16] In him this spirit is allied with a certain nostalgia: the Horatio Alger tradition is gone, there is no fiber in the youth of today, and there are no more coy young maidens. In an interview some years later, Lewis said he chose a Republican as hero because the Republican "represents the old school of honesty and integrity."[17] When his own son begins to talk like Julius Streicher, it is perhaps no more than Doremus expects from a world become sick.

What are the major threats to the free spirit in America? Radio oracles of the Father Coughlin type, after-dinner speakers who praise the purity of the American home, the D.A.R., the Rotary Club—these and others like them are both menaces in themselves and instruments which clever demagogues can use. In previous Lewis novels, we have seen sinister groups of book-burners and morality hounds who are threatening to band together and take over the country—the Good Citizens' League in *Babbitt*, the League of Cultural Agencies in *Arrowsmith*, the Napap in *Elmer Gantry*, and so on. We could never regard them as serious threats, in spite of Lewis's insistence that we ought to; and we cannot do so in this book—not even when they appear in uniforms imported directly from Nazi Germany. Lewis attributes to these groups a maliciousness, a spirit of cooperation for nefarious ends, a unanimity of perverse opinion, which the reader cannot credit.

Since Lewis is writing quickly and with a sense of urgency, he uses the slapdash methods of the journalist.[18]

[16] *It Can't Happen Here* (New York: Doubleday, Doran, 1935).

[17] Allen Austin, "An Interview with Sinclair Lewis," *University of Kansas City Review*, XX (1958), 205.

[18] Martin Light, "A Study of Characterization in Sinclair Lewis's

The choice of Buzz Windrip as Democratic candidate for President in 1936 and his subsequent election require the violently improbable disposal of existing politicians and political issues. Though he makes Doremus Jessup complain about the complexity of the American system of government, Lewis has it succumb to a dictator with a wave of his pen. He does not put his revolutionaries in a distinctive American form; the sadistic and perverted secret police, the racial persecutions, the concentration camps, and the methods of torture are all recognizably German in origin. In other words, Lewis has not taken the trouble to visualize a native fascist movement and its probable road to power. It is all too fantastic; it could convince only those already convinced, and to anyone else its improbabilities would be reassuring evidence that there was nothing to worry about. The ridiculous names like "Buzz Windrip" and "Effingham Swan" do not contribute to an air of verisimilitude. In fact, "Hector Macgoblin" decides things for us once and for all: the story is in the realm of fairyland. Lewis can't fool us; those ogres aren't real; it can't happen here.

Because it was timely, the book seemed more important than it actually was, and it caught the public eye. The "Moscow choir-boys," wrote Mencken, took to it with enthusiasm. Couch prefaces his discussion of its reception with a judgment by Merle Curti to the effect that "When Sinclair Lewis published his own personal alarm call to the nation, *It Can't Happen Here*, there was widespread discussion of the book, and few leaders of American thought stood up to call it foolish." [19] Couch quotes

Fiction" (Ph.D. dissertation, University of Illinois, 1960), pp. 279–280, remarks that the book closes with one of the worst sentences ever to come from a satirist's pen: "And still Doremus goes on in the red sunrise, for a Doremus Jessup can never die." Light also calls attention to the slapdash morality, which does not bother to consider the implications of Doremus's having a mistress as well as a wife.

[19] Merle Curti, *The Growth of American Thought* (New York: Harper, 1943),

some of the more surprising encomiums. Granville Hicks, who had considered *Work of Art* proof of Lewis's loss of contact with the central issues of American life, declared that with this novel Lewis had once more waded into the main stream. John Middleton Murry described the book as not merely an absorbing story but "probably the wisest and most human, the most searching and suggestive piece of realistic political thinking that has been done in America or England for a dozen years." Charles and Mary Beard wrote in 1939 that "In all the years of depression and turmoil, no novel written in the United States portrayed more dynamically the ideals of democracy pitted against the tyranny of the demagogic dictator." [20]

It Can't Happen Here attracted additional attention when a controversy arose over its movie version. Metro-Goldwyn-Mayer had brought the rights, engaged Sidney Howard to prepare the film script, and announced that Lionel Barrymore would play Doremus Jessup. Then on February 15, 1936, came the news that the movie was not to be made after all. In swift succession, in fact, came a flurry of announcements, giving different reasons for the abandonment of the film. According to one, it had been forbidden by the Hays office (the movie industry's own censorship board) for "fear of international politics and fear of boycotts abroad." Louis B. Mayer, however, denied that the Hays office had imposed a ban, and said that the film was temporarily off schedule because of high costs of production. Lewis was enraged; he had no financial interest in the film, he made it clear, but he was irate at this attack on freedom of expression. When he returned to New York from Hollywood, Sidney Howard

---

p. 735, cited in William Couch, Jr., "The Emergence, Rise and Decline of the Reputation of Sinclair Lewis" (Ph.D. dissertation, University of Chicago, 1954), p. 190.

[20] Charles and Mary Beard, *America in Midpassage* (New York: Macmillan, 1939), p. 602, cited in Couch, "Reputation", p. 190.

announced that the Hays office was responsible and that he had seen a long memorandum from Joseph I. Breen, director of the Production Code Administration, which suggested the elimination of many sections of the script and called it inflammatory and filled with dangerous material. Howard's documentary evidence was not convincing; Breen, it was reported, had long resented Hollywood's supine attitude and had declared that there was nothing wrong with Lewis's story, provided it was not turned into political propaganda for the forthcoming Presidential election. The real reason probably was that all M-G-M films would have been banned from Germany and Italy if the movie had been made. Berlin and Rome hailed the ban; a spokesman for the German film industry even went so far as to call Lewis a " full-blooded Communist."

In January, 1935, Lewis accepted an honor he might have been expected to decline: he became a member of the National Institute of Arts and Letters, the parent body of the Academy which he had denounced so vehemently in his Nobel Prize speech. In June, 1936, followed another distinction, which he deeply coveted and appreciated, when his alma mater, Yale, conferred upon him an honorary degree. William Lyon Phelps, reading the citation, described him as an undergraduate who had never bowed down to the idols of the place—never an extreme radical, but an individualist with a passion for literature and a burning zeal for mental illumination. In representing the complacency of trivial people in a trivial environment, Phelps said, Lewis convicted them of sin; he seemed to say, "In this spectacular universe, it is shameful for you to live in such a way." [21]

In her memoir Lewis's first wife tells how their son Wells spent a large part of the summer of 1936 with his

[21] New York *Times*, June 18, 1936, p. 14.

father on the Vermont farm and found him excellent company. The father could now be quite natural with his eighteen-year-old son, and the son found the father, "with his encyclopedic but living knowledge and his avoidance of clichés in thought as well as phraseology," the best of people to listen to.[22] Responding to the mood of his peaceful valley, Lewis even developed an admiration for Thoreau, and in a review he wrote in 1937 he exhorted people to learn from this man who had built his own shack and lived in it "with a dignity vaster than any harassed emperor."[23] According to Maule and Cane, the notion of a retreat from the world had a strong appeal for him at this time; he would argue the reasons why he should remain in an ivory tower, and he thought of writing a novel to be entitled *The Quiet Mind*.[24]

This newly found serenity was only intermittent, however, as another letter from Wells to his mother, during the Christmas season of 1936, makes clear: "After eleven months of complete sobriety Father has returned with a whoosh to the bottle."[25] The immediate causes of his compulsion to drink are not far to seek. Between 1935 and 1940, Lewis had only one novel published. He did a spell of book reviewing for *Newsweek* in the latter part of 1937 and the early part of 1938, and he wrote an occasional article; but he turned out very little fiction.

[22] Grace Hegger Lewis, *With Love from Gracie: Sinclair Lewis: 1912–1925* (New York: Harcourt, Brace, 1955), p. 320.

[23] "One-Man Revolution," a review of Henry Seidel Canby's edition of *Walden*, *Newsweek*, November 22, 1937, reprinted in *The Man from Main Street*, pp. 240–242. Mark Schorer in *Sinclair Lewis: An American Life* (New York: McGraw-Hill, 1961), p. 25, and Sheldon Grebstein in *Sinclair Lewis*, United States Authors Series (New York: Twayne, 1962), pp. 31–32, give differing estimates of the influence of Thoreau on the early Lewis. When he was a boy, Lewis said, no book had a more peculiar enchantment for him than *Walden*, but surely Schorer is correct when he says that it is hard to take this statement at its face value.

[24] *The Man from Main Street*, p. 241.   [25] *With Love from Gracie*, p. 320.

Here was a writer who had declared exuberantly to Harcourt in the 1920's that his head was brimming with ideas for novels, and who now found that he had almost nothing to say. Fear that his inspiration was drying up was undoubtedly one of the chief reasons for his insurmountable misery; Vincent Sheean writes:

> It can be said of most writers . . . that work is their one salvation, but never have I seen anybody of whom it was more true than it was of poor Red. He could work like a regiment of engineers, . . . but when he did not have work to do (which, in his mind, meant a very big novel, nothing less) he lost his power altogether and became a weak, tremulous thing for whom one could feel only pity.[26]

His wife saw this and evidently said it to him: "I know what is eating you and always, periodically, has eaten you. It is the fear that your creative power is waning."[27]

In addition, his second marriage was failing. In the published extracts from her letters and journals, Dorothy Thompson gives the impression of a person of acute mind and sensibility going over and over all the troublesome episodes in their life together, every major quarrel, every source of difficulty, in an effort to understand whether anything could have prevented their breakup. As early as 1929 we find her writing, "Oh, my God, I really don't know whether I love or hate him—but tonight I was *bored* with him."[28] Like Grace Lewis, she found herself constantly being humiliated by him; it is no wonder then that she did what she could to create a separate life of her own. Though her own psychological difficulties, as they are revealed or suggested in *Dorothy and Red*, make it

[26] Vincent Sheean, *Dorothy and Red* (Boston: Houghton Mifflin, 1963), pp. 171–172.

[27] In a long letter of April 29, 1937, *ibid.*, p. 297.

[28] From a diary entry of February 13, 1929, *ibid.*, p. 124.

appear that the story is more complicated than might at first appear, there is undoubtedly a large measure of truth in her final judgment of her husband: "I think you have thrown down the sink the best things that life has ever offered you . . . ." [29]

The almost inevitable separation came when Lewis walked out of their Bronxville house in April, 1937. His emotional situation, as Schorer describes it, was similar to what it had been ten years before, when he was abandoning his first wife; once again he needed treatment in a sanitarium. But somehow or other he found the strength to finish the novel upon which he was working, *The Prodigal Parents*, and it was published in January, 1938.

This is another problem novel, the problem this time that of the younger or "Gimme" generation. Fred Cornplow is blessed with a son, Howard, who is a drunken playboy, and a daughter, Sara, who is a supercilious radical, a "lady Storm Trooper." Nothing good can be said about these two. They demand everything and give nothing. They look on Fred and his wife Hazel as old fogeys who are keeping their inheritance from them; yet in every crisis they come crying for help. They flutter from the dream world of the communist to the mad world of the psychiatrist; except when it caters to their whims, they concede no reality at all to the sane world of Fred Cornplow.

The problem is treated without subtlety in either characterization or writing. As Lewis envisaged the theme, it involved an ironic reversal of accepted ideas; the early twentieth-century revolt of the younger generation, he thought, had been succeeded after 1914 by a growing revolt of parents against their rebellious children. But he shows so little desire to understand the younger generation that his satire becomes peevish and spiteful.

[29] *Ibid.*, p. 308

Howard is made so feeble of intellect that he says, "He's *got* to help us ! The world and the government and your own folks owe everybody a living" (131).[30] A Communist agitator is portrayed as so villainous that he steals money out of the pockets of some boys knocked unconscious in an automobile accident. The same crudity of execution must be responsible for the clumsy jokes with which Lewis tries to add sparkle to his writing:

> A better family is one that has had money or land longer than most; there is nothing more to the trick, and titles and armorial bearings are merely to fool the eye. Nor is it always good taste to ask where the family got the land and money in the first place. The truth about the Norman families of England is that William the Conqueror, a folio edition of Al Capone, stole the country from the Saxons (who had stolen it from the Early English) and divided it among his gang, not yesterday, which would make it criminal, but back around 1100, which is aristocratic, and renders Norman lineage even more important than your golf handicap.
>
> If it had been the Eskimos who had seized England and picked out pretty titles as earls 800 years ago, then the Best Families, both British and American, would today be claiming descent from Oley the Blubber [33].

Besides illustrating the quality of the writing, this passage serves to introduce the dominant theme of the book—the importance of Fred Cornplow. In Maxwell Geismar's terms,[31] Lewis vulgarizes or bourgeoisizes the conflict between East and West and between established family and rising family; here the conflict is reduced to a question of land or money. Thus Lewis carries a step further the defense of the bourgeoisie which he had made in *It Can't Happen Here*. In that book, the dictator Buzz Windrip

---

[30] *The Prodigal Parents* (New York: Doubleday, Doran, 1938).

[31] Maxwell Geismar, *The Last of the Provincials: The American Novel, 1915–1925* (Boston: Houghton Mifflin, 1949), p. 133.

was described as a professional Common Man; his revolution was ostensibly in behalf of the downtrodden proletariat, and during his election campaign he drew crowds of "hungry miners, dispossessed farmers, Carolina mill hands . . . ." His mammoth rally in Madison Square Garden was crowded with "Manhattan peasants" who were "facile material for any rabble-rouser." Well on in the book, Doremus Jessup reflected

> that he did not believe in a dictatorship of the proletariat any more than he believed in a dictatorship of the bankers and utility-owners; he still insisted that any doctor or preacher, though economically he might be as insecure as the humblest of his flock, who did not feel that he was a little better than they, and privileged to enjoy working a little harder, was a rotten doctor or a preacher without grace [375].

The homely name "Cornplow" indicates what manner of hero Lewis has selected for this novel—a middling sort of man. Fred has an automobile agency, which he runs successfully; he is a Republican, a church goer, and an opponent of labor unions. That we may have no doubts about his significance, Lewis explains to us, in a lengthy passage, that there is nothing weightier in the world than Fred Cornplow's changes of mind and that he has been the most important actor in the drama of human history:

> For who in the world has ever been more important than Fred Cornplow?
> He has, at times, been too noisy or too prosy; he has now and then thought more of money than of virtue and music; but he has been the eternal doer; equally depended upon—and equally hated—by the savage mob and by the insolent nobility.

After listing some of the incarnations of Fred Cornplow through the ages—as an Egyptian planning the pyramids, a Roman centurion conquering and ruling a corner of the Empire, an abbot developing agriculture in the "bright Dark Ages"—Lewis declares:

> From Fred Cornplow's family, between B.C. 1937 and A.D. 1937, there came, despite an occasional aristocratic Byron or an infrequent proletarian John Bunyan, nearly all the medical researchers, . . . the poets, the builders, the singers, the captains of great ships. Sometimes his name has been pronounced Babbitt; sometimes it has been called Ben Franklin; and once, if Eugene O'Neill may be trusted, he went by the style of Marco Polo. . . .
>
> He is the eternal bourgeois, the bourjoyce, the burgher, the Middle Class, whom the Bolsheviks hate and imitate, whom the English love and deprecate, and who is most of the population worth considering in France and Germany and these United States.
>
> He is Fred Cornplow; and when he changes his mind, that crisis is weightier than Waterloo or Thermopylae [98–100].

This paean moved Malcolm Cowley to describe *The Prodigal Parents* as "not merely a botched copy of *Babbitt*" but "*Babbitt* upside down." Fred Cornplow, he said, is

> . . . Babbitt triumphant, Babbitt addressing his fellow members of the Zenith Real Estate Board. I turned back to that speech . . . "It's the fellow," Babbitt proclaimed, "with four to ten thousand a year say, and an automobile and a nice little family in a bungalow on the edge of town, that makes the wheels of progress go round." If Babbitt's speech to the realtors was funny, (and Lewis thought it was), then his own solemn address to Fred Cornplow must be funny too. It is the same speech.

The only explanation Cowley can find is that Babbitt killed Sinclair Lewis and wrote the book himself:

> That explains *The Prodical Parents* as no other story, true or false, can explain it. Babbitt gets apologies,

Babbitt gets himself glorified, and his victim, the late critic of middle-class stupidity, gets blamed for publishing a novel so stupid that the middle class won't read it.[32]

Louis Kronenberger gave much the same opinion: Lewis convinces us of nothing here except his own philistinism, and philistinism, in a writer, is the sin against the Holy Ghost.[33] But Lloyd Morris acutely saw the book as interesting because it revealed Lewis's values clearly. Only professional critics, he said, could have been so blind as to miss what Lewis had been saying ever since *Main Street*. The better way of life which he implied but never explicitly proposed was not a new one but the life of American yesterdays, "the old, free, democratic, individualistic career of the middle class," the American dream of a freedom which would come when the environment had been mastered. The younger generation represented not continuity but abrupt and violent deviation; they were used in the novel as moral symbols, embodiments of the psychological hobgoblins which threatened the peace of old-fashioned Americans, the hallucinatory concepts of communism, moral disintegration, and social and economic collapse. For fifteen years, Morris concluded, Lewis's critics had denied him recognition because he had always failed to include in his picture a definition of the good life; here he had furnished that definition explicitly and fully—but he had never been less an artist.[34]

In 1936, when the Federal Theater of the Works Progress Administration had decided to produce *It Can't Happen Here* as a play, Lewis had been brought back into the theatrical orbit once more. He had hurriedly drama-

[32] Malcolm Cowley, "George F. Babbitt's Revenge," *New Republic*, XCIII (1938), 342.

[33] Louis Kronenberger, "The Prodigal Lewis," *Nation*, CXLVI (1938), 101.

[34] Lloyd Morris, "Sinclair Lewis—His Critics and His Public," *North American Review*, CCXLV (1938), 381–390.

tized the novel—in collaboration—or conflict—with J. C. Moffitt. The play fulfilled one of its purposes admirably —that of giving employment to a large number of actors— there were twenty-three companies in all; and it opened simultaneously in eighteen cities on October 27. Like the book, it had considerable popular impact, even if it was not first-rate drama, and it enjoyed a long run in New York. Besides encouraging Lewis in further abortive attempts at play-writing, his renewed contact with the theater tempted him into becoming an actor himself: he agreed to play the role of Doremus Jessup for the South Shore Players of Cohasset, Massachusetts. The play opened on August 22, 1938 and Lewis showed himself capable of enacting the role of a small-town newspaper editor. As the early excitement and applause dwindled into routine, however, he became bored; he was never to become a professional man of the theater. For his next venture in dramatic composition, he had the assistance of a well-known actress, Fay Wray. Their play, *Angela Is Twenty-Two*, opened in Columbus, Ohio, on December 30, 1938, with Lewis playing the male lead opposite Flora Campbell. According to Schorer, the play, though "loose in conception and cloudy in motivation," was generally well received—because Lewis was acting in it. But after two months on tour, he had had enough; he turned over his role of middle-aged lover to another.

Some time later, when Lewis was rehearsing for an appearance in *Ah, Wilderness!*, he impressed a New York *Times* reporter with the thorough way in which he got up the play; there was no doubt that he was "putting all his amazing energy into a new, and for him completely fascinating, job." [35] At the same time he told the interviewer that he liked the gregariousness of the stage; he obviously appreciated it for the opportunities for companionship it offered, especially with young people, and most especially with pretty girls. One of these, eighteen-year-old Marcella Powers, whom he met at Provincetown in August, 1939, was to mean a great deal to him.

Out of his experiences in the theater came a novel, *Bethel Merriday*, published in March 1940. After the decline of the thirties, it gave further evidence that Lewis was no longer to be regarded as a serious novelist. It was readable but insignificant, reminiscent of but inferior to Maugham's *Theatre* and Priestley's *The Good Companions*. As usual, Lewis anatomizes his subject completely, but here his treatment is sympathetic to the point of sentimentality. A character with the name Zed Wintergeist sounds as if he ought to be satirized; instead he is presented as a budding young genius. There is only incidental satire of drama students, character actors, small-town reviewers, and so on. Edgar Johnson correctly described it as a book in which the sentimental values of the popular novelist are presented with a surface of tough-minded realism and satiric commentary. It is "a story to delight the soft-boiled hard guy."[36]

Other critics referred to it as a novel "full of figures and empty of life," as having "an odd, bloodless quality about its romantic episodes" and a silly and entirely predictable plot. The style, Johnson noted, resembled that of the promising author of *Our Mr. Wrenn*, especially in the portrayal of character types through Dickensian caricature. Lewis made far too much use of his trick of mixing incongruous elements together—Zed Wintergeist, to judge by his appearance, "might have been a butcher, a Communist poet, a fundamentalist evangelist,

[36] Edgar Johnson, "Sinclair Lewis's Understudy," *New Republic*, CII (1940), 413.

a prize fighter or a researcher in physics," for example—
and the jokes were entirely labored and juvenile. Still
Lewis was able to communicate something of his own
enthusiasm for the theater, and the book contained some
good reporting; but, as Clifton Fadiman put it, it was
"not so much the story of a stage-struck young girl as the
story of a stage-struck middle-aged novelist who uses the
young girl as a ventriloquist's dummy." [37] And the
novelist had so little regard for his story that he kept
interrupting it for the purpose of social commentary.
There is even a reference to the possibility of war, and
the necessity of every artist's taking "even his tiniest
job more seriously than ever, so that civilization may have
a chance to go on." [38]

[37] Clifton Fadiman, review of *Bethel Merriday*, *New Yorker*, XVI (March
23, 1940), 83.
[38] *Bethel Merriday* (New York: Doubleday, Doran, 1940), p. 389.

7. New Life and Endless Exile

For a brief period in the fall of 1940, Lewis held an unpaid and ill-defined position as director of a class in writing at the University of Wisconsin. From Madison, at Dorothy Thompson's urging, he announced his support for a third term for Franklin D. Roosevelt; in a radio broadcast on October 30 he asserted that no man in the world was less likely to want to become a dictator than the President. He had leased a house in Madison until the next July, but he left abruptly at the beginning of November. After a trip to Cuba with Miss Powers, he costarred with her in a production of *Angela Is Twenty-Two* in Miami. At the end of the play's one-week run he made a public farewell to lights and grease paint and said that he was turning to the planning of a new novel. This was not a last farewell to the theater, however; in October, 1941, he backed and directed the Broadway production of a play called *The Good Neighbor*. One offshoot of this was an article in the New York *Times* of Sunday, October 19, in which he described directing as the most exciting of activities and reported that a working day extending from six A.M.

to midnight "has kept me out of the more vigorous forms of dissipation."[1] Since the play quickly closed, the joys of directing were short-lived. The year 1941 was more notable for its failures than its successes: in November Dorothy Thompson filed suit for divorce on the grounds of desertion, and the divorce was granted on January 2, 1942.

Having parted from his wife, Lewis felt free to portray her satirically in a novel, just as he had done with Grace shortly after she had divorced him. For the writing he returned to Minnesota, spending the summer chiefly in resort areas and taking a house in Minneapolis for the winter. Schorer relates that at the beginning of July he had hardly started writing, but by the beginning of August he had almost completed a first draft. That fall he finished revising the manuscript, simultaneously with teaching a class in creative writing at the University of Minnesota. Published in April, 1943, the novel, *Gideon Planish*, had more satiric bite than anything he had written in the 1930's.

Gideon Planish represents a return to the crude but vigorous method of *Elmer Gantry*. The two heroes have obvious resemblances; like Elmer, Gideon is infatuated with the sound of his own voice, and it determines his choice of a career: "He would be a senator or a popular minister, something rotund and oratorical, and he would make audiences of two and three hundred people listen while he shot off red-hot adjectives about Liberty and Plymouth Rock" (3).[2] It is not long before he discovers that he has a Mission:

> He would be a Good Man, a bringer of Messages to the poor old longing world—Messages about brother-

[1] See "Novelist Bites Art," *The Man from Main Street: Collected Essays and Writings, 1904–1950*, ed. Harry E. Maule and Melville H. Cane (New York: Random House, 1953), pp. 228–230.

[2] *Gideon Planish* (New York: Random House, 1943).

hood and democracy and the regular use of green (including yellow) vegetables. He'd show 'em that there was nothing at all to this predatory vice. . . .

Other hand, he perceived that most of the Good Men, such as his college instructors, had little to show for their virtue. The trouble, he decided, was that they fooled their time away, without direction.

He selected virtue as his lot, but virtue had to be organized [32–33].

Lusting for power, Gideon casts aside integrity and, with the help of his wife, Peony, starts rising in the world of promotional activities. In his work with the Association to Promote Eskimo Culture, the Blessed to Give Brotherhood, and the Dynamos of Democratic Direction, he is an "organizator" taking advantage of "philanthrobbers"— rich people who perhaps, very occasionally, have twinges of social conscience but chiefly want to make displays of benevolence.

Though he has a suitable subject, Lewis does not make *Gideon Planish* an effective satire. The book is sociological analysis as much as satire; it is an exhaustive investigation rather than an imaginative treatment, even to the point of including a very long list of terms from the organizator's vocabulary. A main difficulty is that the target is too big; evidently desiring to show that all foundations and charitable groups are fraudulent, Lewis deals with a great many types of organizations. He is extraordinarily suspicious; apparently there is no such thing as a model society, a group which genuinely tries to carry out its ostensible purpose. To unfairness Lewis adds his usual overemphasis; he tries to convince his readers that the organizations he describes are a serious threat to American democracy. The message is, in fact, similar to that in *It Can't Happen Here*, and Lewis employs a "quiet man" to deliver it for him:

Each of these private armies led by devout fanatics—not always on salary—who believe that the way to ensure freedom for everybody is to shut up every one of their opponents in jail for life, and that this is a very fine, new solution.

God save poor America, this quiet man thought, from all the zealous and the professionally idealistic, from eloquent women and generous sponsors and administrative ex-preachers and natural-born leaders and Napoleonic newspaper executives and all the people who like to make long telephone calls and write inspirational memoranda [426].

If these people are worth attacking, they are worth estimating correctly; but Lewis shows them as possessing no complexity and very little intelligence. When he pictures the Reverend Chauncey Pederson smacking his lips as he talks about the "shameless word-painting of naked women" in popular fiction, Lewis is having a great deal of fun with a type of character which always amused him; but we cannot take seriously his assertion that the man is a real threat to America's peace of mind.

Just as Grace was the prototype of Fran in *Dodsworth*, Dorothy Thompson was presumably the model for the portrait of Winifred Marduc Homeward, the Talking Woman:

She was an automatic, self-starting talker. Any throng of more than two persons constituted a lecture audience for her, and at sight of them she mounted an imaginary platform, pushed aside an imaginary glass of water, and started a fervent address full of imaginary information about Conditions and Situations that lasted till the audience had sneaked out—or a little longer [320].

One of her lesser admirers describes how she affects him:

". . . it isn't that she's always giving her own version of the Sermon on the Mount, but that she always carries her own portable Mount right with her and sets it up even at a cocktail party. She's the first lady Messiah, and I'm afraid she's going to get the entire Messiah industry in wrong . . ." [330].

Once again, Lewis ought to content himself with deriving amusement from drawing a caricature; instead, he tries to make his Talking Woman appear sinister. With her magazine *Attention!* and her corps of Black Blouses she is rapidly making herself the real power in a movement, headed by her Hearst-like father, Colonel Marduc, to establish a new Soviet system in the United States. No matter how forceful Dorothy Thompson may have been, this is a gross exaggeration; Lewis ruins his likeness by letting his imagination fly off into his fairy-tale world once more.

To these major flaws in *Gideon Planish* we must add Lewis's belated attempt to convert it into a novel dealing with a husband-and-wife situation. Just as Lewis occasionally endowed Elmer Gantry with a soul, he eventually decides to give Gideon a conscience; after exposing his ruthless scheming throughout two hundred pages, Lewis attempts to win sympathy for this monster by showing him as the victim of an ambitious wife. Peony will stop at nothing; she refuses to let her husband accept relatively honest employment—as a college president—and of course she is unfaithful to him. In other words, the situation resembles that in *Dodsworth*—a good man suffers from a bad wife. But when Lewis demands sympathy for Gideon, the reader has no reason to give it; his change in character is entirely unconvincing. Consequently, what might have been a successful satire becomes, as the *Commonweal* reviewer put it, "a sort of sour fairy tale." [3]

Twin Farms had gone to Dorothy Thompson as part of the divorce settlement, so that once again Lewis was

[3] "Off the Deep End," *Commonweal*, XXXVIII (1943), 78.

without a home. Still trying to resolve the claims of East and West upon him, he leased an enormous apartment in New York in 1943 and bought an enormous house in Duluth in 1944. As usual, however, he was seldom in any one place for any length of time. For a while he was an itinerant debater, arguing with Rabbi Lewis Browne on whether fascism could become a powerful force in the United States, whether modern woman was a success, and other topics. Eventually, when his longing for the New England countryside again became intense, he bought a 750-acre farm near Williamstown, Massachusetts, in the spring of 1946.

He spent most of the summer of 1943 in Hollywood, collaborating with Dore Schary on a film script for M-G-M, which the company finally decided not to use. Entitled *Storm in the West*, the script was based on an idea of Schary's; but since a version of it has now been published, we can see that it must have appealed strongly to Lewis because of its jejune fantasy.[4] Hygatt, an ornery critter with a small black moustache, comes riding into a western valley with two ugly varmints named Gerrett and Gribbles. The residents soon find that you can't do business with Hygatt. He takes over the run-down property of his uncle Gorman and spruces it up; then, with a forged title deed, he gains possession of Chuck Slattery's ranch. His reign of terror really begins, however, after he forms an alliance with Mullison and hires a gunman by the name of Yunker. He murders Poling, knifes Franson, and altogether proves too much for peace-loving Sheriff Ned Chambers. The cigar-smoking Chancel is just the right man for the job of restoring law and order, but he can't do it all by himself; only when Ulysses Saunders, hitherto reluctant to take action, is stirred up by a sneak

[4] Sinclair Lewis and Dore Schary, *Storm in the West* (New York: Stein and Day, 1963).

attack on his daughter Pearl do things take a turn for the better. "The fact that this story was suppressed," says the dust jacket of *Storm in the West*, "is itself a revealing commentary on mass culture in America and what its lords and administrators think of as 'controversial.'" But the fact that the story was ever written is a revealing commentary on the prevalence of certain myths, the fact that it was ever published a testimonial to the magic of the Lewis name. Finally, the fact that the film was never made proves only that the management of M-G-M was not stupid enough to put money into a movie which turned the Second World War into a horse opera.

Early in 1944, Lewis was instrumental in securing a special award from the American Academy (he was now an esteemed member of that once despised body) for an old antagonist, Theodore Dreiser. If he ended or forgot one controversy, however, he was soon involved in another. In April came the publication of Bernard DeVoto's *The Literary Fallacy*, in which the literature of the 1920's was characterized as false because it had been without living relationship to its society: its writers had accepted and passed on judgments derived from books, not from life. Never in any country or age, DeVoto asserted, had writers so misrepresented their culture; never had they been so unanimously wrong. The part of the indictment which hit Lewis particularly was the charge that writers had toyed with myths and abstractions and disdained the common experiences of ordinary Americans, that they had adopted an attitude of superiority to their countrymen.

In reply Lewis wrote an article which appeared in the *Saturday Review of Literature* for April 15. DeVoto had said that an uninstructed gentleness toward writers had been a mistake of contemporary readers, and that words like "fool" and "liar" might very well be brought back into critical discussion. Following this cue, Lewis entitled his article "Fools, Liars and Mr. DeVoto." Since DeVoto had displeased many and displeased long, especially by his vendetta against Van Wyck Brooks, Lewis's stand won him compliments. In two "Speaking of Books" columns which he devoted to the controversy, J. Donald Adams found DeVoto guilty of overstating his case; though he described Lewis as "that most combustible of novelists," he declared that he had a greater share of human sweetness than most and that he had never nursed a grievance.[5] Yet there is little sweetness in Lewis's article, and much sense of grievance. The tone is established by the title—savage and contemptuous. Reading it now, we must be struck by what a shabby performance it is for a satirist with long experience in his craft. Lewis scores some palpable hits, as when he reveals that DeVoto, in spite of his insistence that writers ought to portray the real America, has been guilty of churning out trashy fiction under a silly pseudonym, John August. But the desire to score points is too obvious— Lewis even refers to his opponent's "frog-like face"; he is not able to put himself in the position of giving a calm assessment of an erratic antagonist. There are better ways of dealing with a man than calling him fool and knave, as Dryden said, and Lewis had not learned the lesson. When he goes beyond DeVoto to attack Howard Mumford Jones, Allen Tate, R. P. Blackmur, Yvor Winters, and Edmund Wilson as "talmudists" and "mincing messiahs," he himself gives the impression which he imputes to DeVoto—that of a small boy lashing out spitefully at anyone within range of his puny little fists.

At the end of October, 1944, Wells Lewis, a lieutenant in the United States Army, was killed in action in Alsace. In Dorothy Thompson's account of how Lewis received the news, the peculiar nature of his temperament becomes

[5] J. Donald Adams, "Speaking of Books," New York *Times Book Review*, April 30, 1944, p. 2, and May 14, 1944, p. 2.

apparent. The word came to Wells' mother, Grace, on November 13. Lewis, then on a lecture tour, was at a party in Chicago that night; he was in the highest spirits, and no one knew whether or not he had heard of his son's death. Eventually Dorothy's brother-in-law took advantage of a quiet moment to express his sympathy. Lewis immediately flew into a rage, not only at Dorothy's brother-in-law but also at Harrison Smith, who had sent a message of sympathy, and at Dorothy, who had canceled her radio program when she heard of Wells' death. Whether or not he had heard the news just before he went to deliver his lecture and had never been better in his life, as he boasted, his tirade lingered in the minds of those who heard it as a memorable example of lack of feeling. Dorothy Thompson comments, however, that he repressed his emotions to a point unbearable for those who wished to share them, and had the pride of Lucifer in doing so; his reaction to frustrations and grief was to hit out at those who cared for him most. It was never possible to know whether he really cared at all—for anybody or anything except his work.[6]

That summer, in and about Duluth, he had been envisioning the setting and characters for a new novel, to be located in the fictitious Minnesota city of Grand Republic. In the fall he returned to New York; and late in September he spoke at a political rally in Madison Square Garden, satirizing Dewey and ridiculing talk of Roosevelt's being old and worn-out. He gave another notable address on December 16, a radio broadcast from the Metropolitan Opera House as part of a victory rally series; entitled "The Artist, the Scientist, and the Peace," it was published in the *American Scholar* for summer, 1945.[7]

[6] Dorothy Thompson, "The Boy and Man from Sauk Centre," *Atlantic Monthly*, CCVI (November, 1960), 41.

[7] Reprinted in *The Man from Main Street*, pp. 32–36.

Although it is in most respects a conventional shoulders-to-the-wheel exhortation, it contains, as Schorer observes, something unusual for Lewis—ridicule of the Arrowsmiths who go their lonely way in isolation from their fellow men. "The old-fashioned type of artist-scientist—the Pasteurs and Whistlers and Walter Paters," Lewis said, "felt that their creative work was so superior that they could live in plush-lined clouds *above* the human struggle." But here and there "a Voltaire or a Dickens or a physician like Vesalius knew that he could have no private light to work by if the whole world elsewhere was in darkness . . . ." Consequently, the artist or scientist must know and "somewhat loudly state" whether or not he is on the side of tyranny.

As he was planning and writing one novel, he was thinking about another: in his first contribution to the Books section of *Esquire* magazine, which he took over for seven issues beginning in June, 1945, he showed familiarity with the Negro problem, even with such weighty discussions of it as Gunnar Myrdal's *An American Dilemma*. In preparation for the novel he would eventually write on this topic, he returned to his old method of thoroughly researching the subject and obtaining the widest possible range of points of view. His July contribution to *Esquire* was another interesting one—a discussion of "Obscenity and Obscurity." The "obscurity" part was his usual attack on writers' indifference to clarity, with illustrations drawn from poetry; he admitted that he could not complain if the poets chose to commit suicide by convincing the world that no sensible person would read them, but he claimed a right to object "when they begin to drag the veils of egotism over the hard clarity of prose." On obscenity he tried to follow a middle road; he ridiculed the pious hypocrite who seemed to start at seeing a shocking word in print, but he disapproved of the "literary botcher" and "pious manurists" who had to use such words. Addressing Hemingway, Farrell and Lawrence— whose *Lady Chatterley's Lover* he referred to as "bleached subcellar smut"—he told them that they had really started something: they had succeeded in being both dirty and clever, but their successors were achieving nothing but dirtiness.

Lewis's new novel, *Cass Timberlane*, published in October, 1945, was now running as a serial in *Cosmopolitan* and establishing itself as a sound commercial proposition. According to Schorer, it made Lewis nearly half a million dollars—from serialization, from regular publication, from selection by the Book-of-the-Month Club, and from sale to the movies (it was made into a very successful film starring Spencer Tracy and Lana Turner). It did extremely well for a novel which was not one of Lewis's best.

The story of a judge in his forties who woos and marries a girl in her early twenties, *Cass Timberlane* is evidently, as Schorer shows, Lewis's own thinly veiled love story; and since the age difference in his own case was closer to forty years than twenty, the romantic passages are awkward in the telling. A number of reviewers, notably Marjorie Farber in the *New Republic*, dismissed the novel as a run-of-the-mill woman's-magazine serial.[8] Diana Trilling, in the *Nation*, complained that, whereas in *Main Street* and *Babbitt* Lewis had discovered the existence of stereotypes of which others were almost unaware, now he was restating familiar American sentimentalities and cynicisms—dealing in observations that had been part of American cliché-thinking about love and marriage for many a year.[9] Edmund Wilson, however, credited Lewis with an alert perception of social phenomena; he was

---

[8] *New Republic*, CXIII (1945), 542.
[9] Diana Trilling, "Of Husbands and Wives," *Nation*, CLXI (1945), 381.

moved to declare that Lewis at his best was one of the national poets, and he entitled his *New Yorker* review "Salute to an Old Landmark." He saw that Lewis was trying to deal with a typical bright young woman of the forties, a very different phenomenon from the emancipated woman of the earlier decades of the century. His Jinny Marshland "wants to compete with the man without learning any trade, is rebellious against marriage but does not want a job, leaves her husband but does not stick to her lover." Lewis wants to catch this type but does not really succeed, because he does not like Jinny sufficiently; if the judge had not been so much in love, he might not have cared for her whimsicality, and with a slight change of tone we could have got one of Lewis's female caricatures, like Peony in *Gideon Planish*. [10] (When Cass says, slowly and miserably, "Jinny, I've given you everything I have, and in return, you are trying to destroy me," the situation is reminiscent of that in *Dodsworth*.) If, as Diana Trilling says, the judge appears soft-headed in his love for Jinny, and if Lewis did not realize how obnoxious he had made his heroine, at least he was not relying on novelistic stereotypes, but was trying to convey, as Wilson points out, an accurate social observation.

Nor was his theme a minor one. The subtitle is "A Novel of Husbands and Wives"; and the book is another of Lewis's investigations of American problems. The novel's protagonist states the issue under consideration and asserts that it is not less but more important than the world war then drawing to a close: "If the world of the twentieth century, he vowed, cannot succeed in this one thing, married love, then it has committed suicide, all but the last moan, and whether Germany and France can

[10] Edmund Wilson, "Salute to an Old Landmark: Sinclair Lewis," *New Yorker*, XXI (October 13, 1945), 98.

live as neighbors is insignificant compared with whether Johann and Maria or Jean and Marie can live as lovers" (173).[11] Interpolated into the story of Cass and Jinny is a series of thirteen short accounts of other marriages— "Assemblages of Husbands and Wives." The effect of these is ironic, since they show that appearances are deceiving: those marriages which seem happy actually are not, and the very few which are happy do not give the impression of being so. In Lewis's conception, the ordinary citizens of an ordinary American community are helplessly driven by biological urges toward the disorder of promiscuity and the horrors of homosexuality and incest. Cass is investigating the problem just as consciously as Lewis, and toward the end of the book he delivers his opinion on what he calls "this whole madhouse of love":

> —You cannot heal the problems of any one marriage until you heal the problems of an entire civilization founded upon suspicion and superstition; and you cannot heal the problems of a civilization thus founded until it realizes its own barbaric nature, and realizes that what it thought was brave was only cruel, what it thought was holy was only meanness, and what it thought Success was merely the paper helmet of a clown more nimble than his fellows, scrambling for a peanut in the dust of an ignoble circus [373].

Here speaks a bitter and disillusioned man, a man in his sixties not his forties, a man who blames society rather than himself for his failure to hold two wives and one mistress.

The conclusion, however, is not pessimistic. In fact, the plot resembles that of *Main Street*: a young woman marries a professional man somewhat older than herself, finds the environment into which she marries stifling, flees in desperation, and eventually returns to her husband.

[11] *Cass Timberlane* (New York: Random House, 1945).

There are differences, however. Carol stops short of adultery; Jinny does not. But Lewis rigs the plot—as Edmund Wilson says—in an absolutely Victorian way: he gives Jinny a lover named Bradd Criley who is nothing but a scoundrel, and he afflicts Jinny with a severe case of diabetes, so that she has no alternative but to return to the arms of the waiting judge. There are other curious twists to the *Main Street* story. Sheldon Grebstein maintains that the novel makes a sinister proposal, one which works against the grain of a cherished American tradition: it suggests "that men are better than women, that they love more tenderly, do not hurt their mates so deeply or so frequently, and that they are the strength and redemption of most marriages."[12] Also, whereas Carol submitted to Kennicott's terms, it is the male who is submissive at the end of this novel; Cass "gave up his vested right to be tragic, gave up pride and triumph and all the luxury of submerged resentment, and smiled at her with the simplicity of a baby" [390]. Horrified at this virtual unmanning of the hero, Philip Wylie suggested that Lewis really meant his "happy ending" to be ironic: the happy couple was really doomed to more suspicion and frustration.[13] Schorer's interpretation seems more plausible: the story of Cass and Jinny is treated with sentimental affection, so that although the novelist recognizes that most American marriages are full of problems, this one is different; it is the marriage which Lewis would now make if he could.

Another similarity to *Main Street* is pointed out by Maxwell Geismar: again Lewis has located his community in the state of Minnesota, rather than "in that appalling chain-state of Winnemac . . . ."[14] Thus he has completed

[12] Sheldon Grebstein, *Sinclair Lewis*, United States Authors Series (New York: Twayne, 1962), p. 150.

[13] Philip Wylie, "Sinclair Lewis," *American Mercury*, LXI (1945), 629.

[14] Maxwell Geismar, *The Last of the Provincials: The American Novel, 1915–1925* (Boston: Houghton Mifflin, 1949), p. 141.

his whole cycle of studies of East and West and returned to his earliest origins. Geismar calls attention to some variations on familiar Lewis themes, and there are others which are worth exploring. The judge does not have to be a self-made man in the Horatio Alger tradition; he does not have to work his way into the upper echelon of society as Sam Dodsworth did—he is born into it. And there *is* an upper echelon. As Geismar says, almost for the first time Lewis is able to visualize an aristocracy (or an *haute bourgeoisie*) which is established, rather than an aristocracy on the make. We are told that a truckdriver might call Boone Havock the contractor by his first name,

> but he would never enter Boone's house or his church, and as for Boone's asylum, the Federal Club, neither the truckdriver nor any Scandinavian or Finn with less than $10,000 income nor any recognizable Jew whatever would be allowed even to gawk through the leaded-glass windows (imported) [13].

So "the division between the proprietors and the serfs was as violent in Grand Republic as in London"; and in Cass's social circle it is "as obligatory to dress for party dinners as in London."

In a more critical mood, Lewis might have portrayed a bogus aristocracy, as he showed the well-to-do of Seattle in *Free Air*; in fact, he occasionally satirizes Cass in a mild way: "If he was distinctly more leftwing than Jinny thought, he was distinctly less so than he thought . . . he had not yet gone many years beyond the Good Old Massa dynasty. And golf at the country club is a sweet odor in the nostrils and a dependable anesthetic" (82–83). But Cass is not blind to Grand Republic's class distinctions, race prejudice, fear of culture, and ugliness; he is very much concerned about the Grand Republics and their civilization. The completely satiric view of them, however, is superficial and imperceptive:

Mrs. Kenny Wargate, Manhattan-born and cynical daughter-in-law of the Ruling Family, asserted that Grand Republic had leaped from clumsy youth to senility without ever having a dignified manhood. She jeered, "Your Grand Republic slogan is: tar-paper shanty to vacant parking lot in three generations."

But Judge Timberlane and his friends, loving the place as home, believed that just now, after woes and failures and haste and waste and experiment, Grand Republic was beginning to build up a kind of city new to the world, a city for all the people, a city for decency and neighborliness, not for ecclesiastical display and monarchial power ... [12].

His vision is one that Lewis shares:

"... I have some kind of an unformulated idea that I want to be identified with Grand Republic—help in setting up a few stones in what may be a new Athens. It's this northern country—you know, stark and clean—and the brilliant lakes and the tremendous prairies to the westward—it may be a new kind of land for a new kind of people, and it's scarcely even started yet" [28].

Edmund Wilson writes that "Grand Republic, Minnesota, is a place where one can imagine living, not, like Main Street, a circle of Hell." [15] Far from being a circle of Hell, Grand Republic offers the opportunity for the development of the only paradise which Lewis can envision.

For some critics, however, the pre-apocalyptic Grand Republic does not have a lived-in look. Geismar concedes that in *Cass Timberlane* Lewis at last conveys something of the variety and mystery of ordinary midwestern life—which he had conspicuously failed to do in his previous works. But from Geismar's point of view, Lewis displays an ironic unawareness; he does not realize that the major economic

[15] "Salute," 98.

determinants of his society are the cartels (he had depicted one of these in *Dodsworth*, the Unit Automotive Corporation) and that the middle-class empire is breaking up under their weight. Be that as it may, it is at least true that Lewis turns his back on larger economic questions, just as he turns his back on international complications, to focus upon the question of Jean and Marie or Cass and Jinny. Even here there are some curious features. Diana Trilling said that Lewis had depicted marriage as only the sum of its most sensational personal frustrations or satisfactions; he seemed to have no conception of the day-by-day interactions of two complicated human beings, no sense of a shared moral, social, and economic responsibility. Furthermore, she thought that, though no writer could fall more in love with his characters than Lewis, he had never conceived a character entirely immune to his satire; there was a lack of true human affection in his novels. The victim of his own divided heart, Lewis could not help victimizing his fictional creations—if not by satirizing them, then by robbing them of some of their due share of life.[16] Mary M. Colum was similarly struck by the hollowness of the characters; their interior life seemed nonexistent, their characteristics laid on from the outside, and the material world sufficed for all of them—they had never even in dreams considered any other.[17]

Certainly there is some depth to Cass; Grebstein thinks that the novel is saved by an undercurrent of deep and honest feeling which is present in the novel's hero. But the complaint is justified by the series of caricatures which Lewis draws of Grand Republic personalities. Consider, for example, the portrait of Sweeney Fishberg, the liberal attorney whom Lewis describes as perhaps the most remarkable man in the city:

[16] "Of Husbands and Wives," 381.

[17] "Sinclair Lewis's New Thesis Novel," *Saturday Review of Literature*, XXVIII (October 6, 1945), 8.

> He was a saint and a shyster; part Jewish and part Irish
> and part German; he had once acted in a summer stock
> company, and once taught Greek in a West Virginia
> college; he was a Roman Catholic, and a mystic who
> bothered his priest with metaphysical questions; he was
> in open sympathy with the Communist Party [52].

The characterising details are simply tags or labels; there is no attempt to bring them into any sort of harmony with each other so the result may be a believable personality. It is almost unnecessary to point out that such words as "saint" and "mystic" have no meaning in a passage of this sort, and that "Roman Catholic" is only a label pinned on the man.

Because religious, political, and ideological terms have nothing to do with seriously thought out values in Lewis's mind, he can jumble them all together as he does here. What sources of value exist in this religionless society? Simply the Midwest itself and the concept of its destiny. How human beings can be made fit for the land, how a meaningful future can be conceived, upon what values the new society can be constructed— these issues are raised at times by the novelist, but they seem to be too big for him, and he weakly takes refuge in the hope that love conquers all, at least some of the time. So he finishes his story with a happy ending—an ending which contrives to be happy, though in terms of the problems posed nothing is solved, no ground for hope is offered, and the conclusion might as well be a despairing as an optimistic one.

If Grand Republic was not a circle of Hell in *Cass Timberlane*, that is exactly what it did become in Lewis's next novel, *Kingsblood Royal*. After investigating racial problems in Duluth, New York, and the South, Lewis had begun planning the book early in 1946, and had settled down to write it at his newly acquired home in New England—Thorvale Farm, near Williamstown. The novel, completed at breakneck speed, was published in May, 1947; it was a Literary Guild selection, and probably succeeded in its avowed intention of jolting the nation— at least it must have jolted most of the million and a half persons who bought copies of it.

The reviewers generally regarded *Kingsblood* as an honest and hard-hitting book, whatever its defects as a work of art, and praised it as a social document. The plot is absurd, especially in Neil Kingsblood's decision to call himself a Negro though he has very little Negro blood in him, in the difficulties he faces because of this decision, in the activities of the organization ludicrously called "Sant Tabac" ("Stop All Negro Trouble, Take Action Before Any Comes"), and in the heroic last stand, straight from the Westerns, of the Kingsbloods against a frenzied mob of their fellow citizens. As an exposure of the fact that northern cities like Grand Republic, for all their assumed superiority to southern intolerance, have racial problems of their own, the book possesses merit.

Thus *Kingsblood* is another of Lewis's investigations of social problems. But because there are so many wrong-headed attitudes to this question, the book offers many opportunities for satire. Lewis tries to present—not merely describe, but illustrate in conversation—all the possible shades of opinion: the brutal, imbecilic white northerner who hates "the whole black mess of 'em"; the employer whose firm never has any trouble with Negroes—because it never hires them in the first place; the procrastinator who longs for the day when . . . , but in the meantime wants the Negroes hustled back south as quickly as possible; and the Little Woman who says,

> "I don't know anything about anthropology and . . . all that silly highbrow junk . . . but I tell you there's a darky family lives right down the alley from us where they keep goats, and I know and I'm telling you that

darkies *are* inferior to us, and I'm not going to have 'em
working in any store or bank or office where I have to
go" [313].[18]

But the white side is only half the spectrum; on the Negro
side there are almost as many shades of opinion, from the
old retainer who is tickled to death to serve a high-class
white gentleman, to the young rabble-rouser who advocates a state of surly hostility. In presenting these positions, Lewis shows his familiar lack of restraint; many of
the speakers talk as though they had just been reading up
on the subject. Nevertheless, he does manage to capture a
very wide range of points of view.

After Neil passes over to the Negro side, his growing
awareness of their disabilities and humiliations brings
growing bitterness. Grand Republic is indeed a circle of
Hell, and the fiends in it drop their smiling everyday
masks and indulge their cruelty to the utmost when they
find a suitable object of hatred. As in *It Can't Happen Here*,
Lewis is too much concerned with the situation to write
a satire on it; instead he writes a horror story which is
unsubtle but has considerable impact. Indeed, Sheldon
Grebstein argues that *Kingsblood Royal* should not be
judged as a realistic novel or even as a satire in the
traditional sense. This is Lewis the fanatic, the crusader,
the inquisitor. Grebstein considers that the book shows
how superbly Lewis was equipped as a propagandist—
able to conjure up scenes of stark physical violence, to
stereotype his opponents for easy recognition and classi-
fication and yet give them such hateful things to do and
say that one forgets they are straw men, and to keep up
suspense with one trick after another. He considers it
indefensible as a work of art, but successful as a public
service.[19] One measure of its success was the award of a

[18] *Kingsblood Royal* (New York: Random House, 1947).
[19] Grebstein, *Sinclair Lewis*, pp. 153–155.

plaque to Lewis by *Ebony* magazine for the book of the year which did most to improve interracial understanding. But beside such other horror stories as Koestler's *Darkness at Noon* and Orwell's *1984*, *Kingsblood Royal* appears very ill contrived and badly written. As a discussion of the racial question, it still contains a great deal of interest, but the actual story of Neil Kingsblood is too implausible. Like *It Can't Happen Here*, the novel is less a tribute to Lewis's skill in presenting a major question of the day in fictional terms than to his uncanny sense of what his audience would let him get away with.

In his Nobel Prize speech Lewis had said that his next novel would concern idealism in America through three generations, from 1818 to 1930. But it was not until he had written *Kingsblood* that he took up this theme which had been with him all his writing life. According to his account "Breaking into Print" which appeared in *Colophon* in 1937, even in his college days he had planned a novel to be called *The Children's Children* which was to deal with a migration westward and with the revolt of each generation against the earlier one. Schorer determines that the *Colophon* reminiscence is inaccurate, but he describes and partially prints an outline of the novel from 1910 according to which the last son was to be a political radical involved in the labor movement. Even in 1910, therefore, Lewis had contemplated writing the labor novel which was to have so many false starts. The title originally proposed for that novel was *Neighbor*, and an alternative was *The Man Who Sought God*. The book he eventually wrote was provisionally entitled *Neighbor* and finally called *The God-Seeker*. Although the novel which he wrote late in his career did not tell the story of the labor movement in the United States as he had planned to write it in the 1920's, it at least embodied the idealism and the dedication which he sometimes found in that movement. It presented, in an alternative form to *Arrowsmith*, Lewis's concept of the heroic life of the seeker after truth. Furthermore, it delineated in final form his own quest for sources of value; on a problem which had bothered him ever since his college days, this was almost all he had to say.

The God-Seeker is Lewis's only historical novel; for it he had to do research in Minnesota history, and he spent some time during 1948 working in the library of the State Historical Society in St. Paul. Set chiefly in the Minnesota of a hundred years before, the book relates the story of Aaron Gadd's upbringing in Massachusetts, his experiences as a missionary's assistant among the Sioux, his marriage to the daughter of a trader, and his work as a carpenter and builder in St. Paul. But Lewis invokes the past chiefly to patronize it, not to understand it. His lack of historical perspective is most obvious in the satiric parts of the novel, which are aimed chiefly at the clergy. Writing about Hawthorne's day, he describes the pall of New England Puritanism in much more forbidding terms than Hawthorne had used for the Salem of long before. His complete lack of sympathy for any form of religious belief makes him depict clergymen in this novel almost exactly as he had depicted them in *Elmer Gantry*; and although he deprives his twentieth-century characters of some lifelike qualities, he reduces their nineteenth-century forebears to grotesque caricatures who revealed their inhumanity in every speech: "Life ain't fun. When you think that most of us are doomed by divine grace to roast in hell, to say nothing of mortgages and hail and bad crops and extravagant womenfolks, 'taint any laughing matter!" (17)[20] Great people were needed to open up the West, and Lewis admires the missionaries as men. But though he has high regard for their courage and fortitude, his contempt for

[20] *The God-Seeker* (New York: Random House, 1949).

their religious beliefs makes them seem small in intellect and honesty. Squire Harge, the minister who lures Aaron to the West, is, if not a Gantry, at least a Babbitt of salvation. He inflames Aaron with a vision of whole nations to be saved, but he makes hardly any attempt to regard the Indians as human beings. Harge on Indians sounds like a Grand Republican on Negroes:

> "Good God Almighty, how many times have I got to tell you that when any of these outlaw breeds—niggers or Indians or Jews or the Ytalians or the wild Irish or any of them—seem like they're bright and decent and even religious, they're just imitating us, like monkeys! Except that the merciful Lord has given them one chance that monkeys don't have—I suppose. He has sent us missionaries to them with the wonderful tidings that if they turn to Jesus like little children—and if by God's will they are elect—then they may be saved just like regular folks. What a lavishing of mercy to send us to them!" [217]

Influenced by an Indian named Black Wolf, who contributes an eight-page criticism of the superstition, dirtiness, stupidity, and moral failings of the whites—he seems to have read Mencken—Aaron concludes that the Indians have more true religion and humanity than those who are trying to convert them. He decides that the Christians' sickly cant of humility and self-abasement is only a device to spread prejudice and superstition, and he rejects it. He will cultivate his own garden: "One of the brightest Christian virtues is humility, and so I say with humility, 'There are many things I don't ever expect to know, and I'm not going to devote myself to preaching about them but to building woodsheds so true and tight that they don't need ivory and fine gold . . .'" (380). One would have thought that now the clergy could cease to be Lewis's *bête noire*. But when Aaron starts the first labor union in St. Paul, unenlightened opposition comes from the usual source: there is a Reverend Mr. Neill who believes that obedience is the only true freedom and that the debased trinity of Reason, Humanitarianism, and Progress is responsible for the greatest crimes since Eden. Lewis harries his opposition to the bitter end of the book, and concedes it not one whit of reasonableness.

This novel deals, therefore, not with the seeking but with the rejecting of God. Edward Wagenknecht calls it a story in which evangelism is pitted against humanism and humanism wins;[21] it might be more accurate to say that a caricature of humanism defeats a caricature of evangelism. At any rate, the paradise envisioned is an earthly one; never since the Puritans came to Boston, Aaron thinks, has there been such an opportunity as this opening up of the Northern Midwest. The sources of value are secular— the land itself, respect for the dignity of other people, the American dream—and the attachment of both Lewis and his hero to them is basically emotional. As Howard Mumford Jones said in his review,[22] Lewis goes into a tailspin of sentimentality about a labor union and a fugitive slave that he would have scoffed at had anyone else written it. His love for his native state shines forth in *The God-Seeker*; he has a great deal of respect for the men who redeemed it from the wilderness, but of their springs of action he has only the faintest glimmerings.

One more novel was to come from his productive pen, and again it was to be on the theme of exile. When *The God-Seeker* appeared in March, 1949, Lewis was in Italy; he had gone there the previous October, accompanied by Mrs. Powers, the mother of his former mistress, and had settled down as a member of the Anglo-American colony

[21] Edward Wagenknecht, *Cavalcade of the American Novel* (New York: Holt, 1952), p. 120.

[22] "Mission in Minnesota," *Saturday Review of Literature*, XXXII (March 12, 1949), 11.

in Florence. In his new novel, to be called *Over the Body of Lucie Jade*, he planned to deal with an American girl in Italy. By Schorer's account he began it in Italy, finished it at Thorvale Farm in the summer of 1949, and then found that neither *Cosmopolitan*, which had contracted for it, nor Random House was willing to publish it. He went abroad again, for the last time, in September of 1949, an aging, enfeebled, and crippled cicerone introducing his brother Claude to the glories of Europe. While Claude took a trip on his own, Sinclair settled into a house in Florence, on the Street of the Plain of the Jesters. Here he relieved the misery of his emptiness through two types of anodyne, drink and work. Neither a Florentine doctor who had to be called in when he suffered a heart attack nor Claude, when he returned, could cure him; the Florentine told him that he was drinking himself to death, and Claude, shortly before he left for home, gave him a year to live if he carried on as he was doing. In spite of his declining health, however, he managed to transmute *Over the Body of Lucie Jade* into *World So Wide*, a novel which brought him full circle—Schorer has found curious parallels between it and his first novel, *Our Mr. Wrenn*, and the title of the later novel is taken from a quotation used near the end of the earlier.[23]

The central character of *World So Wide* is a lonely exile, Hayden Clark. After the death of his wife in an automobile accident, he realizes the emptiness of his life as an architect and solid citizen of Newlife, Colorado: "It was a dream of life in which he had been busy and important and well-bedded and well-fed and had glowingly possessed everything except friends and contentment and any reason for living . . ." (30).[24] In search of

[23] There is an excellent discussion of the resemblances in Schorer's article "The World of Sinclair Lewis," *New Republic*, CXXVIII (April 6, 1953), 18.

[24] *World So Wide* (New York: Random House, 1951).

himself, he goes abroad, to Florence: " 'I think most of us are simply patterns of clothes and habits of work and the same way of saying good morning, invariably . . . . I don't know that I have any personality at all, really . . . . May be I'll find a personality here'" (68–69).

Into the book go appropriate—though sometimes badly integrated—passages from Lewis's notebooks on things wrong with America, things wrong with Florence, and things wrong with contemporary life in general. It also includes a satiric run-down of types of Americans abroad. There are the tourists who merely travel restlessly from place to place, seeing nothing:

> He blurted at last, "Well, come on, Heaven's sake, let's get going !"
>
> "Going *where*?" his wife sighed. "We're here !"
>
> "I know, but good God, you can't just sit around all *day*! Let's—we can go back to the hotel and write some more letters, can't we ?" [132]

There are those who are diligently "doing" Europe:

> There is, Hayden found, something like a system of credits for sight-seeing: doing a cathedral thoroughly counts, let us say, 11 points . . . inspecting a mountain village rarely beheld by tourists is 17, dining at a celebrated restaurant is 6, but if you found it all by yourself, the credit is 9 [102].

There is the American colony, "content, month on month, to go to cocktail parties, with amiable friends, to play a little bridge, to dine out, to read the latest books sent over from Home, to look once a month at a gallery or a church, and, all in all, . . . do nothing but wait for death" (95). There are the students, a few of whom "had learned Italian, and had actually met an Italian," and there are the serious scholars, who have bartered their souls "for trifles of learning . . . no more important, in the atomic age, than a list of Assyrian kings."

Still the action does not take the pattern of the hero's exposure to various alternatives, his discovery of their shortcomings, and his rejection of them one after another. For one thing, his search for value in Europe is not fruitless: ". . . it seemed to him improbable that one who had much contemplated Or San Michele or a Botticelli would willingly allow himself or anyone else to become just a file number in a bureaucracy such as Russia now is and America and Great Britain threaten to be" (85). For another, at least one of the ways of life satirized has an attraction for him until the very end of the book. He meets a woman named Olivia Lomond who has escaped from life into research; he tries on the one hand to humanize her and on the other to imitate her devotion to scholarship. Whether the two of them could ever have worked out a reasonable pattern of existence is not decided. Hayden returns to America, not because he is disillusioned with Europe, but because he retains a sentimental devotion to his native land:

> He remembered the spires of Newlife, and was faintly lonely for home. He knew then that he was unalterably an American; he knew what a special and mystical experience it is, for the American never really emigrates but only travels; perhaps travels for two or three generations but at the end is still marked with the gaunt image of Tecumseh [121].

If the New World has not given Hayden Clark a personality, in itself and by itself it has been, as the religious overtones of this passage make clear, the truest source of value that he has ever experienced.

The plot complications bear this out, for Hayden is rescued from Olivia and Italy by a "chunk of Home," Roxanna Eldritch. In a review entitled "From Main Street to the World So Wide," Serge Hughes gave an interesting analysis of her significance:

She is the typical clever, healthy American girl who calls a thing by its right name, and convincingly shows the hero that he could recognize pretense only in its most obvious dress. She makes perfectly clear that Babbitt, with his pitiful lack of taste and breeding, but with a center and with some drive, is infinitely preferable to a cheap estheticism. Better to act stupidly than to rot in a cultivated fashion. The end of the novel finds the two, newly married, on their way to other places, India and the Far East. This time . . . the hero knows that he too will send postcards to the folks back home, buy sweaters for relatives, and take a lot of snapshots.

The problem of Babbitt has come to a dead end. Exile is no answer. Art is no answer. Culture is a racket. Only this much is clear: there are certain traits in Babbitt which are good. Out of all that messy heritage there are elements which can still be utilized and they must be used. For there is nothing outside of the spotty bourgeois heritage but sham and corruption.[25]

At the end of his career, as at the beginning, Lewis is not a satirist attacking from a position confidently held, but an innocent abroad—an innocent gifted enough, however, to bring up perplexing questions. In rational terms, the questions are insoluble. Lewis is able to save himself from their despairing logic only by giving his situations emotional twists to bring about the necessary happy ending—a happy ending, however, which is not merely gratuitous but is based upon the only deeply rooted faith Lewis ever possessed, his faith in America, which he won a Nobel Prize for abusing.

World So Wide was serialized in the *Woman's Home Companion* in January and February, 1951, and published as a book in March. The reviews were elegies: the author had died in Rome on the tenth of January, in exile and alone.

[25] Serge Hughes, "From Main Street to the World So Wide," *Commonweal*, LIII (1951), 650.

8. The Author, the Critics, and the Nightmare World

IN HIS DISCUSSION of *Elmer Gantry*, as we have seen, Mark Schorer presents a compelling image of Sinclair Lewis as a novelist trapped in his own hallucination of the world as a trap. It is the central contention of many critics of Lewis that he was inescapably and irrevocably bound to the life he denounced; the most influential early statement of this is T. K. Whipple's paradoxical conclusion that Lewis was the most successful critic of American society because he was himself the best proof that his charges were just.[1] In similar vein Perry Miller wrote that when he saw Lewis abroad and thought of his relationship to *Dodsworth*, he realized with a start that Lewis was involved in the book not so much triumphantly as hopelessly: he had not mastered Dodsworth but presented him, and now was forced to re-enact him. In fact, when he flung five-thousand-lire notes about in a Florentine restaurant he was less like Dodsworth than like Babbitt on a spree.[2]

[1] T. K. Whipple, *Spokesman* (New York: Appleton, 1928), p. 228.
[2] Perry Miller, "The Incorruptible Sinclair Lewis," *Atlantic Monthly*, CLXXXVII (April 1951), 31.

For Maxwell Geismar, the real fascination of Lewis's career lies precisely in the fact that in the end he is so completely at one with his subject. That subject is not America, but *his* America—his middle-class fantasy of life in America. There are perhaps elements of fantasy in Geismar's own projection of life in the United States—particularly in his emphasis on the deterioration of the hinterland, the appalling nature of the industrial order, the overwhelming importance of the cartels, and the quick passing of the middle-class empire—but he does establish how narrow Lewis's vision was. There is really no upper class in his novels, nor does he attempt to project a single working-class figure of any dimension. He is completely involved with the middle-middle portion of America. But the middle class he portrays, Geismar contends, is without cultural roots, without a home life, without religion, without an economic status, and without a historical context; full of the manners, habits, and idioms of the United States as his writing may be, it captures little of its reality. And where in the whole range of Lewis's novels, Geismar asks, is there a view of life which would sustain a novelist's belief in life, or even in his own novels? Without cultural roots or abiding human values, he wanders homeless between a hinterland with which he feels no ties and an industrial order with which he cannot come to grips.[3]

Following Geismar, T. R. Fyvel emphasizes Lewis's rigid narrowness of range and declares that he has really only one subject—the thriving, philistine, middle-class society from which he sprang. He calls special attention to the nightmarish quality of the Zenith scene. It is a world not only of non-art and non-culture, but also of

[3] This view of Lewis is presented in both *The Last of the Provincials* (Boston: Houghton Mifflin, 1949) and *American Moderns* (London: W. H. Allen, 1958).

non-security and non-love. The characters live on the suffrance of unknown financial forces; one false step can bring ruin. They have almost no family relationships to lean on; it is part of the nightmare that the figures should be utterly solitary. The psychological struggle depicted in Lewis's novels of the early twenties is unchanging: on the one side is a demonic American society from which there is no escape, and on the other is a hero or heroine who is completely isolated. Comparing Babbitt's unsuccessful attempt at revolt with that of Winston Smith in *Nineteen Eighty-Four*, Fyvel sees the horrors of Orwell's Airstrip One as only a projection or development of the horrors of Zenith.[4]

Is Lewis's fantasy of life in America all that terrifying? The emphasis on the loneliness of the individual might make it seem so. For Lewis, the clichés about American fellowship and the warmth of American home life simply are not true. In spite of loudmouthed assertions that we are all pals together and sentimental references to the little woman and the kids, the individual is essentially alone and afraid. Consequently Babbitt's ordinary world is truly a nightmare world. Nevertheless, the comparison of Zenith to Airstrip One has only to be made for it to be seen as preposterous; surely Fyvel, Geismar, and Schorer exaggerate Lewis's pessimism. Perhaps the purest Lewis is the man Schorer describes; outliving his success and his reputation, parted from family and friends, dying miserably among foreigners, he was evidently a man who found no escape from the dilemmas of life. But the critics who see his fictional world as a nightmare one are following the logic of his premises to conclusions to which he took them only sometimes, not invariably; perhaps if he had been more consistent, he would have

[4] T. R. Fyvel, "Martin Arrowsmith and His Habitat," *New Republic*, CXXXIII (July 18, 1955), 16–18.

been gloomier. Yet there is one slogan from *Nineteen Eighty-Four* which epitomizes his life: Freedom is Slavery.

Discussing Faulkner's return to faith in *A Fable*, Maxwell Geismar writes that Faulkner

> belonged to that generation of the 1920's which grew up to scorn the society around them but which was forced, somewhere around middle life, to fall back upon it as a central source of moral support. The later books of Sinclair Lewis are false and flat precisely because of this dilemma. What Lewis had satirized without full comprehension he tried to apotheosize without conviction.[5]

With a sigh of relief Geismar turns from the contemplation of the mid-century drift toward conformity to recall the pioneering accomplishments of Theodore Dreiser in the early 1900's. Battling against the self-styled custodians of public morals, Dreiser won the final victory in the long struggle for literary expression in the United States:

> This was the "coming of age," in Van Wyck Brooks's phrase, of the modern movement. For what has been called the "Sexual Revolution" in our native letters was actually, during this period, the freedom to discuss human character and human relationships in terms of those primary needs and drives which actually do determine our success or failure in life, which create our happiness and our follies.[6]

Resuming his attack on conformity, Geismar declares that the central tradition of American conscience and belief is one of social protest, and that dissent is the democratic condition. Surely Lewis upheld that tradition to a fault. When he said in his Nobel Prize speech that Dreiser's *Sister Carrie* came to house-bound and airless America like a great free Western wind, and gave it the first fresh air since Mark Twain and Whitman, he made his allegiance

[5] *American Moderns*, p. 12.
[6] *Ibid.*, p. 23.

plain. His novels, read consecutively, do not show the basic change in outlook Geismar suggests; from first to last his attitude remains much the same. Though the biological naturalism which Dreiser espoused and Geismar also adopts was too narrow a creed for Lewis, if he apotheosized anything it was the American tradition of freedom and dissent. Nothing emerges more clearly from a study of his life than his desire to carry this freedom to absurd lengths—to be free from intellectual, moral, marital, and other consequences.

When we turn from the books to Lewis himself, trying to discover what he revealed about his underlying attitudes toward his novels and their subject matter, we find that his public personality often gets in the way. He was a man in the news, constantly giving interviews or making pronouncements; and like those of most public figures, his comments were affected by the impression which he wished to create at the particular time. He was capable, therefore, of describing himself at one time as a romantic escapist and at another as a careful chronicler of domestic rows. Nevertheless, his statements, if they are examined with care, offer useful clues as to his intentions. He often denied being a reformer; once in doing so he contrasted himself with Upton Sinclair: "'Upton has little remedies. I'm the diagnostician. I don't know what to do about anything. I'm not a reformer. I really don't care.' He excepted only 'Kingsblood Royal' .... 'Well,' he says, 'maybe I did care there, but not in the others.'" [7] But elsewhere he suggested that Upton Sinclair was no more emotionally involved in the writing of *The Jungle* than he was in the writing of *Main Street*; he suspected that both of them wrote their books "because it tickled their sense of mischief to write thus," and that when they found their

[7] Joseph Barry, "Sinclair Lewis, 65 and Far from Main Street," New York *Times Magazine*, February 2, 1950, pp. 13, 27.

fulminations ineffective both of them probably went on to other manners and themes without much grief.[8] Perhaps he was speaking in more serious vein when he told Leonard Feinberg that he thought satire could be moral, amoral, or immoral; he took Mencken as an example of an amoral satirist, but he refused to be put in the same category himself: "I am a hedonistic missionary. I am irritated by the fact that people could be so much happier than they are."[9] From these various statements, we can distill at least this much: Lewis was irritated by many things which he observed in his society, he wanted to convince people that they could lead fuller and happier lives than they were leading, and he did not—for the most part—prescribe remedies or therapeutic measures for individual or social ailments but stuck to the necessary preliminary work of diagnosing them.

Of course, he went too far when he said that, except in *Kingsblood Royal*, he had not really cared about the situations in his novels; apparently at this moment it suited him to present an image of lofty unconcern. Still the question of how much he really cared is open to dispute. He once told Allen Austin, "I'm not a cynic. I'm an old evangelist—a moral evangelist preaching to my people."[10] The books, however, have convinced many readers that he viewed his people with very little sympathy. John Farrar declared that Lewis saw life as a circus parade of the things he hated; he made no attempt to understand these animals, for if he did so they would cease to serve his ends.[11] T. K. Whipple said that detestation had barbed Lewis's satire and tipped it with venom; he was

[8] Leonard Feinberg, *The Satirist: His Temperament, Motivation, and Influence* (Ames: Iowa State University Press, 1963), p. 14.

[9] *Ibid.*, p. 36.

[10] Allen Austin, "An Interview with Sinclair Lewis," *University of Kansas City Review*, XX (1958), 204.

[11] John Farrar, ed., *The Literary Spotlight* (New York: Doran, 1924), p. 37.

"as watchful as a wild animal on the lookout for its foes, or as a Red Indian in the enemy's country." [12] Indicating his agreement with Whipple, Robert Cantwell called attention to Lewis's detachment from the scene he viewed and the heartlessness of his approach. [13]

Yet Lewis said that he loved the Babbitts and could even love Gantry. William Rose Benét testified to Lewis's concern for his fellow man with his story of how he and Lewis once met a traveling salesman and Lewis drew the man out in conversation, entering right into his life, while Benét sat disapproving. "That's the trouble with you, Bill," said Lewis afterwards, "you regard him as *hoi polloi*, he doesn't even represent the cause of labor or anything dramatic—but I understand that man—by God, I love him." Benét also told how Lewis used to turn from intense hilarity,

> turn as grave and didactic as a Baptist minister and proceed to lay down the moral law, according to his own highly individual ideas, with an almost snarling earnestness that seemed to bode hell-fire for the unbelievers. It appeared as if Shelley himself could never have been more deeply stirred by the injustices and tyrannies of the economic order . . . . [14]

He did not always view his neighbor, then, with a lofty detachment and a cold heartlessness. One of the most vivid episodes testifying to the contrary was undoubtedly that described by Frazier Hunt, of Lewis standing in tears in the Glasgow slums and cursing the society and the religions which permitted such poverty. [15] As mentioned

[12] *Spokesmen*, p. 219.

[13] Robert Cantwell, "Sinclair Lewis," *New Republic*, LXXXVIII (1936), 299.

[14] William Rose Benét, "The Earlier Lewis," *Saturday Review of Literature*, X (January 20, 1934), 421–422.

[15] This incident is related by Hunt in his *One American and His Attempt at Education* (New York: Simon and Schuster, 1938), pp. 252–253.

earlier, at the height of his enthusiasm for his labor novel Lewis wrote a pamphlet defending the cause of strikers in a Southern mill town; and at about the same time he took part in protest meetings in the Pittsburgh area on behalf of a miner, Salvatore Accorsi, who had been accused of murdering a state trooper. Yet his interest in the downtrodden was neither consistent nor sustained; furthermore, although he could occasionally espouse a humanitarian cause, it is doubtful that he could love human beings for any length of time. Beside Dorothy Thompson's assertion that it was impossible for even those closest to him to tell whether he cared for them or not, we can put Paul de Kruif's statement that, while he owed a great deal to Lewis, "that great satirist's contempt for certain human weaknesses among plain people was something I could not imitate because it was something I did not feel." [16] It seems probable that he had a greater affection for his compatriots than many of his critics thought, but much less than he, in warmly expansive moods, sometimes professed.

"While Lewis could be called *immature* as both man and writer," says Sheldon Grebstein, "immaturity launches satire. The immature reaction is immediate, intense, rebellious; the mature man is deliberate, resigned, accepting." [17] There is no question, first of all, that Lewis was rebellious. Dorothy Thompson said that his reaction to frustrations was to hit out at those who cared most for him, and for whom he cared most; she spoke as well of his flaring and cruel temper, and of his way of dealing blows with words of mockery, vituperation, and scorn. It is certainly possible that he enjoyed giving displays of temperament; Vincent Sheean writes that he loved

[16] Paul de Kruif, *The Sweeping Wind* (New York: Harcourt, Brace, 1962), p. 159.

[17] Sheldon Grebstein, *Sinclair Lewis*, United States Authors Series (New York: Twayne, 1962), p. 155.

getting angry in a righteous cause. Immaturity, however, does not launch mature and sophisticated satire, satire employing the full range of weapons in the satirist's armory. Pope was a waspish person who undoubtedly reacted swiftly and intensely to any slights upon himself; yet his reaction, as it was expressed in satire, was a controlled one. He could be called neither resigned nor accepting, but he was deliberate—he must have held his anger firmly in check as he spun a web of the utmost intricacy for his intended victim. For Lewis, on the other hand, the writing of a novel was a sustained, intense, and concentrated labor; it could be, or could appear to be, the sustained expression of an angry mood. Moreover, he felt so strongly—for the time being—and he wrote so energetically that he may sometimes have made his distaste appear greater than it actually was. At any rate, he did not often give an impression of tolerance, charity, and humility. Walter Lippmann thought, for example, that only for a moment in *Main Street* did Lewis avoid self-righteousness and show some courtesy for the souls of other people.[18] Some satirists have had the ability to appear calm and dispassionate—capable of an objective estimate of whatever it was they were attacking; such detachment was foreign to Lewis's temperament. His strength lay in force and persuasiveness, not in Olympian serenity.

Reacting perhaps against the opinion that he distorted and exaggerated for the purpose of satire, Lewis sometimes maintained that he only wanted to get the facts right. He once wrote, "I don't make exposés. If I happen to write things as I see them, and people don't like it, that's not my fault. Why doesn't someone call *The Bridge of San Luis Rey* an exposé of Peruvian bridge builders?"[19]

[18] *Men of Destiny* (New York: Macmillan, 1927), p. 78.
[19] Feinberg, *The Satirist*, p. 291.

As we have seen, he called himself a diagnostician. From the first he had the journalist's or documentary writer's impulse to find out all he could about a situation and present his interpretation of it. His long discussion of Carl Ericson's origins and significance is like a news magazine feature story on aviators or astronauts, based as it is on observation of a certain type of person, and only slightly fictionalized. The ability to sum up or diagnose a situation in the way Lewis does is in some ways anti-fictional, as Grant Overton wrote in 1925; he remarked further that "there is a strain in Sinclair Lewis which allies him to the statistician and the census-taker."[20] In his concern for accuracy, he sometimes allowed his notebooks to disgorge too much of their contents, while the story stood still. But this at least was the defect of a virtue. Martin Light stresses the importance of the scene in *Main Street* where Carol unpacks and as she does so, begins to learn that the idyllic picture found in novels dealing with village life is untrue; going to the window "with a purely literary thought of village charm—hollyhocks and lanes and apple-cheeked cottagers," she is confronted with the side of the Seventh-Day Adventist Church, "a plain clapboard wall of sour liver colour."[21] Lewis wanted to present an unillusioned view of that segment of America which he took as the subject for a particular novel.

Upton Sinclair had little remedies, and Wells had great ones; but Lewis, in preaching his gospel of hedonism, placed more emphasis on the negative than on the positive side. From time to time he made practical recommendations—in *Ann Vickers* there are suggestions for prison reform, in *Kingsblood Royal* for the improvement of race relations, and so on. But a Lewis novel is not likely to propose a

[20] Grant Overton, "The Salvation of Sinclair Lewis," *Bookman*, LXI (1925), 182.

[21] Martin Light, "A Study of Characterization in Sinclair Lewis's Fiction" (Ph.D. dissertation, University of Illinois, 1960), p. 72.

specific course of action; the positive element in it is more likely to be represented by a certain type of man, a man combining practical action with a worthy ideal. Arrowsmith is such a man; Dodsworth, Frank Shallard in *Elmer Gantry*, and Aaron Gadd in *The God-Seeker* are others; so, in a way, is Fred Cornplow, since he is described as the eternal doer, and to his class of people are credited most of the inventions and discoveries which have taken place since the building of the pyramids. Like Wells and Veblen, Lewis wondered how the enormous progress in science and technology could be made to bring about a great leap forward by the whole of humanity. Perhaps by research work or social work or the design of touricars or the building of new types of houses, his heroes are contributing to that advance; at any rate, they are men of action. Whipple thought that Lewis was one of the shock troops attacking American practicality; though he said this before *Dodsworth* and *Work of Art* conclusively proved him wrong, Lewis had always sided with practicality, from *Our Mr. Wrenn* on. Rebecca West had reason to wish that he would sit still so that life could make a deeper impression on him; neither he nor his heroes could have been farther from the contemplative's precept, "Be still and know."

Lewis stated the main theme of his sermons in his Nobel Prize speech, when he referred to himself as "a writer whose most anarchistic assertion has been that America, with all her wealth and power, has not yet produced a civilization good enough to satisfy the deepest wants of human creatures." [22] His subject was thus the frustration of possibilities. The positive goals of his more admirable characters may be somewhat confused, but invariably we are told what hampers them or ties them down. Such novels as *Arrowsmith* show that American

[22] *The Man from Main Street: Collected Essays and Other Writings, 1904–1950*, ed. Harry E. Maule and Melville H. Cane (New York: Random House, 1953), p. 6.

society places many types of obstacle in the way of the enterprising individual, not the least of these being its criteria for success. Dodsworth, displaying his contempt for the leisure-class symbols of distinction prized by people like his wife Fran and Joyce Lanyon (in *Arrowsmith*), says, "I'm a builder. I don't have to depend on any title or clothes or social class or anything else to be distinctive." [23] Too often, apparently, Americans have been deceived by false values; they have chosen the artificial over the real, the insubstantial over the solid. Lewis chronicles the triumph of mediocrity.

Perhaps the greatest impediment to progress and the greatest threat to the level of culture America had achieved was Main Street's injunction, "Be thou dull!" Mencken's war on herd morality and conformity was Lewis's war; he would probably have accepted Mencken's estimate that "among a hundred Americans, at least ninety-five will be found to hold exactly the same views upon all subjects that they can grasp at all . . . ." [24] Herbert Croly's call for critics who would "stab away at the gelatinous mass of popular indifference, sentimentality, and complacency" was a demand, Grebstein says, which Lewis pre-eminently met. [25] To Lewis and Mencken, however, in the twenties the mass was not entirely gelatinous; the fundamentalist part of it possessed limbs and a will, so that it was an active and menacing phenomenon. Mencken thought that the United States might very well achieve the utopia dreamed of by "seven millions of Christian bumpkins" and that civilization might "gradu-

[23] Arthur B. Coleman discusses this in his "The Genesis of Social Ideas in Sinclair Lewis" (Ph.D. dissertation, New York University, 1954), pp. 169–170.

[24] H. L. Mencken, *Prejudices*, Fourth Series (New York: Knopf, 1924), p. 26.

[25] This passage, from Croly's *The Promise of American Life*, published in 1909, is discussed by Grebstein, *Sinclair Lewis*, p. 165.

ally become felonious everywhere in the Republic . . . ."
To the reply that such fears were surely exaggerated, he
declared that since the triumph of prohibition there was
no end to the forms of tyranny which might be imposed.[26]
Pope's fear of a reign of chaos or of universal dullness was
Lewis's fear too. In *It Can't Happen Here* he compiled a
long list of evidence to show that America, though it
called itself the land of the free, was ripe for dictatorship.
Huey Long's one-man rule of Louisiana, the strength of
Father Coughlin's following, the toleration of graft and
racketeering, the depredations of the Ku Klux Klan, the
influence of William Jennings Bryan in getting state
legislatures to pass laws forbidding the teaching of
evolution, the popularity of evangelists such as Billy
Sunday and Aimee Semple McPherson, the arrest of
labor leaders, the seeming American enthusiasm for
lynchings—these and many more items are adduced in
support of Doremus Jessup's statement "God knows
there's been enough indication we *can* have tyranny in
America."

This perspective explains Lewis's extraordinary distrust
of organizations. Wells felt that progress could be effected
only through such elite groups as his Samurai; but as
Lewis saw and described it, even the most harmless local
boosters' club harbored a gang of potential gauleiters.
Everything that is worth while, Doremus reflects, has
been accomplished by the free, inquiring, critical spirit.
For Lewis, this spirit is the real defense of liberty; he has
little understanding of the ineffectiveness of individuals
unless they combine, and he considers that any organization they do form, no matter how worthy the purpose
for which it is conceived, will exercise illegitimate pressure
to make others act in conformity with its conception of
how they ought to act. The figure from the American

[26] Mencken, *Prejudices*, Fourth Series, pp. 58–59.

past who gripped his imagination was the independent pioneer; he had more respect for the virtues of this image than he had for any political or other institutions in the American heritage. Naturally, he disliked appeals and manifestoes; probably one of the few with which he would have sympathized was the famous one which appeared in the first issue of the *American Mercury*, declaring that the editors had heard no voice from the burning bush, that they would not offer any sovereign balm for the world's ills, and that they doubted whether any such balm would ever be found. Doremus Jessup, believing that it is the highest wisdom to profess allegiance to nothing except a skeptical, inquiring spirit, would agree. In *The God-Seeker*, as Coleman points out, Aaron Gadd turns away from missionary work partly because it is too wrapped up in the zeal for reform to do any good; the lesson of the book is moderation, including moderation in one's beliefs and plans, for man is limited in his vision and capabilities, his experience and his knowledge.[27]

Perhaps Lewis had reason, then, to describe himself, as he did in the autobiographical sketch he wrote for inclusion in Sherman's pamphlet, as "a rather nebulous radical." Near the end of his career he gave much the same advice as he had at the beginning. In *The Job*, after Mr. Fein has declared that all systems are choked with ignorance and clumsy, outworn methods, he puts change in such a long perspective that it seems the highest wisdom not to worry about it:

> "... It's taken the human race about five hundred thousand years to get where it is, and presumably it will take quite a few thousand more to become scientific or even to understand the need of scientific conduct of everything. I'm not at all sure that there's any higher wisdom than doing a day's work, and hoping the subway

[27] Coleman, "Genesis," p. 148.

will be a little less crowded next year, and in voting for the best possible man, and then forgetting all the Weltschmertz, and going to an opera . . ." [309].

In spite of his repeated endeavors to shock the middle class out of its complacency, Lewis continued to encourage it to look with suspicion on most possible means of intellectual, artistic, or moral advancement. In 1931 he wrote:

> If it is necessary to be Fabian in politics, to keep the reformers (left wing or rigid right) from making us perfect too rapidly, it is yet more necessary to be a little doubtful about the ardent souls who would sell Culture; and if the Tired Business Man is unlovely and a little dull, at least he is real, and we shall build only on reality.[28]

He could ridicule reformers just as enthusiastically as he could reactionaries; he could defend, as well as ridicule, comfortable catchwords and stock attitudes. His pious reiteration that virtue stands in the middle way is really an exhortation to mediocrity. It is likewise interesting to examine the references to science in Mr. Fein's speech. John Dewey distinguished two ways of viewing science—either as an intelligently controlled approach to nature, or as a kind of self-enclosed entity and end in itself, "a new theology of self-sufficient authoritatively revealed inherent and absolute Truth."[29] Clearly in the passage we have quoted, and in most places where he uses the term, Lewis's understanding of science is closer to the second than to the first meaning. It does not really serve for him as a means of analyzing and organizing experience in some meaningful way. Nor does he advocate any other tradition of human thought—

[28] "Minnesota, the Norse State," *The Man from Main Street*, p. 279.
[29] John Dewey, *Individualism Old and New* (New York: Minton, Balch, 1930), pp. 97–98.

a religious, philosophical, political, or other framework—
as a basis for a comprehensive view of man's situation. He
prized freedom above intellectual commitment, and made
facetiousness a substitute for reflection.

Reviewing Carl Van Doren's autobiography, *Three
Worlds*, in 1936, Lewis quoted with approval the following
passage: "If this were fiction I might say that I went into
a retreat to think things out. It still is history. I have
never in my life thought things out, nor have I known
anybody who ever did. I have always had to live them out,
thinking as I went along." [30] This discovery Lewis
commended "to all who are accustomed to go off and
brood about their incomparable wrongs, in the belief
that they will just 'begin to get things straight' before they
pop into the psychoanalyst's shop . . . ." Thinking things
out, in other words, is made to seem a neurotic or psy-
chotic activity; in the irony with which it is handled,
there is a provisional defense by Lewis of his own conduct
—it is apparently a grand and glorious thing to be
lacking in intellectual discrimination and consistency.

If the review of *Three Worlds* provides an example of
Lewis's refusal to formulate matters intellectually, he
still calls Van Doren a veteran of the Battle of Intellectual
Irritation which took place in the 1920's, "when the
jeering rebels led by such assorted anarchists as Mencken,
Millay and Masters, unlike except in alliteration, plunged
pitchfork or tuning fork into the tenderest exposures of
all who were rotund and respectable." [31] The alliteration,
the irony, the bantering superiority are intended to con-

[30] This review is reprinted in *The Man from Main Street*, pp. 129–134.
Cf. Henry F. May, *The End of American Innocence: A Study of the First Years
of Our Own Time, 1912–1917* (New York: Knopf, 1959), p. 219: "If the
Liberation had a characteristic doctrine, it was a simple and old one, very
close to the central assertion of earlier romantic periods, the assertion that
life transcends thought."

[31] *The Man from Main Street*, p. 129.

vey that the writer not only was on the right side in this battle but was fully aware of what was what. The clumsy joking and flippancy are carried on into the next sentence, where we are told that some of the literary guerrillas are dead, some have retired to suburban gardening, and "some have turned Bourbon." Nowhere in the review is there any indication that Lewis actually did know what the issues were; though he describes the battle as an intellectual one, he seems to recall nothing about it except his own side's war cries and the terms of abuse they used to hurl at the opposition.

In most of his other references to the intellectual disputes of his time, Lewis also takes refuge in rhetoric. This is true even when he discusses the influence of his great master, H. G. Wells; Wells had

> suggested to our young minds the gaudy fancy . . . that mankind can, by taking thought, by real education, acquire such . . . enchanted qualities as cheerfulness, kindness, honesty, plain decency, refusal to make ourselves miserable and guilty just to please some institution that for a century has been a walking and talking corpse.[32]

Even where he points out the necessity of taking thought, Lewis shows little disposition to take it himself. Although Wells flailed away at old institutions in his writing, he spent fully as much time elaborating on the forms which new ones should take; and of these there is no mention in Lewis's article. His restless impatience with all discipline, his hatred of prohibitions of any kind, made him conceive of happiness chiefly in terms of the removal of restrictions. The process of taking thought seems largely critical, destructive, and negative; it also seems to mean the flippant evasion of complexities rather than their serious discussion.

[32] "Our Friend, H. G.," *ibid.*, p. 247.

He once wrote that he asked only three utopian ideals for the Babbitts:

> that they should know a little more about history; that they should better comprehend the difference between Irish stew in America and fried mushrooms at Schoener's in Vienna; and that they should talk of the quest for God oftener than of the quest for the best carburetor.[33]

But his own view of history, when it was not simply a romantic vision of troubadours and damsels and knights in shining armor, resembled that of Mark Twain's Connecticut Yankee, looking at the medieval world and saying, "My, weren't they dumb?" In spite of the number of his trips abroad and the bland sophistication of his mention of a Viennese restaurant, he acquired only a superficial acquaintance with Europe; to the other evidence we have had on this score, we can add Vincent Sheean's declaration that Lewis did not really understand German, he found French incomprehensible, and he was never able to say the simplest Italian word correctly.[34] Finally, if he talked of the quest for God more often than he talked of the quest for a new carburetor, he talked of the two in the same terms. He trusted to facetiousness to get him by.

Lewis's mind, said Dorothy Thompson, was swift as light. But though it was capable of speed and extraordinary virtuosity, it was not capable of dealing with ideas in any profound way. Whipple called him a man of multiple personality, a man who "shifts his point of view so often that finally we come to wonder whether he has any."[35] De Kruif said that, whereas the scientific researcher is predominantly one-track, Lewis had infinite tracks mentally and emotionally—in fact no tracks, so

[33] "Mr. Lorimer and Me," *Nation*, CXXVII (1928), 81.

[34] *Dorothy and Red* (Boston: Houghton Mifflin, 1963), p. 211.

[35] Whipple, *Spokesmen*, p. 221.

that he was not like any wheeled vehicle, but rather like a jet out of control.[36] He resembled his own description of Edith Cortwright in *Dodsworth*:

> And she, she talked of many things. She was a reader of thick books, with a curiosity regarding life which drifted all round its circumference. She talked of Bertrand Russell and of insulin; of Stefan Zweig, American skyscrapers, and the Catholic Church. But she was neither priggish nor dogmatic. What interested her in facts and diagrams was the impetus they gave to her own imagination. Essentially she was indifferent whether the world was laboring towards Fascism or Bolshevism, toward Methodism or atheism [348].

If this was his conception of Dorothy Thompson's intellectuality, she herself marveled at the fact that Lewis read the newspapers chiefly in search of items to stimulate his imagination, without being concerned about the drift toward totalitarianism which she was so passionately combating. As Raymond Williams says in his discussion of Dickens, there is something juvenile about an airy unconcern with direction or system; what Lewis presents as a pattern of the mature mind is actually the retained position of an adolescent.[37] Although the disparagement of priggishness and dogmatism, together with the approval of Carl Van Doren's principle of living things out, seems to invoke a major American philosophical approach—pragmatism—a glance at John Dewey's *Individualism Old and New*, published the year after *Dodsworth*, will show what a watered-down version of pragmatism it is. The stereotyped idea of individuality which Dewey calls an empty thing is very close to Lewis's concept; and, on

---

[36] Grace Hegger Lewis, *With Love from Gracie: Sinclair Lewis: 1912–1925* (New York: Harcourt, Brace, 1955), pp. 231–232.

[37] Raymond Williams, *Culture and Society, 1780–1950* (London: Chatto and Windus, 1958), p. 96.

the other hand, though Lewis, like Dewey, is concerned with the frame in which individuality must exist and develop, he ridicules most of the definite social relationships and publicly acknowledged functions which Dewey says are the only foundation for an assured and integrated individuality. Adapting one's values to life situations means, for Dewey, not an avoidance of intellectual commitment, but a continuous exploration of its implications.[38]

Lewis's view of life is given the dignity of systematic formulation by Walter Fuller Taylor in his *History of American Letters*:

> It is a simple philosophy that Lewis proposes as a substitute for the standardized ethics which he attacks. He holds simply that an interesting life is better than a dull one, and that life is interesting in proportion as one outgrows a conventional, standardized mode of conduct, and lives with the object of satisfying his deepest desires and impulses. But Lewis does not propose an ignorant, altogether undisciplined realization of desire; he proposes an enlightened one. And enlightenment is to come wholly, if slowly, from fundamental research, particularly research in the natural sciences.[39]

But even this simple formulation is too elaborate. We look in vain for consistency and coherence in Lewis's thought. The desire for a disciplined and enlightened standard of conduct is undoubtedly to be found at times, but few of the consequences of such a standard are envisaged. Instead, Lewis puts his emphasis upon freedom, and his concept of it is so broad and ill-defined as to be almost a parody of any genuine idea of it. The concept could be invoked, for example, to defend in a noble and high-sounding way a line of conduct which had been decided

[38] *Individualism Old and New*, especially pp. 52–55, 78, 81, and 146.

[39] Walter Fuller Taylor, *A History of American Letters* (Boston: American Book Co., 1936), p. 390.

on. We have seen that Lewis refused the Pulitzer Prize with an eloquent statement that such prizes infringed upon the artist's freedom—even though he had previously intrigued for the Pulitzer and was currently intriguing for the Nobel Prize in every way he could. Similarly, his lofty refusal, in a statement he wrote for *La grande revue* in 1930,[40] to commit himself to any school or -ism shows him not really defending artistic liberty, but presenting a carefully cultivated image of himself.

From the first, the profession of writer meant for Lewis escape from conventional routine. But Grace Hegger Lewis suggests that this was not entirely salutary for him: " . . . isn't it possible that freedom like ours encouraged in Hal an independence which would brook no opposition, so that as fame and fortune grew he became a law unto himself . . . ?[41] His disregard for the social conventions grew—sometimes he may have been reacting against his wife's concern for them—and the stories about his behavior became notorious. It was not merely a matter of his going his own way; other people had to go his way too. Schorer calls attention to his psychological need for uncritical adulation; he would fly into a rage at the suggestion that something he had written needed revising. Perhaps the best illustrations of the imperious nature of his demands on others are the many examples of his making someone else drop his own plans and come with him to whatever place struck his fancy. The most famous fictional account of such an episode is Thomas Wolfe's in Chapters 33 through 37 of *You Can't Go Home Again*, where George Webber, after a long period of anticipation, meets Lloyd McHarg in London and suddenly finds himself McHarg's companion in grotesque vagabondage, driving

---

[40] See *From Main Street to Stockholm: Letters of Sinclair Lewis 1919–1930*, ed. Harrison Smith (New York: Harcourt, Brace, 1952), p. 289.

[41] *With Love from Gracie*, p. 134.

through the wilds of Surrey with one of the most distinguished American novelists slumped beside him in comatose oblivion.

The parody concept of freedom is particularly evident in Lewis's dealings with his first wife. In the midst of their marital difficulties in 1924, he was hypocritical enough to tell the reporters that they had worked out a perfectly satisfactory arrangement which left him free to travel as he pleased. Later on, when the decisive break occurred in 1926, his letters to his wife stress his need for independence, but his desire for a marriage relationship as well. He sees a future in which they will have separate establishments, "except for occasional vacations when we elope together," in which they will be able to see each other exactly as they see their other friends, "with no vexing claims," and in which each will have complete independence to live, drink, travel, and have love affairs. He cannot contemplate divorce or any other ugly break, but he knows that "unless the two Hawks, you and I, are left to fly absolutely as we desire," such a break will take place.[42] Denying his wife the stability of a home, confining her to the role of Joyful Companion, he could proclaim this a glorious emancipation.

Similarly, his compulsive need to escape could be represented, as it was to the reporters who interviewed him at the start of his trip into the northern wilds in 1924, as simply a desire to travel because he liked a change. Picturing himself as free from the ordinary tourist's urge to score points for visiting cathedrals or museums or to make startling conclusions concerning national characteristics, he concealed the fact that he had become a desperate wanderer. So Thomas Wolfe described him as wandering from place to place in Europe, looking for something, and taking the cure at Baden-Baden—a cure "for life-hunger,

[42] *Ibid.*, pp. 329–330.

for life-thirst, for life-triumph, for life-defeat, life-disillu-
sionment, life-loneliness, and life-boredom ....'' [43] As
Grace Hegger Lewis says, *The Trail of the Hawk* and *Free
Air* reveal his "apprehensive need to escape from orderly,
thought-stifling, conventional living." [44] When he was
waving the banner of freedom, he felt that he was in harmony with his own nature, his art, and his age; but if
conventional living was thought-stifling, escape from it
was not thought-provoking. His freedom was illusory; it
was as enslaving as convention. In *The Strange Necessity*,
Rebecca West made a comment on this to which we have
already referred: "If he would sit still so that life could
make any deep impression upon him, if he would attach
himself to the human tradition by occasionally reading a
book which would set him a standard of profundity, he
would give his genius a chance." [45]

If his freedom was slavery and self-deception, Schorer's,
Fyvel's, and Geismar's view of him as a man caught in a
trap seems borne out. He seems to have been fitted with
one of the most hampering mental and moral strait jackets
it would have been possible to devise. Yet something
escapes; we are forced to protest that this strait-jacketed
Lewis is not the real one, not the whole man. If we com-
pare him with another midwestern writer, F. Scott
Fitzgerald, we will see the need for qualification. In the
classic statement of American disillusionment at the end
of *The Great Gatsby*, Nick Carraway becomes aware of
"the old island that flowered once for Dutch sailors'
eyes—a fresh, green breast of the new world," and

[43] *You Can't Go Home Again* (Garden City: Sun Dial Press, 1942), p. 560.
[44] *With Love from Gracie*, p. 153.
[45] Quoted in *ibid.*, p. 112. Cf. Raymond H. Palmer, "The Nobel Jury
Judges America," *Christian Century*, XLVII (1930), 1448, on the illusion
that irresponsible freedom is the gateway to a rich life and on Lewis's
failure to become acquainted in any real sense with any of the great
disciplines of humanity.

thinks of the last and greatest of all human dreams: "for one transitory enchanted moment man must have held his breath in the presence of this continent, . . . face to face for the last time in history with something commensurate to his capacity for wonder." [46] The influence of these dreams and the myths they engendered have been traced in such recent studies as Henry Nash Smith's *Virgin Land*, discussing the impact of the vast continent upon the consciousness of Americans up to the time of Frederick Jackson Turner's formulation of his frontier thesis; R. W. B. Lewis's *The American Adam*, describing the nineteenth-century conception of the American as an Adamic figure, a figure of heroic innocence and vast potentialities poised at the start of a new history; and Charles L. Sanford's *The Quest for Paradise*, interpreting American history and culture in terms of a dominant myth of an Eden to be rediscovered. When he carries the story on into modern times, Sanford expresses the view that

> The main theme in American literature during the twentieth century has been the dispossession from paradise, America's abandonment of the security and innocence of an earlier day through some essentially sinful act, an act most frequently associated with industrialism and the commercial ethic. The core of this disillusionment has been the Middle West.

His list of disenchanted Midwesterners includes E. W. Howe, Edgar Lee Masters, Zona Gale, Sherwood Anderson, Sinclair Lewis, T. S. Eliot, Theodore Dreiser, James T. Farrell, John Dos Passos, Ernest Hemingway, Ring Lardner, and F. Scott Fitzgerald. Yet he considers that "the myth of Eden survived in the moral indignation which fired their bitterness," and they "sought to raise a new Garden out of the dust of the Wasteland." [47]

[46] *The Great Gatsby* (New York: Scribner's, 1953), p. 182.

[47] *The Quest for Paradise* (Urbana: University of Illinois Press, 1961), p. 255.

For Fitzgerald, the disillusionment was complete; the dream was already behind Gatsby, "somewhere back in that vast obscurity beyond the city, where the dark fields of the republic rolled on under the night"; and the book closes on an ironic vision of people rowing against the current, stretching to grasp the orgastic future which recedes before them year by year. Lewis, however, never lost sight of the dream; we have seen that he conjured it up in novels written at every stage of his career. It provided him with the vision of the one Eden of which he could conceive; the one great objective worth striving for, in an otherwise barren world, was an enlightened and prosperous America. Though at times he viewed its prospects pessimistically, his basic outlook was not one of disillusionment, but of romantic optimism. Even in ridiculing this optimism he added a defense of it, so that when he described his own short stories as "so optimistic, so laudatory . . . so certain that large, bulky Americans are going to do something and do it quickly and help the whole world by doing it," he added to the ironic description the thought that perhaps such optimism is an authentic part of American life. Then he confessed that he himself, though he had been labeled a satirist and a realist, was actually a romantic medievalist of the most incurable sort.[48]

It is noteworthy that the part of America which he most often attacked was that for which he had the greatest hope. His hawklike man, seeking the land of adventure, finds it in the Midwest; no matter what its faults, it is still the land of opportunity. His basic conception is not of people hopelessly entrapped, but of people whose progress toward a glorious future has somehow been impeded. His objective was similar to that which Sanford ascribes to Hamlin Garland: to hasten the age of beauty and peace

[48] Introduction to *Selected Short Stories* (Garden City: Doubleday, Doran, 1935); reprinted in *The Man from Main Street*, pp. 218–219.

by delineating the ugliness and sordidness of the present.[49] "We've somehow drifted away from our early teachings," Lewis said to Allen Austin. "We've forgotten the ideals of our fathers."[50] Thus his books, paradoxical as it may seem, represent a call for a return to the heroic virtues of the pioneers so progress toward the fulfillment of the American dream can continue. Lewis was never, as Carl Van Doren would have it, the voice of the liberal decade before 1929, never the intellectual reformer, never really the urbane analyst of civilizations. But he was always a romantic who curiously located his romantic dreams in the very region he satirized—the American Midwest.

Many critics have seen Lewis as entrapped in a manner similar to but slightly different from the one just described—as condemned, by his deficiency in creative imagination, to being nothing more than a faithful reproducer of the middle-class world. Usually this type of criticism will assert that Lewis's books have the reality of a waxworks museum: everything is lifelike, but nothing is real, especially the people. In his review of *Main Street*, Francis Hackett contended that Lewis's impulse to document and categorize prevented the development of his characters. All the various types—the Booster, the "gentleman-hen" who loves art, the self-effacing millionaires who take themselves and their Gopher Prairie atmosphere to Pasadena—are pinioned and classified, but in the process their personalities are lost. Will Kennicott, for example, does all the things which ought to make him real—amputates in a farm house at night, goes hunting in an elaborate outfit, talks about cars in slangy terms, and so on. But these do not establish the inner life of Will or give us that rapport with him which is the

---

[49] *The Quest for Paradise*, p. 256.
[50] Austin, "Interview," 201.

triumph of imagination. Likewise, Lewis has not enough concern with the individuality of Carol; he fails to give her a full personality because he is too much interested in her as a specimen.[51]

Lewis Mumford praised Lewis's surface accuracy and lamented that there was nothing beyond it.[52] Lewis's satires, Mumford writes, have the value of photography; his best satiric effects are obtained simply by holding in sharp focus something that actually exists, and forgetting for the moment all that historically or spatially qualifies the object. All the phenomena that Lewis shows are real, but by the nature of his method he is unable to depict a more comprehensive reality. E. M. Forster also used the term "photographer" in his chapter on Lewis in *Abinger Harvest*.[53] Like Mumford, he did not use it in an entirely disparaging way: he declared that it was no mean achievement to be a successful photographer, he praised the quickness of Lewis's eye, and he stated that through Lewis thousands who previously knew nothing of the Midwest were now very much aware of it. However, he called photography an occupation for the young, and he made it apparent that he thought of Lewis as one of the quick, spontaneous writers who lose their spontaneity— the type which has nothing to do but reproduce, either sharply or dimly.

Predictably, Virginia Woolf also lamented—or somewhat delectably relished—Lewis's preoccupation with the superficial. Comparing him with the soft and shell-less Anderson, she wrote that Lewis's books were all shell, so that the only question was whether he had left any

[51] F[rancis] H[ackett], "God's Country," *New Republic*, XXV (December 1, 1920), 20–21.

[52] Lewis Mumford, "The America of Sinclair Lewis," *Current History*, XXXIII (1931), 529–533.

[53] E. M. Forster, *Abinger Harvest* (New York: Harcourt, Brace, 1936), pp. 129 ff.

room for the snail. Zenith was the most complete model of a city ever built: "We turn on the taps and the water runs; we press a button and cigars are lit and beds warmed." [54] But in such an atmosphere intimacy is impossible; all that a writer of Lewis's powers can do is be unflinchingly accurate. Similarly, Joseph Wood Krutch wrote that Lewis employed the aims and methods of the documentary best sellers, "pseudo-fiction in which everything is recognizable as true but with the fidelity of a waxwork and no suggestion of any sort of autonomous life." [55]

Perhaps the most thorough discussion of Lewis's novels from this standpoint is that by Robert Cantwell. [56] Attempting to be as precise as he could about Lewis's merits and shortcomings, he described him as one of the most plunging and erratic of American novelists, but also one of the most ambitious, for on the strength of *Main Street*, he had visualized a cycle of novels comparable in scope to those of Balzac and Zola. He had planned nothing less than a catalog of the interwoven worlds of American society—the small towns and cities, business, science, religion, education, labor, professional politics. This spacious and inclusive project, bolder than anything previously attempted by an American novelist, signified the end of the narrowness and swimming-hole sentimentality which had characterized American fiction. But Cantwell questioned whether it was the conception of a novelist who understood the nature of his art. "Apparently Lewis thought at the beginning of his career," he wrote, "that the muse could be embraced and laid aside at will, and that she would not take her revenge by addling

[54] Virginia Woolf, *The Moment* (London: Hogarth Press, 1947), pp. 97–100.

[55] "Sinclair Lewis," *Nation*, CLXXII (1951), 179–180.

[56] "Sinclair Lewis," *New Republic*, LXXXVIII (1936), 298–301.

the wits of her ravisher . . . ."[57] Lewis's vision of a broad survey of American life was one which a super-competent hack writer might conceive, a writer who thought of his writing in terms of the accomplishment of a foreknown task, who felt that it lay within his powers to "collect material" without becoming emotionally entangled in it or acting in response to its implications.

Was Lewis's approach to writing somewhat mechanical? Did he think he could turn his art to anything, rather than have it reflect the pressure of living which played through him and on him? The criticism seems supported by the facts that Lewis usually began a novel as he would a research project and that into all his novels he poured accumulations of detail far in excess of what the plot demanded or allowed. Furthermore, what Overton called his "utter compositeness" is often in evidence in his depiction of character. He conveys the nature of a person's life by a montage of details—snapshots of the man in various attitudes, of people around him, of his home and place of business. He reproduces the person's utterances just as he does the physical appearance and environment; there is some point to Dorothy Canfield Fisher's exclamation, "Really Sinclair Lewis is a phonograph record!" In conversation the man exhibits the range of his prejudices and the clichés which are his substitute for knowledge. Often there is a fairly pedestrian accumulation of similar types, such as the catalog of Americans abroad in *World So Wide*. The development of a novel may likewise proceed by a chapter-by-chapter, point-by-point exposition of its theme. At times Lewis seems the most literal-minded and unimaginative of novelists.

Still the main point of this criticism might be that Lewis's characters are dummies placed in realistic settings. If this is the case, it might be defended. When his

[57] *Ibid.*, p. 299.

interest was chiefly in the satiric possibilities of a situation, it was sufficient for him to delineate characters who represented various types of folly. For this, depth of personality was not needed or desirable. The basic pattern of novels like *Babbitt*, *Elmer Gantry*, and *The Man Who Knew Coolidge* is the presentation, in typical life situations, of a character who is a caricature of ordinary humanity. An alternative pattern, that of *Main Street* and *Arrowsmith* is the parade of a number of such caricatures or half-men past a character representing a more fully developed humanity and a more enlightened point of view. There was no need for Lewis to endow the Holabirds and Pickerbaughs with any great complexity: it was sufficient for them to represent some of the temptations to abandon a worthy purpose or some of the obstacles to its achievement which American society puts in the way of a man like Arrowsmith. Vernon Parrington praises rather than condemns Lewis for filling his pages with the doings of automata, the simulacra of men. As he sees it, to do so is entirely consistent with Lewis's attack on a society from which life has departed; he is conscious of sketching in a morgue.[58]

Lewis's morgue, however, is hopping with life. Parrington is as wrong in his way as Whipple and Cantwell, Forster and Virginia Woolf are in theirs. Where we expect pallid and lifeless creatures—we are told in one book that this is the world of the quiet dead—we find astonishingly vital grotesques. They may be specimens of various types of folly, they may not be rounded personalities who are capable of surprising us, but they are active and exuberant. What Parrington views as a morgue is for Lewis

[58] Vernon L. Parrington, *Our Own Diogenes*, University of Washington Chapbooks, No. 5 (Seattle: University of Washington Press, 1927). Also in *Main Currents in American Thought*, Vol. III (New York: Harcourt, Brace, 1930), pp. 360–369.

the home of "the most fascinating and exotic people in the world—the Average Citizens of the United States ...."[59] Instead of being dummies which occupy the places carefully prepared for them, Lewis's characters leap out of the frame and begin to talk and act as though they were responding to the impulses of their own natures instead of to the manipulations of their author. Cabell was right when he protested that Lewis's verisimilitude has been overstressed; he may have put too much emphasis on the other extreme when he said that the pleasure he derived from Lewis's characters was that of seeing a minimum of reality exaggerated into Brobdingnagian incredibility, and that in each character there was a single grain of truth which had budded into a gaudy efflorescence of the impossible, but at least he emphasized that the characters were imaginative productions.[60]

Although facts and figures got into Lewis's novels and sometimes overwhelmed them, they were nevertheless intended as aids to imaginative activity rather than substitutes for it. When he had saturated himself in an atmosphere, Lewis relied on his creative imagination to supply him with characters who would make the story real for his readers. Ordinarily he began with an idea, he told Allen Austin, but he said that he never undertook the writing until he had found a person who represented the idea.[61] One of the reasons for his never writing the labor novel, for which he had collected more than enough material, was that he could not "see" his labor leader. Furthermore, one is tempted to say of a Lewis novel, as of a Scott novel, that it contains two types of characters— the real and the unreal—and that paradoxically the most unreal are those most grounded in reality. A physician

[59] *The Man from Main Street*, p. 55.
[60] James Branch Cabell, *Some of Us* (New York: McBride, 1930), p. 69.
[61] Austin, "Interview," 205.

of conventional type such as Will Kennicott, a character embodying a reasonable point of view such as Frank Shallard or Paul Riesling, is fairly obviously put together from pieces which fit only too well. Such a character possesses a smaller degree of reality than the imagined— sometimes fantastically imagined—mythological and typological creations which Lewis evoked in the manner of Dickens. Though these characters usually represented attitudes which Lewis wanted to satirize, their garrulousness, their blissful ignorance, their back-slapping camaraderie made them magnificently comic.

Therefore, though he probably had a much greater desire than Dickens did to give a realistic account of the life around him, reality was often only a jumping-off place for his fancy. "A great work of art is a formal creation, not a parcel of information," wrote Herbert J. Muller, "and what many of our realists are recording so conscientiously is simply the forms of our confusion . . . ." [62] Lewis was one of the realists he had in mind—one of those who, in his view, handed out parcels of information, dealt chiefly in evidences of contemporary instability, and were incapable of formal excellence in their writing. Yet Lewis escapes this definition, as he does so many others. At his best, his imagination and his comic sense took him beyond the limits Muller describes; he made of Babbitt, as Sherard Vines writes, a colossal Humor.[63] At his best, too, he partially fulfilled one of Muller's criteria for great works of art—that of intensifying and ordering our whole experience. Muller distinguished between writers like Shakespeare and Hardy, with whom we look down the whole stupendous vista of life and who leave us brooding over the eternal questions of human existence, and those

---

[62] *Modern Fiction: A Study of Values* (New York: Funk and Wagnalls, 1937), p. 46.

[63] *A Hundred Years of English Literature* (London: Duckworth, 1950), p. 262.

who leave us chiefly with some notions about the imperfections of the social order. As I have tried to indicate, Lewis leaves us brooding over some questions which have not lost their point in a changing society. The question of whether Babbitt, content and childish in his tub, or Elmer Gantry, solemnly marking quotable passages in Longfellow and Ella Wheeler Wilcox, is the end result of democratic culture is a question which we shall always have with us.

If we consider, more narrowly, Lewis's meaning to the United States, we can see that he provided an interpretation, not of the segments of the population which Fitzgerald or Hemingway or Faulkner interpreted, but of the vast majority of the whole population: he did try to generalize the soul of the nation. We have noted many instances of failure of artistic control in his attempts to deal with this enormous subject. We have also found good reason to doubt whether he possessed the intellectual and spiritual capacity ever to handle it satisfactorily. We have seen too that he suffered from curious inhibitions; waging war on complacency, he was himself complacent— encouraged by the kind of influences which Geismar admires to be complacent in dissent. Yet he went far beyond most of his more illustrious contemporaries in raising questions of enduring importance to the national life; for this reason, it is difficult to think that his four or five best novels will ever be forgotten. Probably no one has described more graphically the secular pilgrimage of twentieth-century America—the hopes which sustain it and the hazards which face it on its journey to the fulfillment of its destiny.

Selected Bibliography

WORKS BY SINCLAIR LEWIS

Novels

Our Mr. Wrenn. New York: Harper, 1914.

The Trail of the Hawk. New York: Harper, 1915.

The Job. New York: Harper, 1917.

The Innocents. New York: Harper, 1917.

Free Air. New York: Harcourt, Brace, 1919.

Main Street. New York: Harcourt, Brace, 1920.

Babbitt. New York: Harcourt, Brace, 1922.

Arrowsmith. New York: Harcourt, Brace, 1925.

Mantrap. New York: Harcourt, Brace, 1926.

Elmer Gantry. New York: Harcourt, Brace, 1927.

The Man Who Knew Coolidge. New York: Harcourt, Brace, 1928.

Dodsworth. New York: Harcourt, Brace, 1929.

Ann Vickers. Garden City: Doubleday, Doran, 1933.

Work of Art. Garden City: Doubleday, Doran, 1934.

It Can't Happen Here. Garden City: Doubleday, Doran, 1935.

The Prodigal Parents. Garden City: Doubleday, Doran, 1938.

Bethel Merriday. Garden City: Doubleday, Doran, 1940.
Gideon Planish. New York: Random House, 1943.
Cass Timberlane. New York: Random House, 1945.
Kingsblood Royal. New York: Random House, 1947.
The God-Seeker. New York: Random House, 1949.
World So Wide. New York: Random House, 1951.

Selections

Selected Short Stories. Garden City: Doubleday, Doran, 1935.
From Main Street to Stockholm: Letters of Sinclair Lewis, 1919–1930. Selected and with an introduction by Harrison Smith. New York: Harcourt, Brace, 1952.
The Man from Main Street: Selected Essays and Other Writings, 1904–1950. Edited by Harry E. Maule and Melville H. Cane. New York: Random House, 1953.
I'm a Stranger Here Myself and Other Stories. Selected, with an introduction, by Mark Schorer. Dell Laurel editions. New York: Dell, 1962.

WRITINGS ABOUT LEWIS

Although this bibliography does not include all the works listed in the footnotes, it does include all the judgments on Lewis's work, even brief appraisals, which have seemed worthy of attention.

Books

ADAMS, J. DONALD. *The Shape of Books to Come*. New York: Viking Press, 1945.
ANDERSON, CARL L. *The Swedish Acceptance of American Literature*. Philadelphia: University of Pennsylvania Press, 1957.
BEWLEY, MARIUS. *The Eccentric Design: Form in the Classic American Novel*. London: Chatto and Windus, 1959.

BROOKS, VAN WYCK. *The Confident Years, 1885–1915.* London: Dent, 1953.

CABELL, JAMES BRANCH. *Some of Us: An Essay in Epitaphs.* New York: McBride, 1930.

————. *Straws and Prayer-Books.* London: The Bodley Head; New York: McBride, 1924.

COWLEY, MALCOLM. *After the Genteel Tradition.* New York: Norton, 1937.

DE KRUIF, PAUL. *The Sweeping Wind.* New York: Harcourt, Brace, 1962.

FADIMAN, CLIFTON. *Party of One.* New York: World Publishing Co., 1955.

FARRAR, JOHN. *The Literary Spotlight.* New York: Doran, 1924.

FEINBERG, LEONARD. *The Satirist: His Temperament, Motivation, and Influence.* Ames: Iowa State University Press, 1963.

FORSTER, E. M. *Abinger Harvest.* London: Edward Arnold, 1936.

GEISMAR, MAXWELL. *American Moderns: From Rebellion to Conformity.* London: W. H. Allen, 1958.

————. *The Last of the Provincials: The American Novel 1915–1925.* Boston: Houghton Mifflin, 1947.

————. *Writers in Crisis: The American Novel Between Two Wars.* Boston: Houghton Mifflin, 1942.

GREBSTEIN, SHELDON. *Sinclair Lewis.* United States Authors Series. New York: Twayne, 1962.

HAZARD, LUCY LOCKWOOD. *The Frontier in American Literature.* New York: Crowell, 1927.

HOFFMAN, FREDERICK J. *The Modern Novel in America, 1900–1950.* Chicago: Regnery, 1951.

————. *The Twenties: American Writing in the Postwar Decade.* New York: Viking, 1955.

HUNT, FRAZIER. *One American and His Attempt at Education.* New York: Simon and Schuster, 1938.

KAZIN, ALFRED. *On Native Grounds: An Interpretation of Modern American Prose Literature.* New York: Reynal and Hitchcock, 1942.

LEWIS, GRACE HEGGER. *With Love From Gracie: Sinclair Lewis: 1912–1925.* New York: Harcourt, Brace, 1955.

LIPPMANN, WALTER. *Men of Destiny.* New York: Macmillan, 1927.

MAY, HENRY F. *The End of American Innocence: A Study of the First Years of Our Own Time, 1912–1917.* New York: Knopf, 1959.

MILLGATE, MICHAEL. *American Social Fiction, James to Cozzens.* Edinburgh: Oliver and Boyd, 1964.

MOORE, GEOFFREY. "Sinclair Lewis: A Lost Romantic." In *The Young Rebel in American Literature.* Edited by Carl Bode. London: Heinemann, 1959.

MULLER, HERBERT J. *Modern Fiction: A Study of Values.* New York: Funk and Wagnalls, 1937.

NATHAN, GEORGE JEAN. *The Intimate Notebooks of George Jean Nathan.* New York: Knopf, 1932.

PARRINGTON, V. L. *Our Own Diogenes.* University of Washington Chapbooks, No. 5. Seattle: University of Washington Press, 1927. Also in *Main Currents in American Thought,* Vol. III. New York: Harcourt, Brace, 1930.

PATTEE, FREDERICK LEWIS. *The New American Literature, 1890–1930.* New York: Century, 1930.

PRIESTLEY, J. B. *Literature and Western Man.* London: Heinemann, 1960.

ROURKE, CONSTANCE. *American Humor.* New York: Harcourt, Brace, 1931.

RUBIN, LOUIS D., JR., AND MOORE, JOHN REES. *The Idea of an American novel.* New York: Crowell, 1961.

SCHORER, MARK. *Sinclair Lewis.* University of Minnesota Pamphlets on American Writers, No. 27. Minneapolis: University of Minnesota Press, 1963.

————. *Sinclair Lewis: An American Life.* New York: McGraw-Hill, 1961.

SCHORER, MARK, ED. *Sinclair Lewis: A Collection of Critical Essays.* Englewood Cliffs: Prentice-Hall, 1962.

————. *Society and Self in the Novel.* English Institute Essays, 1955. New York: Columbia University Press, 1956.

SHEEAN, VINCENT. *Dorothy and Red.* Boston: Houghton Mifflin, 1963.

————. *Personal History.* Garden City: Doubleday, Doran, 1936.

SHERMAN, STUART P. *The Significance of Sinclair Lewis.* New York: Harcourt, Brace, 1922.

SMITH, HENRY NASH. *Virgin Land: The American West as Symbol and Myth.* Cambridge: Harvard University Press, 1950.

SPILLER, ROBERT E. *The Cycle of American Literature: An Essay in Historical Criticism.* New York: Macmillan, 1955.

SPILLER, ROBERT E., *et al. A Literary History of the United States.* New York: Macmillan, 1948.

TAYLOR, WALTER FULLER. *A History of American Letters.* Boston: American Book Co., 1936.

THORP, WILLARD. *American Writing in the Twentieth Century.* Cambridge: Harvard University Press, 1960.

VAN DOREN, CARL. *The American Novel, 1789–1939.* New York: Macmillan, 1940.

————. *Sinclair Lewis: A Biographical Sketch.* Garden City: Doubleday, Doran, 1933.

VINES, SHERARD. *A Hundred Years of English Literature.* London: Duckworth, 1950.

WAGENKNECHT, EDWARD. *Cavalcade of the American Novel.* New York: Holt, 1952.

WEST, REBECCA. *The Strange Necessity.* New York: Doubleday, Doran, 1928.

WHICHER, GEORGE F. Part IV: The Twentieth Century, in *The Literature of the American People*. Ed. by A. H. Quinn. New York: Appleton-Century-Crofts, 1951.

WHIPPLE, THOMAS K. *Spokesmen: Modern Writers and American Life*. New York: Appleton, 1928.

WILSON, EDMUND. *The Shores of Light*. New York: Farrar and Strauss, 1952.

WOLFE, THOMAS. *You Can't Go Home Again*. Garden City: Sun Dial Press, 1942.

WOOLF, VIRGINIA, *The Moment*. London: Hogarth Press, 1947.

Periodicals

ANDERSON, SHERWOOD. "Four American Impressions," *New Republic*, XXXII (1922), 172–173.

AUSTIN, ALLEN. "An Interview with Sinclair Lewis," *University of Kansas City Review*, XXIV (1958), 199–210.

BACON, LEONARD. "Yale '09," *Saturday Review of Literature*, XIX (Feb. 4, 1939), 13–14.

BARRY, JOSEPH. "Sinclair Lewis, 65 and Far from Main Street," New York *Times Magazine*, Feb. 5, 1950, p. 13.

BECK, WARREN. "How Good is Sinclair Lewis?" *College English*, IX (1947–1948), 173–180.

BENÉT, WILLIAM ROSE. "The Earlier Lewis," *Saturday Review of Literature*, X (Jan. 20, 1934), 421–422.

BREASTED, CHARLES. "The 'Sauk-Centricities' of Sinclair Lewis," *Saturday Review*, XXXVII (Aug. 15, 1955), 7.

CABELL, JAMES BRANCH. "A Note as to Sinclair Lewis," *American Mercury*. XX (1930), 394–397.

CANTWELL, ROBERT. "Sinclair Lewis," *New Republic*, LXXXVIII (1936), 298–301.

DAVIS, ELMER. Review of *Elmer Gantry*, New York *Times Book Review*, March 13, 1927, p. 1.

FENTON, CHARLES. "The American Academy of Arts and Letters Versus All Comers: Literary Rags and Riches in the 1920's," *South Atlantic Quarterly*, LVIII (1959), 572–586.

FLANAGAN, JOHN T. "A Long Way to Gopher Prairie: Sinclair Lewis' Apprenticeship," *Southwest Review*, XXXII (1947), 403–413.

FYVEL, T. R. "Martin Arrowsmith and His Habitat," *New Republic*, CXXXIII (July 18, 1955), 16–18.

GANNETT, LEWIS. "Sinclair Lewis: Main Street," *Saturday Review of Literature*, XXXII (Aug. 6, 1949), p. 31.

GRATTAN, C. HARLEY. "Sinclair Lewis: The Work of a Lifetime," *New Republic*, CXXIV (April 2, 1951), 19–20.

GREBSTEIN, SHELDON. "Sinclair Lewis and the Nobel Prize," *Western Humanities Review*, XIII (1959), 163–171.

———. "Sinclair Lewis's Unwritten Novel," *Philological Quarterly*, XXXVII (1958), 399–409.

GURKO, LEO AND MIRIAM. "The Two Main Streets of Sinclair Lewis," *College English*, IV (1943), 288–292.

GUTHRIE, RAMON. "The Labor Novel Sinclair Lewis Never Wrote," New York *Herald Tribune Books*, Feb. 10, 1952, pp. 1, 6.

HUGHES, SERGE. "From Main Street to the World So Wide," *Commonweal*, LIII (Apr. 6, 1951), 648–650.

KRUTCH, JOSEPH WOOD. "Sinclair Lewis," *Nation*, CLXXII (1951), 179–180.

MANSON, ALEXANDER (as told to Helen Camp). "The Last Days of Sinclair Lewis," *Saturday Evening Post*, CCXXIII (March 31, 1951), 27, 110–112.

MARCUS, STEVEN. "American Gothic," *New York Review of Books*, I (Jan. 19, 1964), 3–5.

MILLER, PERRY. "The Incorruptible Sinclair Lewis," *Atlantic Monthly*, CLXXXVII (April 1951), 30–34.

MORRIS, LLOYD. "Sinclair Lewis: His Critics and His Public," *North American Review*, CCXLV (1938), 381–390.

MUMFORD, LEWIS. "The America of Sinclair Lewis," *Current History*, XXXIII (1931), 529–533.

OVERTON, GRANT. "The Salvation of Sinclair Lewis," *Bookman*, LXI (1925), 179–185.

PALMER, RAYMOND H. "The Nobel Jury Judges America," *Christian Century*, XLVII (1930), 1448.

RALEIGH, JOHN HENRY. "The 'Truth,'" *Partisan Review*, XXIX (1962), 270–283.

RICHARDSON, LYON N. "*Arrowsmith*: Genesis, Development, Versions," *American Literature*, XXVII (1955–1956), 225–244.

———."Revision in Sinclair Lewis's The Man Who Knew Coolidge," *American Literature*, XXV (1953–1954), 326–333.

SCHORER, MARK. "The Monstrous Self-deception of Elmer Gantry," *New Republic*, CXXXIII (Oct. 31, 1955), 13–15.

———. "The World of Sinclair Lewis," *New Republic*, CXXVIII (April 6, 1953), 18.

SMITH, HARRISON. "Sinclair Lewis: Remembrance of the Past," *Saturday Review of Literature*, XXXIV (Jan. 27, 1951), 7.

STOLBERG, BENJAMIN. "Sinclair Lewis," *American Mercury*, LXIII (1941), 450–460.

STUART, HENRY LONGAN. "Novels from the Grub Street Days of Sinclair Lewis," New York *Times Book Review*, April 22, 1923, p. 3.

THOMPSON, DOROTHY. "The Boy and Man from Sauk Center," *Atlantic Monthly*, CCVI (November 1960), 39–48.

———. "Sinclair Lewis: A Postscript," *Atlantic Monthly*, CLXXXVII (June 1951), 73–74.

VAN DOREN, CARL. "Revolt from the Village: 1920," *Nation*, CXL (1921), 914–917.

———. "Sinclair Lewis and Sherwood Anderson: A Study of Two Moralists," *Century*, CX (1925), 362–369.

WEST, ANTHONY. Survey of Lewis's career, *New Yorker*, XXVII (April 28, 1951), 114.

WOODWARD, W. E. "The World and Sauk Center," *New Yorker*, IX (Jan. 27, 1934), 24.

WYLIE, PHILIP. "Sinclair Lewis," *American Mercury*, LXI (1945), 629.

Doctoral Dissertations

COLEMAN, ARTHUR B. "The Genesis of Social Ideas in Sinclair Lewis." New York University, 1954.

COUCH, WILLIAM, JR. "The Emergence, Rise and Decline of the Reputation of Sinclair Lewis." University of Chicago, 1954.

FEINBERG, LEONARD. "Sinclair Lewis as a Satirist." University of Illinois, 1946.

LIGHT, MARTIN. "A Study of Characterization in Sinclair Lewis's Fiction." University of Illinois, 1960.

Acknowledgment

I GRATEFULLY ACKNOWLEDGE permission to quote from the following copyrighted works:

To Harcourt, Brace and World for permission to quote from Sinclair Lewis's *Our Mr. Wrenn, The Trail of the Hawk, The Job, Free Air, Main Street, Babbitt, Arrowsmith, Elmer Gantry, The Man Who Knew Coolidge*, and *Dodsworth*; from Grace Hegger Lewis's *With Love From Gracie*; and from *From Main Street to Stockholm*.

To the *Saturday Review* for permission to quote from William Rose Benét, "The Earlier Lewis."

To the *New Republic* for permission to quote from Mark Schorer, "The Monstrous Self-Deception of Elmer Gantry," © 1955, Harrison-Blaine of New Jersey, Inc.

To Malcolm Cowley for permission to quote from "George F. Babbitt's Revenge."

To Houghton Mifflin for permission to quote from Vincent Sheean's *Dorothy and Red*.

To the *Nation* for permission to quote from Sinclair Lewis, "Mr. Lorimer and Me."

To *Commonweal* for permission to quote from Serge Hughes, "From Main Street to the World So Wide."

To Hogarth Press and the estate of Humbert Wolfe for permission to quote from Humbert Wolfe, *Notes on English Verse Satire*.

To Alfred A. Knopf for permission to quote from Henry F. May, *The End of American Innocence*.

To Walter Allen and J. M. Dent for permission to quote from Walter Allen, *The English Novel*.

To Hill and Wang and W. H. Allen for permission to quote from Maxwell Geismar, *American Moderns: From Rebellion to Conformity*.

To the Macmillan Company for permission to quote from Walter Lippmann, *Men of Destiny*, © 1927, © renewed 1955 by Walter Lippmann.

To The Bodley Head Ltd. and the Robert McBride Company for permission to quote from James Branch Cabell, *Straws and Prayer-Books*.

To Random House for permission to quote from Sinclair Lewis's *Kingsblood Royal*, *The God-Seeker*, *World So Wide*, *Gideon Planish*, *Cass Timberlane*, and *The Man from Main Street*.

To Ernst, Cane, Berner & Gitlin for permission to quote from Sinclair Lewis's *Work of Art*, *It Can't Happen Here*, and *The Prodigal Parents*, published by Doubleday, Doran, respectively, in 1934, 1935, and 1938.

D. J. D.

Index

Accorsi, Salvatore, 242
Adams, Henry, 153
Adams, J. Donald, xi
Adventure, 13
Aeschylus, 124
Ah! Wilderness, 203
Alger, Horatio, 25, 28, 41, 192, 221
Allen, Walter, 24
American Academy of Arts and Letters, 168, 170, 171, 173, 195, 213
American Federation of Labor, 161, 163
American Magazine, 37
American Mercury, The, 90, 147, 160, 248
American Scholar, The, 215
Anderson, Carl L., 166–168, 270
Anderson, Margaret, 14
Anderson, Sherwood, 58, 77, 79, 171, 258, 261
Arnold, Matthew, 62, 75
Atkinson, Brooks, 173
Austin, Allen, 63, 131, 192, 240, 260, 265

Bacon, Leonard, 8
Bainter, Fay, 187
Balzac, Honoré de, 262
Bard, Josef, 140
Barrymore, Lionel, 194
Beard, Charles and Mary, 194
Beck, Warren, 116
Benét, William Rose, 8, 12, 241
Bennett, Arnold, 13, 90, 111, 142–143

Bewley, Marius, 151, 157
Birkhead, Rev. L. M., 121, 161
Blackmur, R. P., 214
Book-of-the-Month Club, 217
Bookman, The, 35
Borglum, Gutzon, 124
Bourne, Ralph, 21
Bow, Clara, 120
Boynton, H. W., 62–63
Boynton, Percy, xi
Brace, Donald, 105, 164
Breasted, Charles, 64, 91–92, 124–125
Breen, Joseph I., 195
Bridge of San Luis Rey, The, 244
Brooks, Van Wyck, xii, 21, 214
Browne, Rabbi Lewis, 212
Bryan, William Jennings, 247
Burbank, Luther, 122
Butler, Samuel, 27

Cabell, James Branch, xi, 59, 64–65, 265
Campbell, Flora, 203
Canby, Henry Seidel, xi, 26, 115, 196
Cane, Melville H., 160, 196
Cannan, Gilbert, 27
Cantwell, Robert, 36, 97, 241, 262–263, 264
Cather, Willa, 151
Cecil, Lord David, 24
Cobb, Irvin, 36
Coleman, Arthur B., 19–20, 41–42, 45, 51, 87, 90, 97–98, 154, 246, 248

Collier's, 118
Colophon, ix, 227
Colum, Mary M., 223
Commonweal, 185, 211
Comte, Auguste, 109
Cooke, Alice MacGowan, 11, 12
Cooke, Grace MacGowan, 11, 12
Coolidge, President Calvin, 105, 137, 141, 143
Cooper, Frederic Taber, 35
Cooper, James Fenimore, 90
Cosmopolitan, 160, 180, 189, 217, 231
Couch, William, Jr., 55–56, 76, 114–115, 130, 135, 139, 160, 193–194
Coughlin, Rev. Charles E., 192, 247
Cowley, Malcolm, 73, 142, 147, 165, 173, 182, 201–202
Critic, The, 9
Croly, Herbert, 246
Curti, Merle, 193
Curtis, Glenn, 31

Daughters of the American Revolution, 179, 192
Davis, Elmer, 134–135, 274
De Kruif, Paul, 99–103, 116–117, 161, 242, 252
De Voto, Bernard, 213–214
Debs, Eugene Victor, 98–99, 140, 162
Dell, Floyd, 77–78
Designer and the Woman's Magazine, The, 100, 103, 114–115
Dewey, John, 114, 249, 253
Dewey, Thomas E., 215
Dial, The, 88
Dickens, Charles, 6, 22, 47, 113, 189, 204, 216, 266
Doran, George H., publishing company, 13, 35, 40
Dorothy and Red, xiii, 149, 197
Dos Passos, John, 258
Doubleday, Doran and Company, 181, 188, 191
Dreiser, Theodore, 75, 167, 171–172, 179–180, 213, 238–239, 258

Eayrs, Ellen, 50
Ebony, 227
Eliot, George, 24
Eliot, T. S., 258
Ely, Catherine Beach, 76
Emerson, Ralph Waldo, 172
Encyclopaedia Americana, 93
Esquire, 216

Fadiman, Clifton, 205

Famous Players, 50
Farber, Marjorie, 217
Farrar, John, 94–95, 240
Farrell, James T., 217, 258
Faulkner, William, 172, 238, 267
Feinberg, Leonard, 240, 243
Fenton, Charles, 168–170, 173
Fishbein, Dr. Morris, 99, 116
Fisher, Dorothy Canfield, 263
Fitzgerald, F. Scott, 77, 257–259, 267
Fitzsimmons, Robert, 36
Flanagan, John T., 58
Flaubert, Gustave, 63, 78
Florey, Louis E., 118, 186
Fogelqvist, Tosten, 167
Forster, E. M., ix, 261, 264
Frank, Waldo, 77
From Main Street to Stockholm, xiii, 49, 94, 178
Frost, Robert, 176
Fyvel, T. R., 236–237, 257

Galbraith, J. K., 54
Gale, Zona, 258
Galsworthy, John, 54, 75
Gannett, Lewis, 76
Garland, Hamlin, 9, 20, 42, 59, 259
Geismar, Maxwell, xi, 112–113, 146, 199, 220–223, 236, 238–239, 257, 267
Good Neighbor, The, 207
Goodman, Philip, 105
Gordon, George (Charles Crittenden Baldwin), 58
Grande Revue, La, 255
Grattan, C. Harley, xv
Great Expectations, 120
Grebstein, Sheldon, 116, 130, 163, 175, 196, 220, 226, 242, 246
Grey, Zane, 164
Grosset and Dunlap, 164
Guest, Edgar, 87
Gurko, Leo and Miriam, 97, 157
Gustav, King of Sweden, 169, 174
Guthrie, Ramon, 130, 140, 141, 163

Hackett, Francis, 94, 260
Haessler, Carl, 161, 162
Hamsun, Knut, 166–167
Harcourt, Alfred, 14, 49, 50, 58–59, 82–83, 94, 98, 100, 102–103, 105, 118, 121, 123, 125, 140–142, 148, 150, 164–165, 177–178, 189, 197
Harcourt, Brace and Company (originally Harcourt, Brace and Howe), 49, 60, 118, 121, 126, 140, 142, 172, 177–178

Harding, President Warren, 99
Hardy, Thomas, 266
Harper's magazine, 6
Harper Publishing Company, 16, 44
Harte, Bret, 45
Harvard, 7, 9
Hawthorne, Nathaniel, 90, 151, 228
Hay, Ian, 152
Hazard, Lucy Lockwood, 29–30
Hearst, William Randolph, 211
Helicon Hall, 10, 11
Hemingway, Ernest, 73, 171–172, 217, 267
Henry, O, 14
Hitler, Adolph, 180
Hoffman, Frederick J., xi, 89, 146
Howard, Sidney, 186, 194–195
Howe, E. W., 258
Howells, William Dean, 44, 55, 151, 172
Hughes, Rupert, 180
Hughes, Serge, 233
Hunt, Frazier, 241
Huston, Walter, 187

Independent, The, 147

Jack, Peter Monro, 190
James, Henry, 20, 151, 177
Johnson, Edgar, xi, 204
Johnson, Samuel, xiv
Jones, Howard Mumford, 214, 230

Karlfeldt, Erik Axel, 167–70
Kazin, Alfred, xi
Keats, John, 189
Kelland, Clarence Budington, 100
Kittredge, George Lyman, 172
Koestler, Arthur, 227
Kronenberger, Louis, 202
Krutch, Joseph Wood, 262
Ku Klux Klan, 247

LaFollette, Robert, 105
Lardner, Ring, 258
Lawrence, D. H., 27, 217
Lengel, William C., 180
Lewis, Dr. Claude, 4, 104, 231
Lewis, Dr. Edwin J., 3–5, 25–26, 40, 102, 105, 124
Lewis, Emma Kermott, 3
Lewis, Fred, 4
Lewis, Grace Hegger, xiii, 5, 11, 14–16, 27–28, 34–37, 40–41, 44, 48–49, 60, 63–64, 73, 80–82, 99, 101–105, 117–118, 124–125, 140, 143, 148, 159, 195–197, 208, 210, 215, 253, 255–257

Lewis, Isabel Warner, 3
Lewis, Lloyd, 187
Lewis, Michael, 165
Lewis, R. W. B., 26, 258
Lewis, Sinclair, novels: *Ann Vickers*, 97, 181–186, 244; *Arrowsmith*, 97, 99–103, 105–117, 120, 122–123, 129, 139, 161, 177, 192, 228, 245, 246, 264; *Babbitt*, 17, 47, 54, 73, 74, 81–95, 98, 106, 110, 114, 120, 129, 131–133, 156, 164, 169–170, 177, 182, 192, 201, 217, 236–237, 262, 264, 266–267; *Bethel Merriday*, 204–205; *Cass Timberlane*, 215, 217–224; *Dodsworth*, 15, 71, 97, 117, 150–160, 162, 177, 186–187, 210–211, 217, 221, 223, 235, 245, 253; dramatic version, 186–187; *Elmer Gantry*, 7, 97, 121–122, 125–135, 139, 142, 177, 182, 192, 208, 228, 235, 245, 264, 267; *Free Air*, 50–52, 66, 156, 221, 257; *Gideon Planish*, 208–211, 217; *The God-Seeker*, 227–230, 245, 248; *The Innocents*, 40, 47–48; *It Can't Happen Here*, 191–195, 199–200, 209, 226–227, 247; dramatic version, 202–203; film version, 194–195; *The Job*, 41–47, 55, 137, 182, 248–249; *Kingsblood Royal*, 224–227, 239–240, 244; *Main Street*, x, 17, 47, 51–52, 57–76, 78–82, 93–94, 106, 110, 113, 123–124, 131, 133, 136, 139, 156, 168–170, 177, 188, 202, 217, 219–220, 239, 243–244, 260–262, 264; *The Man Who Knew Coolidge*, 141–148, 264; *Mantrap*, 105, 118–121, 142; *Our Mr. Wrenn*, 16–28, 54–55, 91, 204, 245; *The Prodigal Parents*, 198–202; *The Trail of the Hawk*, xxi, 26, 28–35, 55, 257; *Work of Art*, 188–189, 194, 245; *World So Wide*, 80–81, 231–234, 263; projected novels: *The Childrens' Children*, 227; *Neighbor*, 99, 140, 161–163, 178, 180, 227; *The Quiet Mind*, 196; short stories: *Selected Short Stories*, 189–190, 259; "Go East, Young Man," 190; "The Hidden People," 38–39; "Hobohemia," 49; "Land," 190; "Let's Play King," 190; "A Matter of Business," 38; "Nature, Incorporated," 35–37; "Number Seven to Sagapoose," 37; "A Woman by Candlelight," 38–39; "Young

Lewis, Sinclair, (cont.)
Man Axelbrod," 37; articles: "Adventures in Autobumming," 50; "The Artist, the Scientist, and the Peace," 215–216; "Breaking into Print," 227; "Fools, Liars and Mr. De Voto," 213–214; "How I Wrote a Novel on Trains and Beside the Kitchen Sink," 28; "I'm an Old Newspaperman Myself," 6; "Is America a Paradise for Women?" 160; "A Letter on Style," 73; "Mr. Lorimer and Me," 147; "Obscenity and Obscurity," 216–217; "Publicity Gone Mad," 151; "Relation of the Novel to the Present Social Unrest: The Passing of Capitalism," 27; "Self-Portrait," 5; "Two Yale Men in Utopia," 10; "You Meet Such Interesting People," 6; other writings: Angela Is Twenty-Two (play), 203, 207; Cheap and Contented Labor (pamphlet), 161; From Main Street to Stockholm, xiii, 49, 94, 178; Hike and the Aeroplane (juvenile), 15–16; Jayhawker (play), 187–188, 190; The Man from Main Street, xiii, 160, 196; Storm in the West (film script), 212–213; addresses: "American Literature Comes of Age," 179; "The Artist, the Scientist, and the Peace," 215–216; Nobel Prize speech, 59, 72–74, 93, 170–174, 238, 245

Lewis, Wells, 48–49, 103, 105, 118, 148, 195–196, 214–215

Light, Martin, 22, 34, 51, 66, 98, 115–117, 156, 192–193, 244

Lindbergh, Charles A., 30

Lippmann, Walter, 139–140, 243

Literary Guild, The, 225

Literary Review, The, 131

Little Review, The, 14

Loeb, Jacques, 101, 117

London, Jack, 12

London Daily Express, 103

Long, Huey, 247

Longfellow, Henry Wadsworth, 171, 267

Lorimer, George Horace, 35–36, 100, 147

Lowes, John Livingston, 172

Lowry, Helen Bullitt, 77

Macaulay, Rose, 80

Mackenzie, Compton, 13, 27

Man From Main Street, The, xiii, 160, 196

Manchester, William, 136

Manly, John M., 172

Mannin, Ethel, 121

Marcus, Steven, xiii

Marx, Karl, 13

Masses, The, 56

Masters, Edgar Lee, 58–59, 94, 250, 258

Maugham, Somerset, 13, 204

Maule, Harry E., 14, 160, 196

May, Henry F., 78, 86, 250

Mayer, Louis B., 194

McCormick, Anne O'Hare, 92

McPherson, Aimee Semple, 127, 130, 247

Mencken, H. L., 17, 20, 55, 90, 93, 135–137, 141, 147, 160, 181, 193, 229, 246–247, 250

Metro-Goldwyn-Mayer, 194–195, 212–213

Millay, Edna St. Vincent, 250

Miller, Arthur, 42

Miller, Perry, 22, 80–81, 235

Minnesota, University of, 7, 208

Moby Dick, 148

Moffitt, J. C., 203

Morris, Lloyd, 202

Muir, Edwin, 130–132

Muller, Herbert J., 266–267

Mumford, Lewis, 54, 74–75, 176–177, 261

Murry, John Middleton, 194

Myrdal, Gunnar, 216

Nathan, George Jean, 90, 136, 141, 147

Nation, The, 52, 56, 58, 105, 131, 147, 151, 217

National Institute of Arts and Letters, The, 195

Nautilus, 12

New Humanism, 171–172

New Republic, 50, 56, 217

New Thought, 12, 87

New York Herald Tribune, 150–151

New York Times, 124, 166, 186, 188, 203, 207

New Yorker, 218

Newsweek, 196

Nicholson, Meredith, 57

Nobel Prize, 123, 165–178, 234, 255

Norris, Frank, 27

Novy, Dr. Frederick George, 101

Noyes, F. K., 13

Oberlin Academy, 7

O'Neill, Eugene, ix, 74, 123, 171
Onions, Oliver, 27
Orwell, George, xv, 19, 227, 237
Overton, Grant, 244, 263

Palmer, Raymond H., 91, 113–114, 257
Parrington, V. L., x, 172, 164
Pasteur, Louis, 216
Pater, Walter, 216
Peale, Norman Vincent, 25
Phelps, William Lyon, 8, 71–72, 130, 195
Pictorial Review, The, 160
Pope, Alexander, 243, 247
Powers, Marcella, 204, 207, 230
Priestley, J. B., 179, 204
Proust, Marcel, 154
Pulitzer Prize, 50, 76, 122–124, 165–166, 255
Pulitzer, Ralph, 124

Rabelais, François, 69
Random House, 231
Rascoe, Burton, 183
Redbook, 11, 118, 181, 189
Reed, Daniel, 49
Review of Reviews, 17
Rice, Elmer, 188
Richardson, Lyon N., 114–115
Riesman, David, 54
Robbins, Francis Lamont, 158
Rolland, Romain, 27
Roosevelt, President Franklin Delano, 181, 207, 215
Rotary, 29, 192
Rourke, Constance, xi, 25
Russell, Bertrand, 103

San Francisco *Bulletin*, 12
Sandburg, Carl, 98
Sanford, Charles L., 59, 258–259
Santayana, George, 173
Saturday Evening Post, The, 35, 49, 50, 93–94, 147, 189
Saturday Review of Literature, The, 213
Schary, Dore, 212
Schorer, Mark, ix–xv, 3, 8, 10, 39, 53, 55, 58, 72, 81, 93, 104–105, 118, 120, 132–134, 136–137, 162, 165, 175, 188, 191, 196, 203, 208, 216–217, 220, 227, 231, 235, 237, 255, 257
Scott, Sir Walter, 6, 265
Seligmann, Herbert J., 72
Shakespeare, William, xiv, 266
Shaw, George Bernard, 13, 20, 22, 43, 78, 93

Sheean, Vincent, xiii, 81, 149, 197, 197, 242, 252
Shelley, Percy Bysshe, 188
Sherman, Stuart P., 7, 43–44, 50, 53–54, 75, 78, 98, 117, 248
Sinclair, Upton, 10, 239, 244
Smith, Harrison, 92, 126, 142, 215
Smith, Henry Nash, 26, 258
Snow, Phoebe, 36
Sophocles, 124
Soule, George, 91
Spiller, Robert E., x, 26
Spingarn, Joel, 123
Stearns, Harold, 81
Steffens, Lincoln, 54
Stevens, Betty, 131
Stidger, Rev. William, 120
Stokes, Frederick A., publishing company, 13–14
Stolberg, Benjamin, 162
Straton, Rev. John Roach, 131
Streicher, Julius, 192
Stuart, Henry Longan, 44, 47, 115, 146
Sunday, Billy, 88, 127, 130, 247
Swinnerton, Frank, 80

Tate, Allen, 214
Taylor, Walter Fuller, 70–71, 254
Tennyson, Alfred Lord, 8, 43, 111
Thompson, Dorothy, xiii, 4–6, 13, 25, 80, 91, 136, 140–142, 148–151, 159–161, 163, 177, 179–181, 191, 197–198, 207–208, 210–211, 214–215, 242, 252–253
Thomson, Brig.-Gen. C. B., 103
Thoreau, Henry David, 196
Thurston, Katherine Cecil, 9
Tinker, Chauncey B., 8
Tocqueville, Alexis de, 62
Tracy, Spencer, 217
Transatlantic Tales, 11
Trilling, Diana, 217–218, 223
Turner, Frederick Jackson, 258
Turner, Lana, 217
Twain, Mark, 25, 53, 238, 252

Updegraff, Allan, 10

Van Doren, Carl, x–xi, 14, 36, 49, 52–53, 58, 64, 78–79, 82, 94, 112, 122–123, 137, 155, 172, 250, 253, 260
Van Dyke, Rev. Henry, 168–169, 170, 173
Veblen, Thorstein, 20, 31, 45–46, 54, 154, 245
Vesalius, Andreas, 216

Villa, Pancho, 80
Villon, François, 174
Vines, Sherard, 93, 266
Volta Review, The, 12–13
Voltaire, 216

Wagenknecht, Edward, xi, 88–89, 230
Wagstaffe, W. G., 77
Walpole, Hugh, 13, 80, 94
Ward, Artemus, 25
Waste Land, The, 15
Waterloo *Daily Courier*, 11
Wells, H. G., 13, 17–22, 26, 28, 30, 41, 43, 47, 78, 80, 89, 90, 183, 244–245, 247, 251, 253
West, Rebecca, 80, 132, 245, 257
Wharton, Edith, 76, 123
Whicher, George F., 143
Whipple, T. K., xi, 111–112, 235, 240–241, 245, 252, 264
Whistler, James McNeil, 216
White, William Allen, 126
Whitman, Walt, 238

Wilcox, Ella Wheeler, 267
Williams, Michael, 185
Williams, Raymond, 113–114, 253
Wilson, Edmund, 214, 217–218, 220, 222
Winters, Yvor, 214
Wisconsin, University of, 207
Wolfe, Humbert, 71
Wolfe, Thomas, 73, 172, 255–257
Woman's Home Companion, The, 47
Woodward, W. E., 131, 175
Woolf, Virginia, 89–90, 261, 264
Wray, Fay, 203
Wright brothers, 31
Wylie, Philip, 220

Yale, 7–11, 180, 195
Yale *Courant*, 8–9
Yale *Literary Magazine*, 8–9
Youth's Companion, The, 6

Zangwill, Israel, 9
Zinsser, Hans, 116
Zola, Émile, 262